# Chromebook®

for
# dummies®
A Wiley Brand

# Chromebook®

3rd Edition

## by Peter H. Gregory

A Wiley Brand

# Chromebook® For Dummies®, 3rd Edition

Published by: **John Wiley & Sons, Inc.,** 111 River Street, Hoboken, NJ 07030-5774, www.wiley.com

Copyright © 2023 by John Wiley & Sons, Inc., Hoboken, New Jersey

Media and software compilation copyright © 2023 by John Wiley & Sons, Inc. All rights reserved.

Published simultaneously in Canada

No part of this publication may be reproduced, stored in a retrieval system or transmitted in any form or by any means, electronic, mechanical, photocopying, recording, scanning or otherwise, except as permitted under Sections 107 or 108 of the 1976 United States Copyright Act, without the prior written permission of the Publisher. Requests to the Publisher for permission should be addressed to the Permissions Department, John Wiley & Sons, Inc., 111 River Street, Hoboken, NJ 07030, (201) 748-6011, fax (201) 748-6008, or online at http://www.wiley.com/go/permissions.

**Trademarks:** Wiley, For Dummies, the Dummies Man logo, Dummies.com, Making Everything Easier, and related trade dress are trademarks or registered trademarks of John Wiley & Sons, Inc. and may not be used without written permission. Chromebook is a registered trademark of Google, LLC. All other trademarks are the property of their respective owners. John Wiley & Sons, Inc. is not associated with any product or vendor mentioned in this book.

For general information on our other products and services, please contact our Customer Care Department within the U.S. at 877-762-2974, outside the U.S. at 317-572-3993, or fax 317-572-4002. For technical support, please visit https://hub.wiley.com/community/support/dummies.

Wiley publishes in a variety of print and electronic formats and by print-on-demand. Some material included with standard print versions of this book may not be included in e-books or in print-on-demand. If this book refers to media such as a CD or DVD that is not included in the version you purchased, you may download this material at http://booksupport.wiley.com. For more information about Wiley products, visit www.wiley.com.

Library of Congress Control Number: 2023933155

ISBN 978-1-394-16880-4 (pbk); ISBN 978-1-394-16881-1 (ebk); ISBN 978-1-394-16882-8 (ebk)

SKY10044356_031323

# Contents at a Glance

# Table of Contents

# Introduction

L aptop sales have been declining for years. This decline is mainly due to the rise in popularity of smartphones and tablets in the consumer market. Technology is getting smaller, faster, and more portable, so the world's dependence on full-size, full-featured (and some would say bloated) computers with fixed connections has begun to decrease.

However, in this declining market, the rising star is the *Chromebook* — a low-cost, portable computer powered by Google's ChromeOS, the first popular operating system inspired by and designed specifically for the internet. Unlike Windows PCs and the Mac, which were designed for general computer use with several large applications and local storage, Chromebooks are designed *primarily* for internet use. Instead of a gigantic hard drive, Chromebook relies mainly on cloud-based storage. Instead of lots of expensive memory, Chromebook uses the Chrome browser that doesn't use a lot of memory. And instead of resident applications, Chromebook uses mainly web-based applications that are accessed and book-marked through the Chrome Web Store and the Google Play store.

By offloading the bulk of the functionality to the cloud, Google made it possible for hardware manufacturers to create computers with hardware configurations designed specifically for life on the web. The result is an accessible, user-friendly computer with a much lower price point, making it an excellent option for schools, students, companies, and budget-conscious people needing modern computing power.

It's paying off. With sales in the tens of millions worldwide, Chromebooks make up almost two-thirds of all computers sold to K–12 schools in the United States and over half of those sold in Australia, and they're gaining traction worldwide. This market share — which is expected to keep growing in the education, business, and consumer sectors — means that the future of Chromebooks is bright. What students use in school today, they'll use at home and work tomorrow.

Similarly, more corporations are offering Chromebooks to employees for their corporate workstations. Chromebooks have a lower price point, are easier to manage, and don't have the security problems experienced by Windows (mostly) and Macs (a little, and growing).

Although Chromebooks use Google's ChromeOS operating system, by no means are Chromebooks "Google only" computers. Tools from Microsoft, Apple, and Amazon work on Chromebooks, too. And because Chromebooks are browser-centric, the entire world of the internet is your oyster!

# About This Book

Sometimes the greatest obstacle with new technology is the fear that you won't be able to grasp it fast enough for it to be of use. The good news is that this book is designed to remove all the guesswork. *Chromebook For Dummies*, 3rd Edition, is designed to give you all the tips and tools you need to excel with your Chromebook.

You don't need to have any preexisting experience with Chromebooks, ChromeOS, Android, or the Chrome browser to use *Chromebook For Dummies*, 3rd Edition. You don't even have to own a Chromebook: This book can help you choose the right Chromebook! (See Chapter 1 for an overview of features and Chapter 20 for details on selecting the right Chromebook for your needs.) If you have a Chromebook, this book guides you from the initial setup phase to the features that make Chromebooks unique and easy to use. Later sections of the book give you step-by-step instructions on using popular apps that can make you productive (or entertain you) on day one. By the time you hit the book's advanced settings and features section, you'll probably consider yourself an advanced Chromebook user. It doesn't take long!

Many computer books get bogged down with technical jargon and mumbo jumbo. This book, however, isn't written for the technological elite; it's written for the 99.9 percent of the population who just want a no-nonsense approach to using an easy-to-use computer.

Currently, several hardware manufacturers make Chromebooks. You've probably heard of many of them: HP, Samsung, Lenovo, Dell, Acer, Toshiba, and Asus, to name a few. Google even has its own branded Chromebook, the Google Pixelbook Go. The only difference between these devices is the hardware — not the operating system. For that reason, *Chromebook For Dummies*, 3rd Edition, doesn't reference any specific device or manufacturer. ChromeOS is the same across all of these brands.

Chromebooks are great devices, and their intuitive design makes for a very short learning curve. This book can help ensure that you have all the info you need to use your Chromebook like a rock star.

# Foolish Assumptions

*Chromebook For Dummies,* 3rd Edition, requires no prior computer knowledge or experience. Of course, if you have experience using PCs or Macs, you'll already be familiar with many of the Chromebook's features. If you've never used a laptop before but have used smartphones, you'll find that many concepts carry over. You'll be fine!

This book makes no assumptions about your skill level. Although it's primarily an introductory guide to the Chromebook and ChromeOS, you can also consider it an essential guide to personal computing.

# Icons Used in This Book

Throughout this book, icons in the margins highlight certain types of valuable information that call out for your attention. Here are the icons you'll encounter and a brief description of each.

**TIP**

The Tip icon marks tips and shortcuts that you can use to make your Chromebook experience easier. The tips in this book are timesaving techniques or pointers to resources that you should try so that you can get the maximum benefit from your Chromebook.

**REMEMBER**

Remember icons mark the information that's especially important to know. This icon reminds you of meaningful content you should file away because it may be useful again.

**TECHNICAL STUFF**

Whenever you see this icon, think advanced tip or technique. You may find these tidbits of useful information to be just too boring for words, or they may contain the solution you need to get your Chromebook working just the way you want. Skip these bits of information whenever you like.

**WARNING**

At the risk of sounding like an alarmist, I use a warning icon to point out something you should pay close attention to. Proceed with caution if you must proceed at all.

# Beyond the Book

In addition to what you are reading now, this book also comes with a free access-anywhere Cheat Sheet that gives you access to extra content, including quick-reference information that may come in handy when you're in a pinch. Check out this book's online Cheat Sheet at www.dummies.com and search for Chromebook For Dummies in the Search box.

# Where to Go from Here

The time has come to dive into the world of Chromebooks and ChromeOS. If you're entirely new to computers or maybe just a little timid with them, start with Chapter 1. The first chapters of the book are designed to guide you through the process of powering on your device, logging in, navigating your new computing environment, and even getting familiar with some keyboard and touchpad features unique to the Chromebook.

If you're a little more daring than others, you may skip the book's first few chapters and head directly to the chapter on the Chrome browser. If you already have a Chromebook, you can read this book from cover to cover to pick up knowledge here and there, or go to the table of contents or the index to look up specific information you need. Regardless of how you fancy yourself, this book can serve as an excellent primer for life with a Chromebook. And what a great, easily-managed life it can be!

# 1

# Getting Started with Chromebook

IN THIS CHAPTER

» Understanding what makes a
  Chromebook tick

» Selecting your very own Chromebook

» Using your Chromebook for the
  first time

» Switching to Chromebook from
  Windows, Mac, or Linux

# Chapter 1

# Choosing and Setting Up Your Chromebook

Google rocked the computer world in 2011 with the introduction of the Chromebook because there was nothing on the market quite like it. It was, and still is, an affordable laptop that offers an internet-centric platform. Today, more than 50 million Chromebooks are used in classrooms by teachers and students in blended learning environments that allow students to have unlimited access to educational resources. Chromebooks are also increasingly being used by businesses, remote workers, and digital nomads that need an inexpensive laptop that allows them to work from the office, home, or the nearest coffee shop. The Chromebook has evolved far from its humble beginnings and will likely be the only laptop you need.

In this chapter, I discuss what makes the Chromebook so compelling compared to other personal computers on the market. I also take an in-depth look at how to set up your Chromebook and prepare you to transition to Chromebook from Windows, Mac, or Linux.

A Chromebook is very easy to use and understand. Easier, I'd say, than a Windows computer or even a Mac. In fact, a Chromebook is about as easy to use as an iPhone, iPad, or Android.

# Checking Under the Hood of the Chromebook

In short, a Chromebook is a laptop computer running Google's proprietary operating system, ChromeOS.

**TECHNICAL STUFF**

The *operating system* (OS) is the software that manages and schedules your computer's primary tasks and functions. You may have a little experience with other popular operating systems such as Windows, Linux, or macOS. Smartphones and tablets also have operating systems; Apple's iPhone OS is called iOS, iPadOS runs on Apple iPads, and the OS that runs on Android tablets and phones is called, um, Android.

ChromeOS is an operating system developed by Google to work primarily with web-based software on laptop and tablet computers. Your experience using your Chromebook will be very similar to previous experiences you may have had surfing the web with the Chrome web browser (or any browser). The Chrome web browser shares many similarities with other web browsers on the market, like Firefox, Edge, and Safari. (See Figure 1-1.)

FIGURE 1-1:
The Google
Chrome web
browser.

*Illustration courtesy of Peter H. Gregory*

Except for the Chromebook Pixel Go, Google isn't manufacturing Chromebooks directly. Instead, Google has licensed several major laptop manufacturers to create them. Manufacturers such as Acer, ASUS, HP, Lenovo, Dell, Toshiba, and Samsung are all making their own Chromebooks with their own technical specifications. They all come with ChromeOS pre-installed.

## The software

Much of what you will do on your Chromebook happens in the Chrome web browser. This is because many of the applications you will use on your Chromebook actually reside on the internet. This is one of the things that sets Chromebook apart from other computers: You don't need to install most applications on a Chromebook; instead, you access them from the internet. You find applications through the Chrome Web Store (dubbed CWS) and add them to your Launcher, which, in many cases, means nothing more than creating a bookmark for quick access through your Chrome web browser. This approach can be limiting in some cases, but these cases are rare. Thanks to the vast nature of Google's global computing ecosystem, thousands of great applications are at your fingertips.

REMEMBER

Although some Chromebook applications offer offline features and functionality, you need an internet connection to initially set up your Chromebook and be able to take advantage of everything your Chromebook has to offer. You may assume that Chromebooks are designed for an "always online" lifestyle, but once you have set up your Chromebook, you can definitely do things with it while offline as well.

## The hardware

Unlike all other computers on the market that run macOS, Windows, or Linux, not much software is installed on your Chromebook, which means that your Chromebook doesn't need to have vast amounts of hard drive space, memory, or processing power. Most Chromebooks have 4 gigabytes (GB) of memory, at least 80GB of hard drive space, and a low-power processor.

The reduced technical features mean that Chromebooks use less power, which means longer battery life. It also means that Chromebooks have a drastically lower price tag than other computers. This explains why Google is gaining such a large share of the laptop market. For the things that most people do, a Chromebook is more than adequate and far less costly.

If you prefer a desktop computer running ChromeOS, plenty are available. These computers are called *Chromeboxes*. If you own or are thinking about getting a Chromebox instead of a Chromebook, 99 percent of everything you read in this book will still apply to you because most of what's in this book is about ChromeOS — the same OS that runs on Chromebooks and Chromeboxes.

# Choosing a Chromebook

Given the online nature of ChromeOS, Chromebooks do not require extremely high-powered hardware to provide an excellent user experience. Even so, the great variety of manufacturers, models, and hardware specifications available can make choosing a Chromebook somewhat tricky.

If you are not yet familiar with computer terms like hard drives, RAM, SD card slots, or HDMI ports, you don't really need to understand any of these things to buy a Chromebook that will work for you. If you are shopping for your first Chromebook (even if it's the first computer you have ever purchased), go to a store with a good selection (three or more models) of Chromebooks and knowledgeable salespeople. If you buy the least expensive model with a screen size you can live with, you probably won't be disappointed. If you *do* want to understand the inner details of Chromebooks and make your purchase decision based on RAM, hard drive size, and ports, flip over to Chapter 20 for all those details.

TIP

Another helpful way to decide which Chromebook to purchase is to research models online. *PC Magazine* and other well-known publications have good reviews on Chromebook models that can help you pick one.

# Setting Up Your Chromebook

TIP

You should have a wireless internet service when setting up your Chromebook. If you're using a stationary (home or public) wireless internet network or a portable device with an internet hotspot, you probably need to know the following:

>> The network name (like Smith Family Wi-Fi or ATT034)

>> The network password (usually a bunch of random letters and numbers, often printed on a sticker on your internet router)

If you don't already have a Google Account, you'll also need a landline phone or smartphone handy to verify your new account while you set up your Chromebook.

## Turning on your device

Regardless of the brand you choose, the Chromebook is built for speed — and you'll notice this speed the first time you turn on your device! To turn on your Chromebook, you may simply need to plug in the power cord and open the laptop. If your Chromebook doesn't turn on automatically, locate the Power button, which may be found on the top-right corner of the keyboard itself, or on the side or back of the Chromebook. Look for the familiar power logo consisting of a circle with an intersecting vertical line. Figure 1-2 shows the Power button on the Lenovo C330 and the Samsung 303C. The Power button on your Chromebook is probably similar to one of these.

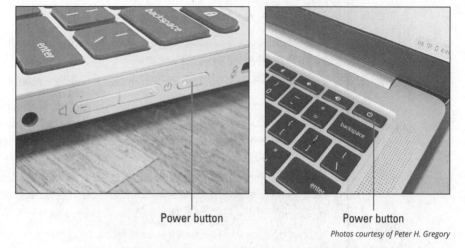

FIGURE 1-2:
The Power button on two different Chromebook models: the Lenovo C330 (a) and the Samsung 303C (b).

Power button                    Power button

*Photos courtesy of Peter H. Gregory*

When you turn on the device for the first time, a Chrome logo pops up on the screen, and within seconds, the computer powers on and displays the Welcome window. Click Get Started to begin setup.

I recently unboxed an HP Flagship 14 Chromebook and went through the setup. In addition to guiding me through the setup visually, it also spoke to me in a friendly, mechanical voice.

## Selecting a language

When the Welcome window appears, it will most likely say Welcome in the English language. If you want to change your Chromebook to work in your language, click on the current language. The Choose Language and Keyboard window displays. When you click on Language, a list of available languages appears, and when you click on Keyboard, a list appears. (I wish it had an option for Pirate English. *"Select your languaaaarge, matey!"*)

## Connecting to the internet

Next, you need to select a network to connect to the internet. If no network is available, I suggest holding off on attempting to set up your Chromebook until you can connect to an internet source.

If you're using a mobile device that can provide an internet hotspot, it's time to turn on the hotspot and find the network name and password.

You need to know the network name and possibly the password to connect your Chromebook to the internet for the first time. Just follow these steps:

1. **Select your network from the list of networks shown.**

   Your Chromebook may detect and display several other nearby home or business networks. You can ignore them.

2. **If your Chromebook requests it, enter your network password.**

   After you select the network and enter a password, if applicable, the Wi-Fi bars onscreen fluctuate as your computer tries to connect. (Figure 1-3 shows the Wi-Fi signal icon.) After the connection is successfully established, the Continue button at the bottom of the dialog window becomes active.

   If your Chromebook does not successfully connect to the Wi-Fi network, you'll see the error message bad password and you can try entering the password again. You can also select a different Wi-Fi network if you prefer.

   You can view the Wi-Fi password you are typing by clicking the little eye symbol to the right of where you are typing in your password.

3. **Click the Connect button.**

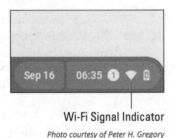

**FIGURE 1-3:**
The Wi-Fi signal icon.

Wi-Fi Signal Indicator

*Photo courtesy of Peter H. Gregory*

## Agreeing to the Terms of Service

You may see a message that says Your Connection is Not Private. This issue is not something to worry about at this point.

If you've installed software or activated a device within the last ten years, you've likely seen a terms-of-service agreement. You can accept it by following these steps:

1. **Review the Terms of Service.**

2. **(Optional) When you're satisfied that you understand and agree to the terms, select or deselect the check box that sends usage stats back to Google.**

TIP

I recommend that you leave this box selected. The data is helpful for identifying and fixing bugs, creating new features, and making the Chromebook better for everyone! (Google and the NSA have all our information anyway, so why not?)

3. **Click Accept and Continue to move to the next step.**

## Adult or child user

Next, the Chromebook asks if you are an adult or if you are setting up the Chromebook for a child. If you are setting it up for a child, you can then configure various rules about usage of the Chromebook, such as what apps can be used, which websites and types of websites that can be visited, and time limits.

# Logging In for the First Time

To unlock all the features your Chromebook offers, you must first log in with a Google username and password. You can use your existing Google Account or create a new account at this time.

## Logging in using an existing Google Account

You can log in by using your Google Account username and password:

1. **Enter your Google Account username into the Username field.**

2. **Enter your Google Account password into the Password field.**

3. **Click Login.**

Your Chromebook informs you about Chrome Sync, where your bookmarks, history, passwords, and other things in the Chrome browser will be synced across your Chromebook and other devices where you use the Chrome browser.

TIP

If you have an Android phone associated with your Google Account, you'll be able to agree to use certain features, such as unlocking your Chromebook with your Android phone. Sounds pretty cool to me.

This completes the initial login process.

**REMEMBER**

If your Google Account uses Google Authenticator or Google Advanced Protection for logging in to Google, you'll need to log in to your Chromebook using those services for the first time. If this is your situation, your first login to your new Chromebook will be like logins you've done in the past on other computers.

## Creating a new Google Account

You can create a Google Account by following these steps:

1.  **Under the userid field, click the More Options link; then click the Create Account option.**

    The Chrome web browser launches and takes you to a set of pages where you can create your Google Account. Google asks you for your name, birth date, gender, and email address.

2.  **Complete each page and click Next.**

    On this screen, Google wants to verify that you are a real human being. I assume that you are!

3. **Enter your phone number and whether you'd rather be called or texted, and click Next.**

   Google will contact you in the manner you selected to provide you with a verification code. You can skip this step (and the next one) if you want. However, I suggest you provide a phone number, as this would be needed if you need to recover your Google Account.

4. **Enter the verification code and click Continue.**

5. **Review the privacy agreement and other agreements and agree.**

Pay attention to the agreement options. For instance, your Chromebook can send your location to apps you may use later. Uncheck this if you don't want your Chromebook revealing where you are. Also, you can choose whether Google Assistant can view your screen if you need help, and whether you want to use the "Hey Google" activated assistant. I checked No, but your preference may vary.

You may be shown a Chromebook tutorial known as ChromeVox. This accessibility feature reads the contents of the screen to you. Watch it if you like, or click Exit Tutorial to skip it.

You are now logged in to your Chromebook.

## Using Chromebook as a guest

Logging in to your Google Account allows you to use all of Chromebook's functionality. However, you can still access many of these functions without logging in. Chromebook allows you to use the device as a guest by selecting the Browse as Guest option.

**TIP**

Letting a friend or family member use your Chromebook for a while is a great use of Chromebook's Guest feature.

If you browse the Chromebook as a guest and then later decide to register or log in as a user, you first need to exit Guest mode. You can log out by clicking the status area (on the bottom-right of your screen, where you see the time, battery, and Wi-Fi status) and selecting Exit Guest from the top of the list. (See Figure 1-4.) Exit Guest takes you back to the login screen.

**FIGURE 1-4:**
The Exit Guest button.

*Illustration courtesy of Peter H. Gregory*

# Transitioning to a Chromebook from Mac, Linux, or Windows

Transitioning from a Mac, Linux, or Windows computer requires a few easy steps outlined in the following list. All these items are covered later in this book:

>> **Get a Google Account.** The section "Creating a new Google Account," earlier in this chapter, shows you how to get a Google Account. Your Google Account is the key to nearly everything you do on your Chromebook moving forward.

>> **Move your files.** In Chapter 6, you can find out how to access your Chromebook hard drive, external storage, and Google Drive (where most of your files will reside after you make the leap to Chromebook).

>> **Get your Chrome bookmarks.** If you've signed in while using the Chrome web browser on other devices, your bookmarks, apps, and extensions will come with you to your new Chromebook! I cover bookmarks in Chapter 3.

>> **Find new apps.** Your Chromebook comes with several applications in your Launcher by default. You can, however, add new apps by navigating to the Chrome Web Store and adding them to your menu. In Chapter 5, you can look at some of the existing apps on your Chromebook and discover ways to locate and add new apps that are useful to you.

# Where to Go Next

Now that you've completed the basics of setting up your Chromebook and logging in, what would you like to do next? Here are a few ideas:

» Find out more about using your Chromebook. Go to Chapter 2.

» Discover more about the Chrome browser. Go to Chapter 3.

» Download and use other Chromebook apps. Go to Chapter 5.

» Use office tools to create documents and worksheets. Go to Part 2.

» Start working with music, photos, videos, and ebooks. Go to Part 3.

» Explore advanced features (are you ready?). Go to Part 4.

A last word: If you find your initial Chromebook experience difficult or frustrating, don't give up! You'll soon develop "muscle memory" for common functions, and before long, you'll love the sheer simplicity and ease of use of your Chromebook.

# Chapter **2**

# Working with the Chromebook Desktop

The Chromebook desktop is displayed after you turn on and log in to your Chromebook. The desktop is a visual interface that uses a system of windows and controls to organize and manage applications, data, and files. You interact with the desktop by using a mouse, touchpad, keyboard, touch screen, or your voice. Your desktop has a launching point from which you can manually navigate your computer's apps and files. Other operating systems have similar launching points: Microsoft Windows uses the *taskbar*, and Macs have the *dock*. On your Chromebook, this launching button is called the *Launcher*, and the region at the bottom of your screen is called the *shelf*.

In this chapter, you explore the Chromebook desktop, Launcher, status area, and shelf. You discover how to find, add, and organize apps, as well as how to modify basic Chromebook settings and navigate the Chromebook window system.

If you're using ChromeOS for the first time, remember to be patient. Soon, your Chromebook will feel as comfortable as your favorite shoes!

# Accessing the Chromebook Shelf

The *shelf* is where all the magic happens on your Chromebook. Your shelf is customized specifically to you. To access it, however, you must first log in to your Chromebook with your Google username and password (refer to Chapter 1 for instructions on creating a Google Account and logging in).

**REMEMBER**

Logging in takes you out of *Guest mode*. When you're in Guest mode, you can't install apps or permanently customize your Chromebook, so it's of limited use. However, Guest mode is a great way to give your friends and family access to your Chromebook without fear of them changing or manipulating your data or personalized settings.

Okay, now that you're logged in, find a row of icons lined up along the bottom of the screen. This area is the *shelf*, which appears by default at the bottom of the screen. You *can* change the location of your shelf, as described in Chapter 17, but for now, just leave it. A quick tour of the shelf reveals two groupings of icons: one on the left and one on the right (see Figure 2-1):

>> The icons on the left include

- **The Launcher (on the far lower left of the screen):** This icon looks like a white circle and functions like the Start button in Windows or the Apple key on Macs. Click the Launcher icon, and a collection of app icons appears, arranged in a grid. Click any icon to launch its app. Click the up-arrow on the screen, and you'll see the entire Launcher as it fills the screen. Click the Launcher once again to close it entirely.

- **App shortcut icons (immediately to the right of the Launcher):** For convenience, you can place any of the apps you see in the Launcher on your shelf. By default, your Chromebook has a few popular app shortcuts already installed on the shelf. You can add or remove any of these as you like.

>> The group of icons on the right is referred to as the *status area.* These icons include the following:

- Clock

- Wi-Fi signal indicator

- Battery icon (indicates battery charge)

- Notifications (if any)

**REMEMBER**

The appearance of the figures on your Chromebook is likely to differ a bit from the illustrations from my Chromebooks in this book. Don't worry if yours are not exactly like mine. In most cases, the differences won't matter at all.

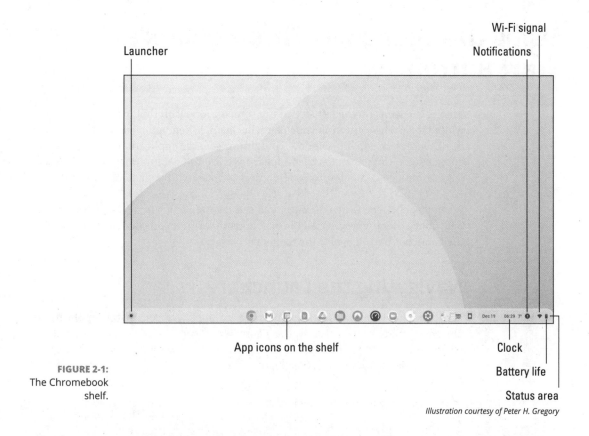

Launcher

Wi-Fi signal

Notifications

App icons on the shelf

Clock

Battery life

Status area

**FIGURE 2-1:**
The Chromebook
shelf.

*Illustration courtesy of Peter H. Gregory*

## CONQUERING THE DESKTOP

With your desktop, you can run programs and create, edit, and otherwise manipulate files by dragging, dropping, and clicking filenames or icons. However, this type of functionality wasn't always the case. Did you know that the first desktop — the graphical user interface (GUI) kind of desktop, not the physical kind — was created back in 1973 by Xerox? This version of the desktop, known first as the Xerox Alto and then later as the Xerox Star, never really took off because the devices and software were too expensive. Microsoft and Apple took note of the innovation, and in the 1980s, both companies rolled out their own versions — Windows and Macintosh System 1 respectively. A parallel effort at MIT resulted in the functionally similar X-Windows system used on Unix computers and today on Linux computers.

The desktop was a revolutionary approach of interacting with a computer because it simplified things (for most people, anyway) by making things visual. These days, of course, the desktop is a staple of all major operating systems, but in the early days of computing, users could interface with computers only by typing obscure commands in a command line. (Remember DOS and CP/M, if you're not too young?) The desktop was a quantum leap in accessibility, and it made possible the digital future we're all living in today.

# Using the Launcher: Chromebook's Start Button

Among the icons on the left side of the screen is one icon that looks like a black or white circle. This button is your Launcher icon. When you click on it, you reveal the *Launcher*, a pop-up window containing several applications. Until you add applications, the only apps that appear here are the default ones that come with your Chromebook and any apps already associated with your Google Account.

When you click the Launcher once, you see several application icons with a search field above them. These are all Chrome apps that run if you click them. If you click the Launcher button again, the Launcher closes.

## Navigating the Launcher

The Launcher window displays the first 20 apps. As you install applications, ChromeOS adds more space to the Launcher to contain your application icons. When you have more than 20 applications, scroll through the Launcher to see additional application icons. (See Figure 2-2.)

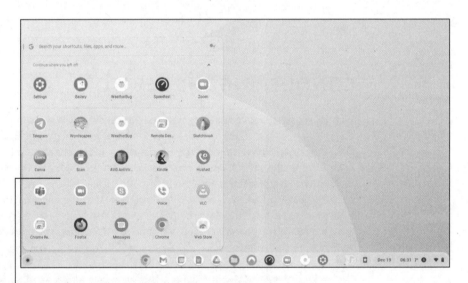

**FIGURE 2-2:**
The Chromebook Launcher.

Scroll up and down to see all the icons.

*Illustration courtesy of Peter H. Gregory*

## Organizing Launcher Icons

If you like to keep things in a particular order, like the way you can arrange glasses and dishes in your cupboard, then you will appreciate being able to organize the icons on your Launcher as you see fit. Simply click applications and drag them around inside the Launcher window until they are in the order you desire. You can move the app icons in the Launcher by following these steps:

**1.** Open the Launcher by clicking the Launcher icon.

**2.** Click and hold the application icon that you want to move.

**3.** Drag the icon to where you would like to place your selected application.

Wait patiently until the window shifts.

**4.** Drop the app icon in the desired location.

When you are done moving app icons around, you can close the Launcher by clicking the Launcher icon on your shelf.

# Setting Up App Shortcuts

Next to the Launcher icon, you see several additional application icons. These are shortcuts to frequently used applications on your Chromebook. If you frequently use applications like Gmail, Calendar, Docs, or Drive, adding shortcuts to these apps on your shelf is a great way to streamline your user experience.

## Pinning app shortcuts to your shelf

You can add application icons to your shelf by following these steps:

**1.** Click the Launcher icon.

The Launcher appears.

**2.** Navigate to the application you want to add directly to your shelf.

Finding the application may require moving among Launcher windows.

**3.** While holding down the Alt key, click the application icon.

If you are using your Chromebook's touchscreen, tap and hold the application icon for an entire second.

A menu with several options appears.

**4.** **Select Pin to Shelf from the list.**

Your application shortcut has been added to your shelf (see Figure 2-3).

**FIGURE 2-3:**
Pinning applica-
tion shortcuts to
your shelf.

A second option for pinning apps to your shelf is the drag-and-drop method. Simply click and hold the icon for any application you want to pin and drag it down to the shelf. You can easily move the icon to any position you desire. Then, just release the click to drop it in place.

After you pin an application to your shelf, you can place your icons in the order you desire by clicking and dragging icons left or right along the shelf.

Don't worry, pinning icons to your shelf doesn't remove the application from the Launcher. It merely creates an *additional* way for you to use the application so that you can quickly move among your frequently used applications.

**TIP**

It can take a little practice if you've never performed a drag-and-drop action before. Although it tends to be a bit easier to do using a mouse, you can also do it with your trackpad. Move the pointer to the object you want to move. At the lower-left corner of the trackpad, use your thumb to click and hold the object; then, keeping your thumb down, press your finger on the trackpad and keep pressing while moving it to drag the object to another part of the screen. Drop the object by lifting your thumb to release the click. Practice makes perfect!

# Removing app shortcuts from your shelf

You have a few options if you want to remove an application shortcut from your shelf. Here's one easy method:

**1. Hold the Alt key and click the application icon on the shelf.**

You see a pop-up menu with several options.

**2. Select Unpin to remove the icon from the shelf.**

Selecting Unpin doesn't delete the application from your machine; it just removes the shortcut from your shelf. You can still find it if you click the up-arrow in the Launcher.

Another easy method: Just click and drag the icon you want to remove from the shelf. (If you have a touchscreen, you can just tap and drag the icon off the shelf.)

# Getting the Scoop in the Status Area

On the lower right corner of your screen are a bunch of icons. This set of icons is called your *status area.* One of the icons in this group is nothing more than a circle with a number in it, and your number may be zero (or it may not appear at all). This icon is the *notification panel* (see Figure 2-4). If you click this icon, your notification window appears. Notifications can be many things, including

>> Calendar event reminders

>> Stock tickers

>> Sports scores

>> Weather updates

>> Email

>> Application updates

>> ChromeOS updates

Google selects its notifications by observing your behavior. As you use Google for repeated searches, Google starts to identify your common searches and automatically funnels those search results into your notification panel.

Notifications

**FIGURE 2-4:**
The Chromebook
notification panel.

For instance, say you're a huge Washington Huskies fan and you keep up with the scores by conducting Google searches. Google picks up on your search habits and begins sending scores automatically to your notification panel.

TIP

The notification icon disappears if you have no new unread notifications.

Next to your notifications is the *Settings area.* This area contains the current time, a Wi-Fi signal indicator, and a battery indicator. Click anywhere in this area to reveal your Settings page. On your Settings page, you can make some basic settings tweaks that include

>> **Wi-Fi:** Click the Wi-Fi symbol to turn Wi-Fi on and off. When Wi-Fi is turned on, the icon is blue; when it is off, it's gray. Click below the Wi-Fi icon to view available wireless networks. If you're already connected to a network and want to view information specific to that connection, simply click the network. A window will pop up, revealing additional and advanced information.

>> **Bluetooth:** In the Bluetooth section of the page, you can enable or disable your Bluetooth signal. In this section, you can browse Bluetooth devices and manage your connections.

>> **Notifications:** Click here to configure which applications are permitted to show notifications and which ones you don't want to hear from. You can also turn off all notifications by clicking Do Not Disturb.

» **Night Light:** This feature dims the blue parts of the display, making them appear more reddish. You can turn this feature off and on, or set up a schedule such as "sunset to sunrise." I talk more about using Night Light in Chapter 17.

» **Cast:** If you have a Google Chromecast device or a monitor with a built-in casting feature, you can use the device or television as an additional monitor to play a movie.

» **Volume:** Easily control volume levels by dragging the slider to the right to increase the volume level and to the left to decrease it.

» **Brightness:** You can control the brightness of the Chromebook display. (Your Chromebook's keyboard likely also has screen brightness keys.)

As you navigate through the different basic settings windows, you always have the option to navigate back to the main Settings page by clicking the left-pointing arrow at the top of the settings window. If you're in the Wi-Fi window, for example, the button at the bottom will look like < Network. If you're in the Bluetooth window, the button will be < Bluetooth. If you want to get into the advanced settings, you can click Settings in the settings panel window.

# Taking Charge of Window Controls

The other main feature of your Chromebook desktop is the window system. When opened, almost all applications will load into a system of windows, much as they would on a Windows or Apple computer.

The following list describes the window controls (shown in Figure 2-5) on your Chromebook. Each window has a little set of controls in the window's upper-right corner.

» **Close:** You can close a window by clicking the X, which is the right-most window control. Closing a window causes the app to exit.

» **Maximize:** You can maximize a window (so that it fills the entire screen) by clicking the middle button that looks like a little box. To return a window to its original size, click the middle control again (which now looks like one box over another).

» **Minimize:** You can minimize a window by clicking the little "underline" button, which is the leftmost of the three controls. Minimizing a window sets it aside, metaphorically; the app is still running. To get it back, click its icon on the shelf, and the window reappears just as it was before.

FIGURE 2-5:
Controls to
minimize,
maximize, and
close a window.

Maximize window

Minimize window | Close window

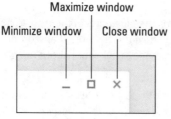

*Illustration courtesy of Peter H. Gregory*

# Multitasking with Multiple Windows

You can multitask by activating several application windows at one time. You can quickly switch from one window to another using one of two methods:

>> **Alt+Tab:** While holding down the Alt key, press the Tab key. A bar appears across the screen with a smaller version of each window. Each time you press Tab, the selection moves to the next window. You can press Tab repeatedly to view all the active windows. When you reach the window you want to view, release both the Alt and Tab keys (see Figure 2-6).

>> **Select from the shelf:** Look at the application icons on the shelf. Each one that is currently running has a small dash beneath it. Just click the icon whose window you want to view. It's that simple!

Your Chrome browser can have two or more tabs. If you want to make a browser tab into a stand-alone window, you can do so by following these steps:

1. **Locate the tab that you want to break out.**

2. **Click and hold the desired tab.**

   This brings the tab to the front and makes it active.

3. **Drag the tab in any direction until it pops out into its own window, as shown in Figure 2-7.**

4. **Release the click.**

While on the subject of window controls, I need to cover one more topic. If, for any given application, you have several windows open, you have an additional way to identify those windows and navigate to the one you want. For example, if you have three different Chrome browser windows and want to open one of them, click the Chrome browser icon on the shelf. The Chrome browser window opens if only one window is active in the app. If, however, two or more windows are active, your Chromebook displays a list of them, as shown in Figure 2-8. Click the one you want to open, and voilà!

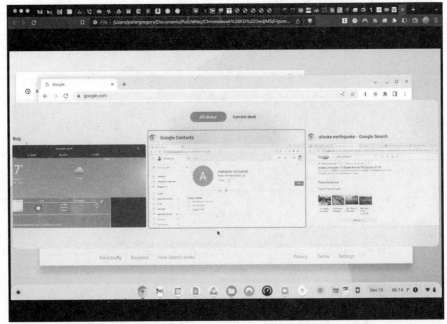

**FIGURE 2-6:** Navigating among applications using Alt+Tab.

*Illustration courtesy of Peter H. Gregory*

Tab dragged out to its own window

**FIGURE 2-7:** The Browser tab is now a new, separate window.

*Illustration courtesy of Peter H. Gregory*

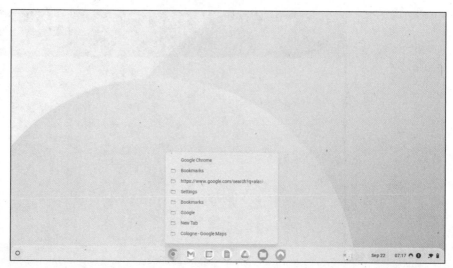

FIGURE 2-8:
Selecting one of
multiple windows
to open.

*Illustration courtesy of Peter H. Gregory*

# Setting Up a Printer

The world is not quite paperless; sometimes you need a hard copy. For example, you may need to print and sign a legal agreement, or you may want to print a recipe to jot notes on.

Many kinds of printers are available, and you have several ways to set them up. I cover the basics here.

**TIP**

When you shop for a new printer to work with your Chromebook, if you stick with major brands (Brother, Canon, Epson, HP, and Lexmark, for example), chances are your printer and your Chromebook will get along just fine. Still, it's probably wise to ensure that any new printer you are thinking of buying will work with your Chromebook with no fuss. It's a good idea to ask a salesperson, read the specs, and read reviews.

## Direct connect printing

Direct connect, the easiest type of printing to set up, involves connecting a USB cable from your printer to your Chromebook. If the instructions that came with your printer vary from the steps here, definitely go with the printer's instructions! Otherwise, follow these steps:

1. **Turn on the printer and connect the USB cable from your printer to a USB plug on your Chromebook.**

2. **On your Chromebook screen, click the status area to open the Settings view and then click the Settings icon, which looks like a tiny gear near the top-right corner.**

   The Settings window opens.

3. **Scroll all the way down in the Settings window and click Advanced.**

   You see the Advanced settings section in the Settings window.

4. **Keep scrolling until you find Print and scan; then click Printers. (See Figure 2-9.)**

5. **Click the stylized "+" sign to the right of Add printer.**

   The Add a Nearby Printer window appears and your printer should appear in a list. (Your printer may be the only one on the list.)

6. **Click the printer that is shown.**

   It should match the make and model of the printer that your Chromebook is connected to.

7. **Click Save.**

   That's all you should need to do.

**FIGURE 2-9:**
Setting up a local printer.

*Illustration courtesy of Peter H. Gregory*

You can rename your printer if you want. For example, I wanted to change my printer's name from "HP Officejet 4630 Series (USB)" to something more useful for me, so I called mine "Office Printer." To change your printer's name, click the three vertical dots to the right of the printer and then, in the little window that appears, click Edit to open the Edit Printer window. Enter your printer's new name in the Printer Name field and click Save. (You should not need to change anything else in the Edit Printer window.)

## Wi-Fi printing

Several brands of printers support Wi-Fi printing so you don't have to connect a USB cable to your printer. One great advantage of having a Wi-Fi–supported printer is that you can print from almost anyplace in your home or office. Be sure to follow your printer's setup instructions for this type of printing in case they vary from the procedure outlined in this section. Here are the basics of setting up Wi-Fi printing on your Chromebook:

1. **Turn on your printer and follow its setup instructions to connect it to your Wi-Fi network.**

   Have your Wi-Fi network identifier and password handy. Your Wi-Fi network identifier is the network name to which you connect your Chromebook in Chapter 1.

2. **On your Chromebook screen,** click the status area to open the Settings view and then click the Settings icon (which looks like a tiny gear near the top right corner of the status window).

   The Settings window appears.

3. **Scroll all the way down in the Settings window and click Advanced.**

   The Advanced settings section in the Settings window appears.

4. **Keep scrolling until you find Print and scan; then click Printers.**

   (Refer to Figure 2-9.)

5. **Click Add Printer.**

   The Add a Nearby Printer window appears. Your printer should appear in a list. Check whether the printer is still turned on if you don't see it.

6. **Click the printer that matches the make and model of the printer your Chromebook is connected to.**

7. **Click Save.**

   That's all you should need to do.

Chapter **3**

# Surveying the Chrome Browser

I n late 2008, after a brief beta run, Google released the first consumer-ready version of its Chrome web browser. Google's goal was to create an alternative to popular web browsers such as Internet Explorer (now known as Microsoft Edge), Safari, and Firefox. The application was launched globally in 43 languages.

Chrome's stripped-down approach, speed, and extensibility proved to be popular with many users, from dabblers to the technologically savvy. It was quickly developed for other operating systems like macOS and Linux, as well as mobile platforms Android and iOS. Today, Chrome accounts for over 65 percent of all web browsing on the internet.

At their core, web browsers are nothing more than vehicles for surfing the web. In this chapter, you take an in-depth look at the Chrome browser for Chromebook. Find out how to create and manage your bookmarks, manage your browser history, and surf without leaving a record in your browser history.

# Navigating the Chrome Browser

Before breaking down the Chrome browser into its different pieces, let me give you a quick tour. Figure 3-1 shows an open Chrome browser window. At the top-left corner is the tab — in this figure, the only tab — featuring the word *Google* and the Google icon; the navigation buttons are below the tab. The navigation bar is to the right, referred to as the *Omnibox*.

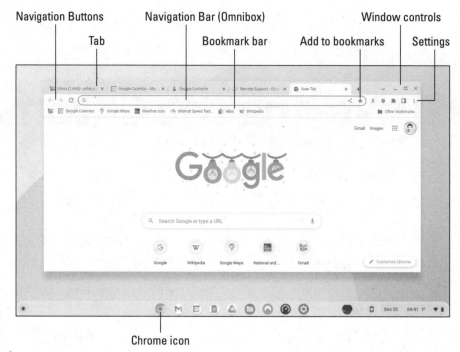

Illustration courtesy of Peter H. Gregory

**FIGURE 3-1:**
The layout of the Chrome browser.

On the far right of the Omnibox is an icon that looks like three little dots — the Settings button. Below the Omnibox is the bookmark bar, and below the bookmark bar is where web pages are loaded.

## Sizing the Chrome window

To launch Google Chrome on your Chromebook, just click the Chrome icon in the bottom left of your screen. (Refer to Figure 3-1.)

The first time you use Chrome, it opens only one browser window containing one tab. You can launch additional windows by holding the Ctrl key and clicking the Chrome icon again, or by pressing Ctrl+N.

Instead of opening additional windows, consider using multiple tabs within a single window to achieve the same effect. (I introduce tabs in the next section.)

You can close an open Chrome browser window by clicking the X-shaped Close button in the top-right corner of the browser window (as I discuss in Chapter 2) or by pressing Ctrl+W.

When a window is maximized, it takes up the entire screen of your Chromebook. If you want Chrome to take up only a portion of your screen, you have a few options. These include

>> **Restoring a window to a non-maximized size:** You can de-maximize a window by clicking the box-shaped Maximize icon at the top-right of the browser window, or by clicking the header space between the tab and the Maximize button. Either method shrinks your window, allowing you to move it around on the screen.

>> **Minimizing a window:** *Minimizing* shrinks the active window, so it's hidden from the screen but not closed. Minimizing is helpful when you want to open a different application or perform some function on your Chromebook without having the Chrome window in the way. To minimize a window, hover your cursor over the Minimize button until a drop-down menu of options appears. Then click the button in the middle.

If you have only one Chrome window open, you can also minimize it by clicking the Chrome icon on your shelf.

## Working with tabs

Using Chrome window tabs is much easier and more efficient than opening and managing multiple windows. The tab system is a lot like tabs on folders in your filing cabinet. Take a look at Figure 3-2 to see what Chrome tabs look like. You can have one website open per tab, and an almost limitless number of tabs in one Chrome window.

When you launch Chrome or open a new Chrome window, one tab is opened. To open additional tabs, click the New Tab button to the right of the last tab in your browser window.

Multiple tabs make it easier to surf the web without losing your place. You can also open additional tabs by pressing Ctrl+T. You can close a tab by clicking the X in the right corner of the tab or by pressing Ctrl+W.

Tab close buttons

New tab button

**FIGURE 3-2:**
Chrome
browser tabs.

The current tab color is different from all others

*Illustration courtesy of Peter H. Gregory*

## Using the Omnibox and the navigation buttons

Chrome's Omnibox and navigation buttons allow you to surf the web. They're located at the top of the Chrome browser window. (Refer to Figure 3-1.) In the Omnibox, you can enter a URL (such as www.bbc.com) or a search term or phrase (such as "hardware stores in Seattle"). Chrome and other browsers work in this way.

From left to right, the navigation buttons found to the left of the Omnibox are

>> **Back:** Allows you to navigate to the web page you were on previous to the current page.

>> **Forward:** Takes you forward one page in your browser history. Chrome isn't psychic, however; this button remains grayed-out and inaccessible until you've used the Back button. Go backward one page, and clicking the Forward button returns you to your original page.

>> **Refresh:** Reloads your current page. Sometimes you may want to use the Refresh button to load new information that may be in the process of launching. Have you ever been tracking a package in shipment? You might click the Refresh button repeatedly to view updates on the progress of your shipment. (We are all guilty of this.)

## Saving your place with the bookmark bar

Just as a bookmark helps you remember your place in a book you're reading, Chrome's bookmarks allow you to quickly pick up where you left off. If you find a place on the internet to which you want to return in the future, you can create a bookmark to get there with a click of the mouse. With Chrome bookmarks, you don't have to write down a URL or record it somewhere else (like a document or worksheet); let Chrome remember it for you!

To create a bookmark in Chrome, navigate to the web page you want to save and click the star icon on the right side of the Omnibox. This action automatically adds the site's name and address to your bookmarks list in the Bookmark Manager. If your bookmark bar is enabled, and if you have space available, your new bookmark also appears there.

You can also bookmark a page simply by pressing Ctrl+D while on the page you want to bookmark.

Chrome can store an almost unlimited number of bookmarks in your Bookmark Manager. Chrome also allows you to save a small number of bookmarks in the bookmark bar in the browser window. The bookmark bar is located directly under the navigation buttons and Omnibox. As shown in Figure 3-3, the bookmark bar has limited space. Keep your best bookmarks — the places you visit most frequently — in the bookmark bar.

**FIGURE 3-3:**
The bookmark bar has limited space.

*Illustration courtesy of Peter H. Gregory*

If you can't see the bookmark bar, it may not be turned on. To turn it on, follow these steps:

1. **Click the Settings button on the right side of the Omnibox.**

   The Settings menu appears.

2. **Hover your cursor over the Bookmarks option in the Settings menu.**

   A submenu appears.

3. **Select the Show Bookmarks Bar option.**

   The bookmark bar appears in your browser window.

Now your favorite places on the internet are only one click away!

You can instantly turn on and off the bookmarks bar by typing Ctrl+Shift+B.

The Chrome browser also remembers where you visit, and Chrome helps you in yet another way. To see how, click the + (plus sign) icon in the Chrome browser to add another tab. Chrome displays icons for up to eight recent or frequently visited sites. Just click one of those to visit the page. (See Figure 3-4.) You can also hover

over any of the icons and click the *x* in the top-right corner of the box that appears around it to remove it from the list.

If, when you open a new tab, you see the Google search bar, click Enable Most Visited Sites to show a grid of icons for websites you visit often.

**FIGURE 3-4:**
Chrome can show recent sites in a new blank tab.

*Illustration courtesy of Peter H. Gregory*

# Customizing and Controlling Chrome

You can access many of Chrome's functions and advanced settings in the Settings menu. The Settings menu contains quite a bit of general-purpose functionality. Within the Settings menu, you can

>> Launch a new tab

>> Open a new window

>> Open a new incognito window (more on this in the section "Going incognito," later in the chapter)

>> View your browser history to find a page you visited in the past

>> View files you have downloaded in the past

>> Access and manage bookmarks

>> Zoom in to make web pages appear larger or smaller

>> Print the current page you are viewing

- » Cast the page to another device, such as a television
- » Find text on a page
- » Copy and paste text
- » View and change Chrome and Chromebook settings
- » Get help

The Settings menu has features and settings for advanced users and developers. With these options, you can

- » View or save the HTML source of a web page
- » Clear browsing data
- » Manage Chrome browser extensions
- » Inspect web page elements
- » View the internal workings of the Chromebook with Task Manager
- » Take a screenshot
- » Use developer tools

REMEMBER

If you're unsure how to do something in the Chrome browser, the Help page is a good place to start looking.

You can access the Help page by clicking the Settings button on the right side of the Omnibox, clicking Help, and then clicking Get Help. The Settings button looks like a vertical stack of three lines, as shown in Figure 3-5.

## Managing bookmarks

The Bookmark Manager is a tool in the Chrome browser used to manage your bookmarks. To access the Bookmark Manager, click the Settings button to the right of the Omnibox and then hover your cursor over the Bookmarks option in the menu that appears. In the resulting submenu, select Bookmark Manager, as shown in Figure 3-6.

TIP

You can instantly access the Bookmark Manager by typing Ctrl+Shift+O (the letter O, not the number zero).

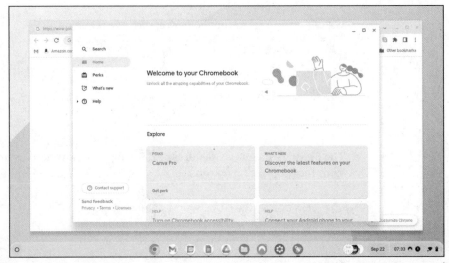

FIGURE 3-5:
The Help page.

*Illustration courtesy of Peter H. Gregory*

Bookmarks Organize button

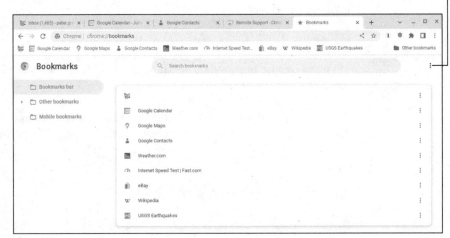

FIGURE 3-6:
The Chrome
browser
Bookmark
Manager.

*Illustration courtesy of Peter H. Gregory*

In the Bookmark Manager, you can perform the following actions:

>> Add or edit bookmarks

>> Delete bookmarks

>> Organize bookmarks into folders

>> Add or remove bookmarks to the bookmarks bar

>> Search for saved bookmarks

The Bookmark Manager window is divided into two main sections: folders for organizing bookmarks on the left and the bookmarks on the right.

You can add new folders to the section on the left by following these steps:

1. **In the Bookmark Manager, click the Organize button to the right of the Search field, as shown in Figure 3-6.**

   (Make sure you click the Bookmark Organize button, not the Chrome browser organizer button!)

   A menu of options appears.

2. **Click Add new folder.**

   A new folder is added to your folder list.

3. **Type in the desired name for your folder and click Save.**

   Your new folder is saved in the Bookmark Manager.

The bookmark folder contents pane is on the right side of your Bookmark Manager window. In this pane, you see bookmarks and subfolders. You can organize your bookmarks in this pane by dragging the bookmarks to any position you want. If you want to add a bookmark to one of the folders in the leftmost pane, just click and drag the bookmark to the desired folder.

To delete a bookmark, simply select it and hit the Delete key.

## Managing your history and downloads

As you surf the internet, you create a breadcrumb trail of activity, otherwise known as your browsing history. The Chrome browser stores your history so you can go back to a page you may not have bookmarked. If you cannot remember a site you want to revisit or your Chrome browser window unexpectedly closes while surfing the web, Chrome remembers all the websites that were loaded into tabs and windows prior to closing.

In addition to tracking the websites you visit, Chrome manages the files downloaded with your Chrome browser. The Download Manager keeps track of files downloaded and logs where they reside on your Chromebook. The Download Manager also gives you options for re-downloading lost files and pausing large downloads for resuming later.

There are advantages to keeping track of your internet and download history. For one thing, it can improve your web-surfing experience: Sometimes, when you visit a website, Chrome saves information about that website on your computer so that it will load faster the next time you visit it. Also, many parents use internet history to keep track of their children's web-surfing habits to keep their kids safe.

To view your internet history, click the Settings button. In the Settings menu that appears, select the History option to open the History page, as shown in Figure 3-7.

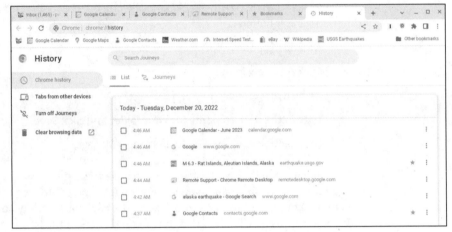

FIGURE 3-7:
The Chrome browser History page.

*Illustration courtesy of Peter H. Gregory*

TIP

You can also instantly access the History page by clicking Ctrl+H.

The Chrome History page is broken up into three distinct sections:

>> **The Search History box:** The top of the page contains the search box for quickly searching through your browsing history.

>> **Device-specific history:** The section below the search box contains the recent web history grouped by the browsing device.

REMEMBER

When you log in to your Chromebook, Chrome imports all your browsing data, bookmarks, and plug-ins to your device. If you use the Chrome browser on your smartphone or another computer, Google tracks your web history and makes it accessible wherever you log in to a Chrome browser.

>> **Complete browsing history:** Below the device-specific section of the History page is your complete browsing history from each of your devices, combined into one list and organized by date and time.

A menu icon on the right side of each history entry looks like three little dots. Clicking this icon allows you to remove the site from your history.

# Erasing your browsing history

Before you sell your computer (or loan it to someone else), you may want to remove any personal information first. Your browsing history certainly qualifies as personal information. To erase your entire browser history, just follow these steps:

1. **On the History page, click the Clear browsing data link.**

   A window with several options appears, as shown in Figure 3-8.

2. **(Optional) Click All time to select from the drop-down list a time in your history you want to delete.**

   All time is typically the default.

3. **Select the Browsing history check box.**

   Deselect all remaining boxes, unless you want to remove those items as well.

   In addition to clearing your browsing history, you can clear out several other items by selecting their associated boxes. These items include

   - **Download history:** A list of files you have downloaded from internet sites.

   - **Cookies and other site data:** Small files that keep track of your login status and other preferences on websites.

   - **Cached images and files:** Images and other files that remain in your Chromebook, helping web pages you've visited before load faster if any large image files are unchanged.

   - **Passwords and other sign-in data:** If you instructed the Chrome browser to save any passwords you entered when logging in to various websites, you can clear them here.

   - **Auto-fill form data:** This is data such as your email address and home address, which Chrome can remember to make filling out forms easier and faster.

   - **Site data:** This data includes HTML5-enabled storage types such as application caches and application data associated with some websites.

   - **Hosted app data:** This includes data associated with any Chrome apps you have used.

   If you're browsing the web quite a bit, these collections of information can get rather large and begin eating up your available storage space. For this reason, try to periodically clear out that information.

4. **Click the Clear data button.**

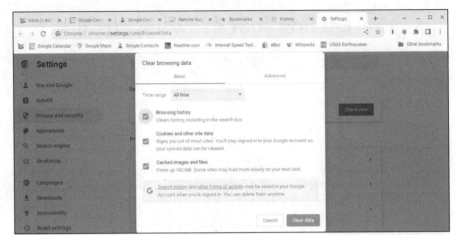

**FIGURE 3-8:**
The Clear
Browsing Data
window.

*Illustration courtesy of Peter H. Gregory*

## Going incognito

Sometimes you may want to browse without the worry of creating a trail of crumbs in your browser for someone to follow. You may be using a public computer or a computer that's not yours. Or maybe you're planning to surprise someone and don't want them to stumble across your surprise when they use the Chrome browser on your computer. Whatever your reason for wanting to not leave a history trail, Chrome gives you the option to go incognito.

Going incognito means opening an *incognito browser window*. This window is separate from any other open browser windows, and it functions differently. In an incognito browser, Chrome doesn't keep a record of the sites you visit or any files you download, and any cookies sent to an incognito browser are deleted when the browser is closed. Although Chrome doesn't keep records of your history in an incognito browser, your internet service provider, employer, or anyone else monitoring web traffic still can. An incognito browser window is simply a good way to surf the web without needing to manually clear the history from your account.

Follow these steps to open an incognito window in the Google Chrome browser:

1. **In Google Chrome, click the Settings button to the right of the Omnibox (search field).**

   Chrome Settings opens in a new browser tab.

2. **Click New Incognito Window.**

   Your incognito browser window opens.

You can also type Ctrl+Shift+N to open a new incognito window.

TIP

You know you're incognito if you see the silhouette of a person wearing a hat and sunglasses in the top-left corner of your Chrome browser window, as shown in Figure 3-9.

The Incognito icon

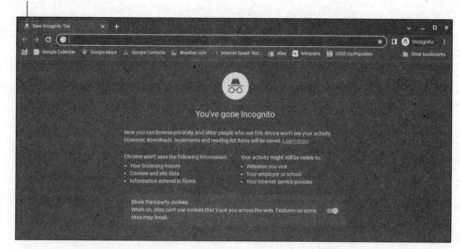

**FIGURE 3-9:**
The incognito window.

WARNING

When your browser is in incognito mode, your browser and your computer do not keep a record of your browsing. However, the sites you visit track you the same way they do when you're not in incognito mode. If you want to visit a website without being tracked, go to Chapter 18 to find out more.

# Changing Search Engine Providers

By default, Google is the search engine used when you type any search term in the Omnibox (search field) in your Chrome browser. For various reasons, you may prefer to use another search engine, such as Yahoo!, Bing, DuckDuckGo, and hundreds of others. There are choices associated with many different retail stores, for instance — setting your browser search engine to one of these if you are a frequent shopper may be handy.

To manage and change your Chrome browser search engine, follow these steps:

1. **Click the Settings button to the right of the Chrome browser Omnibox (search field).**

2. **Click Settings.**

3. **Click Search Engine.**

4. **Click Manage search engines and site search.**

   The Manage search engines and site search window appears, as shown in Figure 3-10. The Default search engines are those that are most often used. The Other search engines are additional search engines that you can also use.

5. **To select any of these search engines as your new default, click the More Actions button (three little dots to the right of the search engine name), and select Make Default.**

**FIGURE 3-10:**
Selecting a new default search engine.

*Illustration courtesy of Peter H. Gregory*

**TIP**

In your browser, the search engine used when you type searches into the Omnibox is identified by a small icon at the left of the Omnibox.

**TIP**

If the site you want to use as your default search engine does not appear in the list, you can bookmark the site and use the site directly for searching.

# Using Other Browsers

Other browsers exist besides Chrome, and they're available for your Chromebook.

Some people just prefer other browsers. For me, it's Firefox. I won't judge you, and I doubt anyone else will, either. Firefox has a great reputation as a reliable, well-performing browser.

To install the Firefox browser, follow these easy steps:

1. **Open the Play Store app.**

2. **In the search window, type Firefox.**

   You see a result that resembles Figure 3-11. Remember, Firefox is from Mozilla, and you should see that company name as the source for Firefox.

3. **Click Install.**

4. **When the installation is complete, click Open.**

   The Firefox browser starts.

5. **If you think you will want to use Firefox often, go to the shelf, Alt-click, and then click Pin to pin Firefox to the shelf.**

   This way, it's always there when you want to use it.

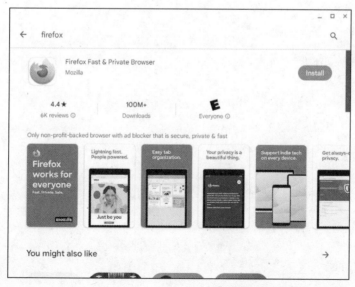

**FIGURE 3-11:**
Installing the
Firefox browser.

*Illustration courtesy of Peter H. Gregory*

Installing the Brave privacy web browser is just as simple as installing Firefox. Search for Brave browser in the Google Play app, click Install, and then click Open. Pin it to the shelf if you like.

TIP

The Firefox Focus web browser is popular with people who don't like to be tracked. Unlike Google Chrome, which sends information about your web surfing history to Google, Firefox Focus performs no tracking at all. However, using any browser (even in incognito mode) does not stop websites you visit from tracking your visits.

Chapter **4**

# Getting Your Hands on the Keyboard and Touchpad

t's hard telling whether Christopher Latham Sholes thought that his design and letter layout of the QWERTY keyboard would still be in use well into the 21st century. Regardless of his original intent, his legacy is alive and well today. When Sholes devised the layout and functionality of the keyboard that we use today, he intended to reduce typewriter jams and thereby speed up the typist. ("Glass half empty" people argue that the arrangement of letters really slowed down the typist and thus also reduced typewriter jams.)

Over the last 140 years, keyboard arrangement has changed very little. The basic layout of letters and numbers is the same; the only significant additions have been multipurpose keys like the ?/ key or the :; key. With the advent of word processors and computers, keys like Alt, Caps Lock, Num Lock, and Esc appeared, as well as function keys (you know, the F keys located at the top of some keyboards).

In this chapter, you explore the Chromebook keyboard and touchpad in all their glory. You discover how to customize the language of your keyboard, adjust the function of some keys, and save time with keyboard shortcuts. You also find out how to add an external mouse or keyboard and how to customize external devices.

# The Chromebook Keyboard at a Glance

Google didn't stray too far from the norm when it created the keyboard for the Chromebook. Figure 4-1 shows the keyboard on the Lenovo C330. Check out the top row: If you've done much work on a Mac or a PC, you probably remember the function keys (F1 through F12) used as shortcuts for various operating-system-specific functions. On Chromebook, the function keys are gone, replaced by a series of more intuitive keys called *shortcut keys*.

*Illustration courtesy of Peter H. Gregory*

Moving left to right, the top row of keys are as follows:

>> **Esc:** The "get me out of here" key, often used to stop something you're doing. In the web browser, it stops a page from loading.

>> **Back (indicated by a left arrow):** Navigates to the previous web page.

>> **Forward (indicated by a right arrow):** If you navigated back a page, use forward to navigate forward.

- » **Refresh/Reload (indicated by a circular arrow):** Reloads your current web page.

- » **Full Screen (indicated by a box with little arrows in two corners):** Makes the current window full screen, without the menu bar or other ancillary window controls.

- » **Reveal All Windows (indicated by a box with two bars to the right):** If you have multiple windows open, clicking this key reveals them all on the screen at one time so you can quickly click and navigate between windows. If you have more than one "desk," they will be shown at the top.

- » **Dim (indicated by a small sun):** If you're in a dark environment, you may want to reduce the screen's brightness so that the light emitted doesn't disturb others. This feature is also a great way to extend battery life if you're using your Chromebook with its internal battery, away from electric power.

- » **Brighten (indicated by a bigger sun):** If you're in a bright environment, you may want to brighten your screen because the screen may be too dim to see.

- » **Mute (indicated by a speaker with a slash through it):** Quickly eliminates all sound coming from your Chromebook.

- » **Volume Down (indicated by a speaker with a single sound wave):** Decreases your machine's volume incrementally.

- » **Volume Up (indicated by a speaker with two sound waves):** It's time to party. Turn up the volume!

- » **Lock:** Locks your Chromebook if you are stepping away and don't want others to tamper with it (requires that you have your screen lock setting turned on).

- » **Power:** Turns your Chromebook on and off.

Chromebooks generally have either the Lock key *or* the Power key, but not both.

**TIP**

The remaining keys on the keyboard are more or less what you'd expect — with the exception of the Search key, as shown in Figure 4-2.

As is typical of laptop manufacturers, you can find some minor variations in the layout of keys among various makes and models of Chromebooks. The two Chromebooks I use differ a bit, and you may notice that your keyboard varies slightly from what I show in Figure 4-1.

**REMEMBER**

Pushing the Search key opens the Launcher and puts your cursor in the search bar so you can quickly submit a search query. If you're searching for an application, like Gmail, type in **gmail**, press Enter, and your Chromebook opens the Chrome web browser and loads your Gmail. Maybe you want to quickly do a Google search. This search can even find one of your Google Docs documents. To do a Google search, enter your query in the search bar and press Enter. Chromebook opens a Chrome browser and loads Google.com (or your default search engine, if it's something else) with your search results teed up.

Search key

**FIGURE 4-2:**
The Chromebook
Search key.

The last thing you should notice about the keyboard is that the bottom row of keys includes no Start key, Fn key, or Command/Apple key. Instead, it simply has a Ctrl and Alt key on both sides of the spacebar. Ctrl and Alt are used quite a bit in short-cut combinations, so you may as well get used to having them there!

# Using Shortcut Key Combinations

In addition to shortcut keys, several key combinations perform a litany of tasks on your Chromebook without making you navigate and click your way through the ChromeOS menu system. Table 4-1 shows some of the more interesting and help-ful shortcut key combinations that will make your experience on a Chromebook more intuitive and efficient. (You can find a complete list in the Cheat Sheet for this book at www.dummies.com.)

**TABLE 4-1**     **Shortcuts for Chromebook, Chrome Browser, and Chromebook Apps**

| Shortcut | Function |
|---|---|
| Ctrl+Alt+/ | Open the list of available keyboard shortcuts |
| Ctrl+/ | Open Help center |
| Ctrl+Shift+W | Close the current application window |
| Alt+= | Maximize the application window |
| Alt+- | Minimize the application window |
| Alt+Tab | Go to the next window you have open |
| Alt+Shift+Tab | Go to the previous window you have open |
| Ctrl+Shift+= | Zoom in entire screen |
| Ctrl+Shift+- | Zoom out entire screen |
| Ctrl+Shift+0 (zero) | Reset screen zoom level |
| Reveal All Windows | Display all windows; click again to revert |
| Ctrl+Alt+(Reveal All Windows key) | Take a screenshot of a single window |
| Ctrl+(Reveal All Windows key) | Take a screenshot of the entire screen |
| Full Screen key | Toggle full screen |
| Alt+Shift+S | Open the Status area |
| Alt+Shift+N | Display notifications |
| Search key | Open/Close the Launcher |
| Search+L | Lock your Chromebook (requires your Chromebook password or PIN to unlock) |
| Ctrl+Alt+Shift+(Refresh Key) | Rotate current window |
| Ctrl+Shift+Q | Log out of your Chromebook |
| Shift+Search+L | Put your Chromebook in sleep mode |
| Ctrl+N | Open a new Chrome browser window |
| Ctrl+Shift+N | Open a new Chrome browser window in incognito mode |
| Ctrl+T | Open a new Chrome browser tab |
| Ctrl+click a link | Open the link in a new Chrome browser tab in the background |

*(continued)*

**TABLE 4-1** *(continued)*

| Shortcut | Function |
| --- | --- |
| Ctrl+H | Open the History page in the Chrome browser |
| Ctrl+P | Print your current page in the Chrome browser |
| Refresh/Reload or Ctrl+R | Reload your current page in the Chrome browser |
| Ctrl+D | Save your current web page as a bookmark in the Chrome Browser |
| Ctrl+J | Open the Downloads page in the Chrome browser |
| Ctrl+A | Select everything on the page |
| Ctrl+C | Copy selected content to the Clipboard |
| Ctrl+V | Paste content from the Clipboard |
| Ctrl+X | Cut (copies selected content to the Clipboard and deletes the content) |
| Alt+Search | Turn Caps Lock on and off |

When you see a keyboard shortcut like Ctrl+N, it means you should press the Ctrl and N keys at the same time. When you see a keyboard shortcut like Ctrl+Shift+N, press the Ctrl, Shift, and N keys at the same time.

When using external keyboards: If you use a Windows keyboard, use the Windows key when Chromebook specifies the Search key. If using a Mac keyboard, use the Command key for Chromebook's Search key.

The good news is that when you don't have this copy of *Chromebook For Dummies* nearby, you can use Google's built-in Help tool for quick reference. To access the visual helper, press Ctrl+Alt+/. The Keyboard Shortcuts window appears. The main categories of keyboard shortcuts appear on the left; select one and view the individual shortcuts on the right. (See Figure 4-3.) Use the Keyboard Shortcuts screen for a quick reminder as you use your Chromebook.

Don't be intimidated by the long list of keyboard shortcuts. You are not obligated to memorize any of them! Even everyday Chromebook experts use a small number of these shortcuts.

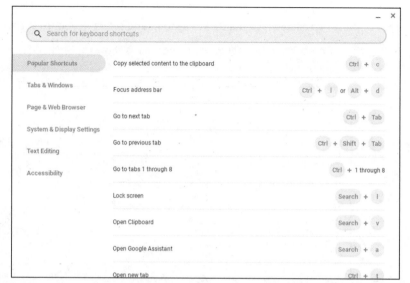

FIGURE 4-3:
The Keyboard
Shortcut Help
page.

# Configuring Keyboard Settings

The first time you turn on your Chromebook, you complete a basic setup process that includes selecting your language and desired keyboard language layout. You can edit this setting, among other keyboard settings, after the fact. To access your keyboard settings, follow these steps:

1. **Click the status area located in the bottom-right corner of your desktop.**

   You may recall that the status area contains your clock, Wi-Fi, and battery charge level indicator. It is also pictured in Figure 4-4.

   Your settings panel appears.

2. **Select Settings (click the gear).**

   A window launches and loads your Chromebook Settings page.

FIGURE 4-4:
The Chromebook
status area.

**3.** **Scroll down to the Device section and select Keyboard Settings.**

A Keyboard Settings window appears, as shown in Figure 4-5.

In the Keyboard Settings dialog box, you can

>> Reconfigure your Search, Alt, Ctrl, Esc, and Backspace keys.

>> Turn your shortcut keys into function keys (F keys).

>> Change your keyboard language configuration.

I discuss these options more fully in the next few sections.

## Reconfiguring keyboard keys

By default, the Alt, Ctrl, Search, Esc, and Backspace keys perform their intended tasks: You use the Alt and Ctrl keys in combination with other keys (and the track-pad or mouse) to access additional functionality, and you use the Search key to quickly access the search function in the Launcher, as well as to unlock additional functionality when used in combination with other keys. The Esc key is the "get me out of here" key with somewhat different meanings, depending on what you're doing at the time. You use the Backspace key to delete characters to the left of the cursor.

You can modify these keys so that they serve different purposes. For instance, you can change your Search key to behave like a Caps Lock or set your Ctrl key to act like the Alt key. To change the function of the Alt, Ctrl, and Search keys, follow these steps:

**1. Click the status area in the bottom right of your desktop.**

The settings panel appears.

**2. Click Settings (click the gear).**

Your Chromebook loads the Chromebook Settings page.

**3. Scroll down to the Device section and select Keyboard.**

The Keyboard dialog box appears.

**4. Click the corresponding box for the key you want to reconfigure.**

A drop-down list appears with options for changing the selected key's function, as shown in Figure 4-6.

**5. Make your desired changes and click OK.**

This feature allows you to configure your keyboard in a manner that is convenient to you. You can reconfigure your keys as many times as you like.

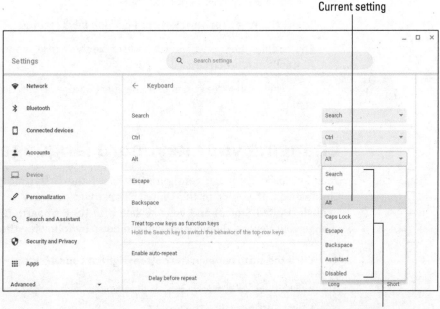

Current setting

List of available choices

*Illustration courtesy of Peter H. Gregory*

**FIGURE 4-6:**
Reconfiguring
the Alt key.

The reason why the Search, Ctrl, Alt, and other keys can be modified is that these keys appear in slightly different positions on different kinds of keyboards. As advanced users move between different computers and keyboards, this helps give everything the same feel.

## Turning shortcut keys into function keys

On most Chromebooks, the function keys (F1 to F10) common to Macs and PCs have been replaced by shortcut keys. Few Chromebook models come with F11 or F12, and depending on your model, you may not even have a reference to the function key on each shortcut key.

If you need function keys, don't fret; you can disable the shortcut keys and enable function keys in your keyboard settings by following these steps:

1.  **Click the status area in the bottom right of your desktop.**

    The settings panel opens.

2.  **Select Settings (click the gear).**

    Your Chromebook Settings page appears.

3.  **Scroll down to the Device section and select Keyboard Settings.**

    The Keyboard Settings dialog box appears.

4.  **Select the Treat Top-Row Keys as Function Keys setting.**

    This disables the shortcut functionality of the shortcut keys and enables their functions as function keys.

    To re-enable shortcut keys and disable function keys, simply deselect the setting.

## Changing your keyboard language

Your keyboard language configuration is set the first time you log into your Chromebook. If you're in the United States, you probably set your language to English (United States) and your keyboard to US Keyboard. If you would like to change your keyboard language, you can do so by following these steps:

1.  **Click the status area in the bottom right of your desktop.**

    The settings panel appears.

2.  **Select Settings (click the gear).**

    Your Chromebook Settings page loads.

**3.** **Click Device.**

**4.** **Click Keyboard.**

**5.** **Scroll down and click Change input settings.**

The Inputs and keyboards page appears, as shown in Figure 4-7.

**6.** **Click Add input methods to display available languages and keyboard options.**

You'll see a list of keyboard options in your current language and other languages, as shown in Figure 4-8. You'll see here that numerous types of keyboards are available for computers in various languages and layouts.

**7.** **Select the desired language and keyboard layout.**

**8.** **Click Add.**

The Inputs and keyboards page reappears with the keyboard layout and language you just selected. Note that your prior input method is still the one in use, indicated by the word "Enabled."

**9.** **Click on the new keyboard layout and language you selected to enable it.**

Your input method is changed to the new selection, indicated by the word "Enabled."

TIP

You can view additional settings specific to your selected keyboard layout and language, as shown in Figure 4-7.

Click here to select from available languages and layouts

Click here to view additional options

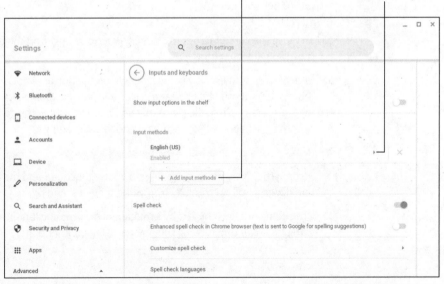

FIGURE 4-7:
The Input and
keyboards
dialog box.

*Illustration courtesy of Peter H. Gregory*

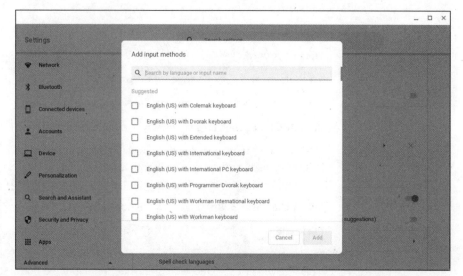

FIGURE 4-8:
The Add input methods dialog box to configure your language and keyboard layout.

# Using the Touchpad

Over the years, numerous different laptop mouse controllers have appeared. The trackball was cool until you got too much of your lunch stuck under the ball. The pointing stick was nice if you didn't mind that it was the size of a pencil eraser. Then came the touchpad. The touchpad on the Chromebook is a lot like most touchpads used on Windows, Linux, and Mac computers. Here are some basic gestures to get you going:

>> To move the cursor across the screen, place one finger on the touchpad and move it in any direction.

>> Click buttons and links by pressing down on the bottom left corner of the touchpad until you feel or hear a click. Or, if you like *tap-to-click* instead, just tap the touchpad to click. (Note that you need to enable this feature; see the upcoming section "Adjusting the touchpad click settings.)

>> Right-click by tapping with two fingers.

>> Scroll vertically by placing two fingers on the touchpad and moving them up and down; scroll horizontally by moving them left and right.

>> Drag items or highlight text by simultaneously pressing (and holding down) with one finger and moving the pointer using another finger.

# Finger gestures

Google aimed to make the Chromebook one of the easiest and most intuitive devices on the laptop market. Naturally, Google has included several advanced features for the touchpad to make using the Chromebook fluid and intuitive. Some of these features include the following:

» You can reveal all available windows by placing three fingers on the touchpad and swiping up simultaneously. You can click the desired window to make it active and bring it to the front. Or click anywhere else to revert to the prior view.

» While you are in the Chrome browser, use three fingers to swipe from left to right or right to left across the touchpad to go to a different browser tab.

# Touchpad and keyboard combinations

Google has implemented several ways to perform the same function, mainly to accommodate users transitioning from other devices. Some quick ways to use the touchpad and keyboard together are

» **Right-click:** Hold down the Alt key and click the touchpad. Right-clicking helps reveal common functions without using a menu or shortcut keys.

» **Highlight content:** Click one side of the content you want to highlight. Then, holding down the Shift key, click the other side of the content. The text is highlighted. This feature is handy when you want to copy a body of text. Alt+click the highlighted text to reveal options like Copy or Cut.

# Customizing Touchpad Settings

The touchpad is not without customization capability. You can change the touchpad settings from within the Chromebook Settings page. To open the touchpad settings, follow these steps:

1. **Click the status area in the bottom right of your desktop.**

   The settings panel opens.

2. **Select Settings (click the gear).**

   Your Chromebook Settings page opens.

3. **Select Device.**

4. **Select Touchpad.**

The Touchpad dialog box appears, as shown in Figure 4-9.

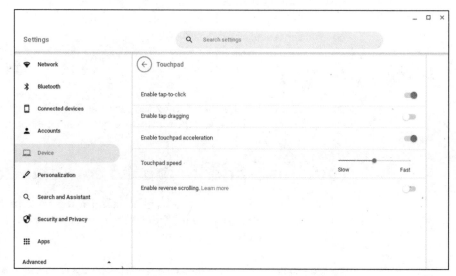

*Illustration courtesy of Peter H. Gregory*

**FIGURE 4-9:** Configuring the Touchpad.

In the Touchpad dialog box, you can make the following customizations:

>> Change the touchpad speed.

>> Adjust your click settings.

>> Change scroll directions.

I discuss these settings in the next few sections.

## Changing the touchpad speed

Found in the Device section of your Chromebook Settings page, the Touchpad Speed slider allows you to adjust the speed of your touchpad — that is, the distance your cursor moves onscreen in relation to the distance your finger travels on the touchpad. To move the cursor faster, move the slider to the right. To move it slower, move the slider to the left. Figure 4-9 shows the Touchpad speed control.

TIP

Note that this setting takes immediate effect. Move the cursor around a bit to see how it feels. Move the slider left or right to adjust to your liking.

## Adjusting the touchpad click settings

Clicking the touchpad requires you to press down on the bottom half of the touchpad until you hear a click. If you want to use less effort to click, you can also turn on the tap-to-click feature. After you engage this feature, your touchpad treats any quick tap or touch of the touchpad as a click. To enable this feature, follow these steps:

1. **Click the status area in the bottom right of your desktop.**

   The settings panel opens.

2. **Select Settings (click the gear).**

   Your Chromebook Settings page opens.

3. **Scroll down to the Device section and select Touchpad.**

   The Touchpad dialog box appears.

4. **Select the Enable tap-to-click check box.**

   After you enable this option, you can immediately tap the touchpad to click links, buttons, and so on. You can also double-click by tapping twice.

## Changing scroll directions

You can accomplish scrolling on the Chromebook in a few ways:

» Move your pointer over to the right side or bottom of the screen to reveal the available scroll bars. You can then scroll by clicking the scroll bar and dragging up and down (to scroll vertically) or left and right (to scroll horizontally).

» Place two fingers on the touchpad and move them up and down to scroll vertically, or left and right to scroll horizontally.

By default, the Chromebook is set up to scroll traditionally, meaning that swiping your fingers up on the touchpad makes the window scroll up, and swiping your fingers down makes it scroll down.

You may, however, be more familiar with the opposite action, meaning that when you swipe up, it's as if you're pushing your finger on the screen and pulling more content from the bottom of the screen, and vice versa if you swipe down. You can activate this feature by taking these steps:

1. **Click the status area in the bottom right of your desktop.**

   The settings panel appears.

2. **Select Settings (click the gear).**

   Your Chromebook Settings page opens.

3. **Scroll down to the Device section and select Touchpad.**

   The Touchpad dialog box appears.

4. **Select the Enable reverse scrolling radio button.**

5. **Click OK.**

   Your scroll has now been changed.

# Connecting a Mouse or Keyboard

Sometimes you have to work on your computer for hours using a laptop keyboard and touchpad, which may make your mobile-computing experience a bit of a grind. To make things easier, it's nice to have a separate keyboard or mouse that you can plug in and use with your laptop. With your Chromebook, you can add a physical keyboard or mouse using USB or Bluetooth.

To connect a USB keyboard or mouse to your Chromebook, you just need to locate the USB port on the side of your computer and insert the USB connector for your device into the port. (Your USB connector can go in only one way, so don't force it.) Your Chromebook automatically detects the new keyboard or mouse and applies all existing settings to it. You may not see any messages as you would on a Windows computer; instead, it will just begin to work automatically.

If your keyboard or mouse and your Chromebook are Bluetooth enabled, no cable is necessary! Connect your Bluetooth keyboard or mouse by following these steps:

1. **Click the status area in the bottom-right of the desktop and then click the Settings icon.**

   The settings panel opens.

2. **Select Bluetooth.**

3. **If your Bluetooth is disabled, click to enable it.**

4. **Click on Pair new device.**

Chromebook begins searching for available Bluetooth devices.

5. **Ensure that your Bluetooth keyboard or mouse is enabled and wait for it to appear in the Bluetooth list.**

6. **Select your keyboard or mouse from the list and follow any instructions for "pairing" them to your Chromebook that appear.**

7a. **When connecting a keyboard, enter the randomized pin on the keyboard to ensure that it's the correct device.**

Upon successfully pairing your keyboard with your Chromebook, your Bluetooth keyboard assumes all existing keyboard settings, and you can start typing immediately.

7b. **When connecting a mouse (optional): After your mouse has been plugged in or paired and Chromebook has identified it, you can configure its settings by following these steps:**

1. **Open the settings panel and choose Settings.**

2. **Scroll down to the Device section and select Touchpad Settings.**

The Mouse and Touchpad dialog box appears. (See Figure 4-10.)

3. **Select and change the desired option.**

Like touchpad settings, changing mouse configuration settings takes immediate effect, enabling you to check it out to see whether you like the change you made.

**FIGURE 4-10:** Configuring a mouse.

*Illustration courtesy of Peter H. Gregory*

Chapter **5**

# Finding and Exploring Chromebook Apps

Because Google's original vision for Chromebook was to create a computer that did most of its work over the internet, a lot of a Chromebook's functionality is achieved through the Chrome web browser. Unlike Windows or Mac computers, few applications are installed on the Chromebook; instead, apps are stored on remote computers and accessed over the internet. Google has numerous applications to help you with work, school, personal development, entertainment, and more. This concept — using online applications and reducing the need to install, store, and run software locally — increases simplicity and reduces costs for both Google and the consumer because the Chromebook doesn't require expensive hardware to run the applications.

In this chapter, you get a brief overview of the applications that come with your Chromebook, as well as the lowdown on how to find and add new applications to your Launcher. Keep in mind that adding apps to your Chromebook often requires little more than adding a shortcut to your menu and adjusting a few settings.

TIP

Your Chromebook holds many built-in apps, and more are available in the Chrome Web Store, which means that you can do a lot with your Chromebook! But don't feel you must understand all these apps to get the most out of your Chromebook. If you just want to check Turner Classic Movies schedules with your browser and play Mahjong, that's fine!

# Exploring Chromebook's Pre-Installed Apps

Apps, short for *applications*, are computer programs made for a particular purpose. For people using laptop computers, including Chromebooks, examples of apps are the Chrome browser, Gmail, Calendar, and Solitaire. Apps make computers useful and fun.

On a Chromebook, a few applications are pre-installed on the system. Many of the applications on your shelf are like links that open web applications in the Chrome web browser. You can view the applications on your computer in a couple of different ways:

>> **Press the Search key.** This opens the Launcher and places a cursor in the search bar. You can then scroll through your windows in the Launcher using two fingers to swipe up or down on the touchpad.

>> **Click the Launcher.** This is located on the bottom-left corner of your desktop on your Chromebook shelf.

Your Chromebook comes with shortcuts for several applications already in place. These shortcuts may differ slightly from Chromebook to Chromebook. If I cover an application that doesn't already exist on your Chromebook, you can easily add it through the Web Store. The next few sections give you a quick look at some of the more important applications.

## Storing data in the cloud with Google Drive

Google Drive is your hard drive in the cloud. You can create files through Google web-based office tools, and store those and other important files in Google Drive. Your Google Drive folder syncs to every device you own that has Google Drive installed. You can even access your files through a web browser on any computer with a web connection. Google Drive is a necessity for any Chromebook user.

You can find a lot more detail about Google Drive in Chapter 7.

## Word processing with Docs

*Docs* is Google's word-processing application. If you have done any work with Microsoft Word or Apple Pages, you'll be at home with Google Docs. Create text documents; format your text; add links, images, videos, tables, and more; use templates to quickly create preformatted documents; and save in numerous formats, including Microsoft Word, OpenDocument, Rich Text Format (RTF), or

Portable Document Format (PDF). Documents created with Google Docs are automatically saved to Google Drive and accessible from any device that can access the internet. You can even invite others to collaborate on your Docs files without having to email files and worry about duplication of efforts or lost work. This feature means that two or more users can be working on a Google Doc simultaneously.

More information on using Google Docs appears in Chapter 8.

## Using spreadsheets with Sheets

*Sheets* is Google's spreadsheet application, and it's a lot like Microsoft Excel. With Sheets, you can build lists, keep track of personal finances, analyze data, and so much more. A templates library helps you by creating worksheets that are already formatted. Build formulas for performing complex calculations and data analysis. Filter, sort, and otherwise organize your data with ease. As with Docs, all spreadsheets are saved in Google Drive and easily shared with collaborators.

Starting a new business? You should consider using Sheets for your cash-flow projections. You and your business partners can work on it without fear of losing information or overwriting each other's work!

Find out more about Google Sheets in Chapter 9.

## Making presentations with Slides

*Slides* is another of Google's web-based office products. With it, you can create beautiful slide presentations with all sorts of prebuilt or custom themes. Import images, videos, and other interactive content; link to web content like YouTube videos; and more. Slides is a powerful presentation tool that allows you to present through the web or export to PowerPoint, PDF, and other globally supported formats. If you've used Microsoft PowerPoint, Slides will be familiar to you. Collaboration is also made easy with Google Drive.

You can find out more about Google Slides in Chapter 10.

## Taking notes with Keep

Whether you're a student, stay-at-home mom or dad, or a remote or office-based worker, note-taking is an important part of life. Google Keep is designed to make note-taking a breeze. Use Keep to take written notes or voice notes. Easily add pictures and videos, or set a reminder. Save your notes to Google Drive to share with other users and collaborators. You can even export your notes to services like

Dropbox (www.dropbox.com), OneDrive, or Box.com, or you can download them to your computer or storage device. In the usual Google style, your Keep notes will be available on all of your devices. Google Keep's minimalist interface makes it fast and easy to use. Take notes more efficiently than paper and pen with Keep. Figure 5-1 shows a Google Keep session.

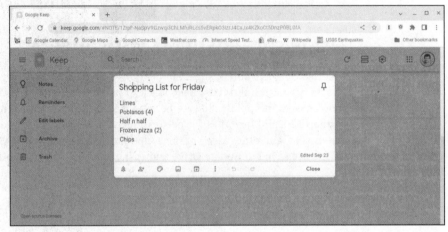

**FIGURE 5-1:**
Take notes with Google Keep.

*Illustration courtesy of Peter H. Gregory*

## Organizing and playing music with YouTube Music

Formerly known as Google Play Music, Google's YouTube Music is the one-stop music service on your Chromebook. When you move your music collection to YouTube Music, it's accessible to you anywhere in the world. Organize your songs into playlists, share your playlists, or listen to your friends' playlists. Stream countless themed music channels for free. Shop through the YouTube Music database of songs to purchase and expand your collection. You can even subscribe to get access to stream more than 70 million songs at any time. YouTube Music syncs with all your devices. Explore YouTube Music in all its glory in Chapter 12.

## Communicating with Google Voice

You don't need any fancy hardware or additional software to make calls using your Chromebook. Simply launch Google Voice, and you can quickly call any phone number worldwide. Domestic calls are usually free, and international calls cost a fee, but you don't need a phone to call your family anywhere in the world! Communicate via text, and take and send pictures.

Chapter 15 explores Google Voice in much more detail.

## Emailing with Gmail

 Gmail is Google's powerful free email platform. With Gmail, you can send and receive emails; attach files, pictures, videos, and links; and quickly save attachments to your Google Drive cloud storage. Gmail for Chromebook also has an offline feature to check emails, write emails, and queue them up to send the next time you get online. Native Gmail apps are also available for Android and iPhones and on all other laptop and desktop computers through their browsers. Google also offers Gmail for businesses so you can have hosted email from your company domain. Find out more about Gmail in Chapter 6.

## Organizing your schedule with Calendar

 Google Calendar is a versatile calendar system. You can easily create events on your calendar, set them to repeat periodically, set alarms, invite others to attend your events, and more. You can create multiple calendars within your Google Calendar and share the calendar with your family, friends, and coworkers. Organize your calendar and view it by day, week, month, or year. You can also sync your calendar with any modern smartphone. If you need to access your Google Calendar from a Mac, you can sync it with your Mac's Calendar. You can even bring your Google Calendar content into Microsoft Outlook. Explore Google Calendar in Chapter 6.

## Remotely accessing with Chrome Remote Desktop

 Chrome Remote Desktop is a handy tool for accessing your other computers or for accessing your Chromebook from anywhere. Install Remote Desktop on your Chromebook to access your Chromebook remotely from your Mac or Windows PC; conversely, you can access them from your Chromebook anywhere in the world. Of course, the computers you want to access must be turned on and connected to the internet, and you'll need to generate one-time codes to make a connection. Accessing your files, running applications, and working remotely is a breeze with Chrome Remote Desktop.

## Reading with Google Play Books

 If you enjoy reading ebooks, you will love using Google Play Books, which offers 5 million titles. You can use Google Play Books to read ebooks, audio books, textbooks, and even comic books. Shop for books at low cost and store them in your Google Play Books account. Easily sync your books to any device you own that has Google Play Books installed. Then you can read your favorite novel or business book on the beach, in bed, at the office, or anywhere else you like — and you can choose from your phone, tablet, or Chromebook.

## Getting directions with Maps

Google Maps is one of the most powerful map programs currently available. Look up point-to-point directions or route a road trip with multiple destinations. Wherever the wind takes you, Google can make sure you're on the right road. Search for businesses, locations, or popular destinations within Google Maps; share maps with friends; and even zoom down to the street view. Switch your views to satellite view and see whether you recognize the cars parked near your dwelling. You can even download offline maps for use when you don't have an internet connection. Google Maps isn't just functional, it's FUNctional.

# Finding More Apps with the Chrome Web Store

The Chrome Web Store has many more apps to offer than those that appear by default on your Chromebook. You can search for apps and add them with great ease by taking these steps:

1. **Click the Launcher icon located in the bottom-left of your screen.**

   The Launcher, a window containing your applications, appears.

2. **Find and click the Web Store icon.**

   A Chrome browser window appears and loads the Web Store.

3. **Click on Apps to view Chrome apps.**

4. **Browse applications by category or search by name.**

5. **Click the desired application.**

   A window appears that contains information specific to the selected application.

6. **To add an application, click the Add to Chrome button near the top-right of the application window.**

   The application is added to your Launcher. (See Figure 5-2.)

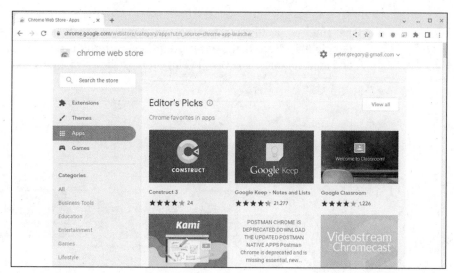

**FIGURE 5-2:**
Finding and installing apps at the Web Store.

The method for launching applications that you've added from the Web Store is the same as that for apps that come by default with your Chromebook. Just follow these steps:

1. **Click the Launcher icon in your screen's bottom-left corner.**

   The Launcher opens.

2. **Scroll through the Launcher window until you locate the icon of your recently installed application.**

3. **Click the application icon.**

   The application launches.

**REMEMBER**

If you're curious whether a particular app is useful or popular, you can read the customer reviews in the Web Store. These reviews, although public opinion, can help you decide between different apps. Most apps in the Web Store are free, so you take little risk in simply trying an application. You can always uninstall it if you don't like or use it.

# The Google Play Store

Google Play Store is functionally similar to the Web Store, so why do you have two stores for getting apps? Originally, only the Web Store was available for Chromebook users; the Web Store has apps that run on Chromebooks as well as extensions for the Google Chrome browser on Windows, macOS, and Chromebooks. The Google Play Store is the app store for users with Chromebooks, Android tablets, and smartphones. The Google Play Store is shown in Figure 5-3.

**FIGURE 5-3:**
Exploring apps on the Google Play Store.

I tell you about YouTube Music earlier in this chapter. Yes, this same Google Play Store, which is Google's main distribution point for digital content, offers gazillions of Android apps as well as music.

Some apps available in the Google Play Store include Facebook, Instagram, Disney+, Netflix, WhatsApp, Slack, Wikipedia, Adobe Reader, and more than I can list in this book.

TIP

Whenever you're looking for an app for your Chromebook, I recommend you first search through the Web Store; if you don't find what you're looking for, consider the Google Play Store. And remember, you can always try an app from either source; if you don't like it, you can just remove it!

## Installing apps

To install an app from the Google Play Store, click the app's logo and then click the Install button. The app downloads and is automatically installed. You can open it right away by clicking Open. If it's an app that you want to run frequently, you can pin the app to the shelf, as discussed in Chapter 2.

# Checking app safety

Google keeps a watchful eye over all of the apps on your Chromebook. You can always scan your apps by going to the Google Play Store, Manage apps, then Go to Play Protect and scan your apps. You'll also see messages there about any problems found earlier.

When you visit Play Protect, you may also see a message that tells you that app permissions have been removed from apps you haven't used in more than 3 months. This is a precaution taken to protect your information. If you use those apps again, you'll just need to give them permission again the next time you use them. No big deal.

**TECHNICAL STUFF**

You can configure your Chromebook so that Play Protect does not automatically remove app permissions. Go to Play Protect, click See apps, then click Auto-remove off. You can even set this per app by clicking on the app you want to change, and then toggle the remove permissions setting.

# Managing installed apps

You can use the Google Play Store app to manage all the apps you have installed on your Chromebook. Just open the Google Play Store app (see the previous section for how-to info) and click your photo (or avatar) near the upper-right corner of the app. Then click Manage Apps and Device. The Overview page shows general information, and a list of your apps appears if you click Manage, as shown in Figure 5-4.

**FIGURE 5-4:**
Managing your installed apps with the Google Play Store.

*Illustration courtesy of Peter H. Gregory*

## Updating apps

The Updates Available function in the Google Play Store shows apps where software updates are available. You want to periodically check this feature and install any available updates because doing so is a good security practice. Chapter 18 provides more details on Chromebook security.

One thing about updates: If you decide to update an app, checking first to see whether it is running is a good idea. The update will stop the app and install a new version. Depending on the app, you may get a warning that you have unsaved work, but to be on the safe side, just stop the app if you're not sure.

## Finding out what apps you have installed

Click the Installed button to see what apps are installed on your Chromebook. Doing so shows the apps you've installed and how much storage each has used. Figure 5-5 shows an example.

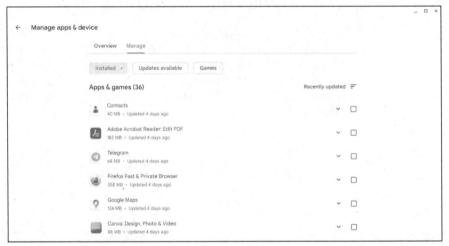

FIGURE 5-5:
Checking installed apps.

*Illustration courtesy of Peter H. Gregory*

## Removing apps

If you want to remove an app, Google Play (interestingly enough) doesn't provide this feature. Instead, you go to the Launcher to do this. To remove an app, click the Launcher and scroll through it to show all your apps. To delete an app, right-click or Alt-click the app and click Uninstall. It's that simple!

# Chapter **6**

# Working with Gmail and Google Calendar

n the beginning, Google created a search engine. Over time, however, Google has created or acquired hundreds of software tools and platforms and connected them together to make up what is commonly referred to as the Google ecosystem. Gmail was an early innovation that quickly took root and gained international appeal. At first, Gmail was nothing more than a free email platform that offered users 1GB of email storage. However, Gmail's easy-to-use interface made the perfect recipe for growing a user base. Over the past 18 years, Gmail has acquired 1.8 billion users (yes, that's billion with a *b*), making it the most popular email service in the world. Today, users receive 15GB of free storage in Gmail, and with a paid subscription, users can store up to 1TB of data. Best of all, Gmail and Chromebooks were made for each other.

In this chapter, you find out how to launch Gmail on your Chromebook, sort your emails with labels, send emails to multiple recipients, and attach files to email messages. You can explore how to write emails and schedule your messages to be sent later. You can also explore how to customize your Google Calendar and share it with others.

# Gmail for Chromebook

Before accessing your Chromebook, you must log in using your Google Account username and password. Your Google Account gives you access to almost all of the Google platform, which includes Gmail. Your Chromebook comes with a Gmail app icon that you can use to send and receive email.

**TIP**

If you have a non-Gmail email address that you've used for a long time, you can still use it on your Chromebook. If your non-Gmail email is a webmail service (such as Hotmail, Yahoo! Mail, or Pobox.com), you can simply use your Chrome browser to access any or all of those email services.

## Launching Gmail

Before you get started, have your Gmail username handy. Chances are, this is the account you used to initially set up and sign in to your Chromebook. You use that Gmail username (also known as your email address) in the procedures here.

Google automatically creates a Gmail account for you. Your Gmail email address will be your Google Account name followed by "@gmail.com."

To launch Gmail, click on the Gmail icon on the Shelf, or open the Launcher and click the Gmail icon. When you do so, Gmail launches in a new window, as shown in Figure 6-1.

Gmail initially includes a "Get Started with Gmail" pane with icons that help you get started. The icons you see may include:

>> **Customize your inbox.** You can choose how Gmail displays email messages, as well as select a Theme (colors and styles that are a part of the Gmail app when you use it).

>> **Change profile image.** Here, you can include a photo for your email profile (this will also be the photo used for all of your Google services).

>> **Import contacts and mail.** This includes information and instructions for copying over your contacts from another email account (for instance, if you used Hotmail or Yahoo for email in the past and want to begin using Gmail instead).

>> **Get Gmail for mobile.** This includes information and instructions for getting and using Gmail on an Android phone or tablet, iPhone, or iPad.

Selecting any of these opens a pane where you can provide information and select options. Close the pane by clicking the X in the upper-right corner. You can also close the Get Started with Gmail pane by clicking the X in the upper-right corner.

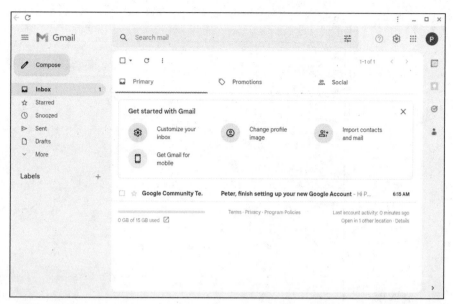

FIGURE 6-1:
The first time you
launch Gmail.

# Navigating Gmail

When you log into Gmail, you see Gmail's minimalist interface. (See Figure 6-2.) The Gmail interface is broken up into two main areas. On the left is a list of folders, including your Inbox. In Gmail, these folders are called *labels.* Directly to the right of your list of labels is the email area. Above the email area is the Gmail toolbar, and above the toolbar is the Search bar.

Gmail gives you a default set of labels for categorizing your email. Labels are much like folders, except messages, unlike files, can have multiple labels. (See more on categorization in the section "Organizing your Inbox" later in this chapter.)

The basic labels in Gmail are the following:

>> **Inbox:** Your Inbox is where your new mail is delivered. The Inbox doesn't include spam, trash, or sent mail.

>> **Starred:** Give your messages a special status by using a star so you can more easily find them.

>> **Snoozed:** These are email messages you don't want to be notified about now.

>> **Sent:** Any email you send to others is labeled Sent.

>> **Drafts:** Emails you write but don't send are labeled Drafts.

>> **Spam:** Junk mail that Google automatically identifies as spam.

>> **Trash:** Email that you delete is labeled trash and can be erased from existence.

Labels                                                                    Settings

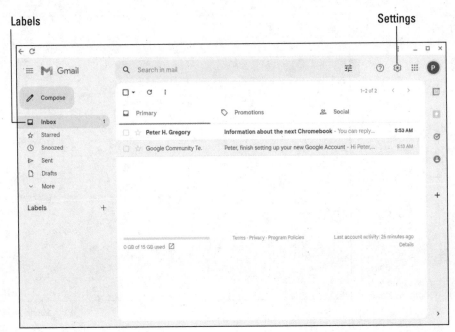

**FIGURE 6-2:**
Gmail's user
interface.

*Illustration courtesy of Peter H. Gregory*

Spam will not appear until you or Gmail mark an incoming email as spam. Similarly, trash will not appear until you have deleted email messages.

Your Gmail view defaults to the Inbox label. When you have unread emails in your Inbox, a number appears directly to the right of the label. Both read and unread emails appear in the main email message area. Unread emails appear in bold, as shown in Figure 6-2. Directly above your email messages, by default, are three tabs — Primary, Social, and Promotions. Gmail automatically sorts the emails in your Inbox based on what it believes the incoming email to be. Google places emails from social outlets into your Social tab, emails judged to be advertisements into your Promotions tab, and the remainder into your Primary tab.

## Customizing your view

You have several ways to customize the look and feel of Gmail. By default, Gmail leaves a good deal of space between lines, emails, and so on. However, if you prefer, you can condense this space to make room for more information on your screen. To compact the space, follow these steps:

1. **Click the Gmail Settings icon near the upper-right corner of the Gmail window.**

   The Settings icon looks like a little gear.

The Quick settings pane opens, as shown in Figure 6-3. Density pertains to your Gmail display, where you can select Default, Comfortable, and Compact options. Density options determine how close together messages in your folders appear.

**2.** **Pick a Density option.**

Your Gmail display automatically reconfigures itself and refreshes the spacing of email messages.

**FIGURE 6-3:**
Customizing your
Gmail view.

You can also change how your Gmail account handles the messages in your Inbox. By default, messages are grouped in the order they are received, regardless of whether they're read, and they are filtered based on the tab settings you're using. You can, however, change your Inbox view to assign different priorities to the messages you receive. Configuring your Inbox to keep all unread messages at the top can help you avoid missing a message. You can reconfigure your Inbox by following these steps:

**1.** **Click the Gmail Settings icon near the upper-right corner of the Gmail window.**

The Settings icon looks like a little gear.

2. **Scroll down until you see the Inbox type table.**

3. **Choose Unread First.**

   Your Inbox is reconfigured to keep all unread emails at the top. All read emails are sorted by date, as shown in Figure 6-4.

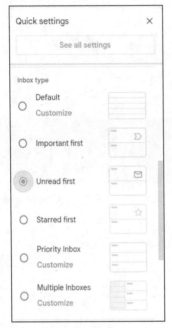

FIGURE 6-4:
Configuring your
Inbox view,
specifying Unread
emails to appear
first.

*Illustration courtesy of Peter H. Gregory*

# Adding a theme

Gmail has several themes for adding color and images to your account screen. Add flavor to your Gmail with a theme by following these steps:

1. **Click the Settings icon near the upper-right corner of the Gmail window.**

   The Quick settings pane appears.

2. **To the right of Theme, click View all.**

   Gmail loads the Themes pane that contains images of several themes. You can scroll down to see many more.

3. **Browse the selection of color themes. Select a theme by selecting the theme, and then click Save.**

   Gmail automatically applies the theme to your Gmail and returns to the Inbox display. Do you like the theme you selected? If not, go back and find another!

You can also select any of your own photos and use one as your Gmail theme. Click on My photos in the Pick your theme pane to select one.

# Sending Email with Gmail

All email consists of the same core elements — it must have a sender, a receiver, and a message — and email sent using Gmail is no different. The message typically comprises a subject line and a body of text. You can have multiple recipients and, in addition to text, your message can include documents, music, videos, and more.

## Checking out the New Message window

The New Message window has three main parts. The *header* of the email window is located at the top of the email message. The header contains the window controls for the email message you will compose. The footer contains the editing tools for formatting and styling your email, and the middle portion is the email itself. Figure 6-5 shows a blank email message in Gmail. The email message is composed of the following parts:

>> **To:** Specify the recipient(s) by entering an email address (or email addresses) here. You can add recipients using the carbon copy feature. Carbon copy sends a message to someone who isn't the primary intended recipient. You use a *carbon copy* (or *Cc,* as it's commonly referred to) to start dialogues among multiple people over email. You use a *blind carbon copy,* or *Bcc,* to send an email to one or many recipients, where none of the recipients knows who any other Bcc recipients are (if any).

>> **Subject:** Add a subject line to your email. Subjects are usually 50 characters or fewer.

>> **Body:** You type your message in the body, which is the big, white, blank area below the Subject line.

## Writing an email

Writing an email with Gmail is similar to writing a letter using Google Docs or any other word processor. To write an email in Gmail, take the following steps:

1. **Click the Compose button at the top-left of your Gmail window.**

   A new, blank message appears on the bottom-right of the Gmail window.

New Message

To                                                    Cc Bcc

Subject

Send

**FIGURE 6-5:**
Sending an email
message in
Gmail.

*Illustration courtesy of Peter H. Gregory*

2.  **Click the To field at the top of the Email Editor and enter the email address of the person to whom you want to send your email.**

    Email addresses follow the format of *name@domain.something;* for instance, the email address I use for Chromebook work is `peter.kromebook@gmail.com`.

3.  **Click in the Subject field and enter a subject line for the message.**

    It's always good advice to keep your subject line short and to the point.

4.  **Click in the Body of the email and type your message.**

5.  **When you finish writing your email, click Send.**

    The New Message pane vanishes, indicating that the email has been sent.

## Styling text

Gmail provides several advanced features for spicing up your emails, such as word-processor features to style your text. You can make your text bold or italicized by using the formatting toolbar at the bottom of the composition area, as shown in Figure 6-6.

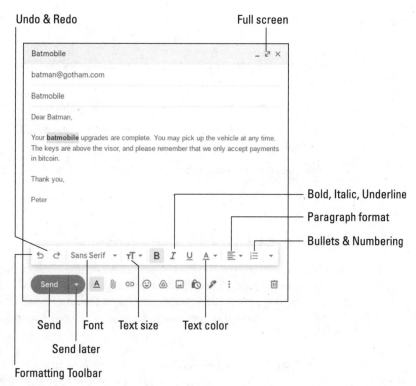

Undo & Redo

Full screen

Bold, Italic, Underline

Paragraph format

Bullets & Numbering

Send

Font

Send later

Text size

Text color

Formatting Toolbar

**FIGURE 6-6:**
The formatting toolbar in an email message.

*Illustration courtesy of Peter H. Gregory*

To apply boldface, italics, or underline to the text in your email, follow these steps:

**1.** Select the text you want to format by clicking and dragging your pointer.

**2.** Click the underlined A button next to the Send button in the footer of the Email Editor.

Clicking it again makes the formatting options bar disappear.

**3.** Select the B button (to make the selected text bold), the I button (to make it italic), or the U button (to add an underline).

The selected text changes appropriately.

TIP

You can also use keyboard shortcuts to apply formatting to text in your emails. While your text is selected, use the following shortcuts to apply the associated style:

>> **Bold:** Ctrl+B

>> **Italics:** Ctrl+I

>> **Underline:** Ctrl+U

To change the color of the text in your email, follow these steps:

1. **Select the text whose color you want to change by clicking and dragging your pointer.**

2. **Click the underlined A button on the left side of the formatting toolbar.**

   A menu appears, allowing you to select a color to apply to your text or to apply as a highlight on your text.

3. **Select your desired color from the available options.**

   Your text changes to the selected color.

## Attaching files to an email

Email has come a long way since the early days of the internet. Now you can send more than just a digital letter; you can also send files with your emails. Want to send photos to Mom and Dad? Maybe you need to submit your homework to your teacher? Or perhaps you're just swapping files with your friends. Email is a great way to do it.

Most email service providers limit the file size of attachments that can be sent or received to 10–30MB (megabytes) or less. If you need to send a larger file, you may be forced to find a different way to send it. Gmail's limit, by the way, is 50MB — the total allowed size for all attachments.

You can attach a file to your email by following these steps:

1. **Click the Attach Files icon (the paperclip) in the footer of your email.**

   The Select one or more files window opens.

2. **Navigate to the location of the file you want to attach. Select the file.**

3. **Click Open.**

   The file uploads and appears at the bottom of your email, as shown in Figure 6-7.

You can also attach files from your Chromebook by dragging and dropping the files directly from the Files app onto the body of the message.

## Customizing your email view

By default, the New Message window appears as a window on the bottom-right of your Chrome browser while you're in Gmail. You can, however, change the view so that the New Message window is full screen (actually, it's only three-quarters of a full screen, but who's counting?). Using the New Message window in Full

Screen mode is helpful for writing emails that are longer in content. You can write emails in Full Screen mode by clicking the arrows icon in the top-right corner of your New Message window (it is indicated in Figure 6-6). To take your New Message window out of Full Screen mode, click the same arrow icon in the top-right corner of the full-screen New Message window.

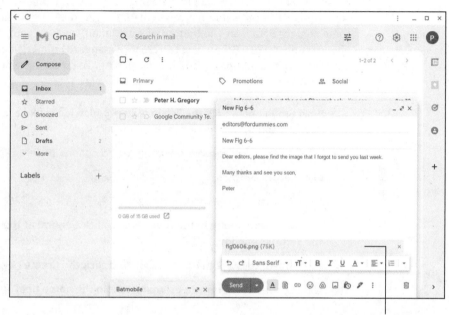

To tell Gmail to default to Full Screen mode every time, follow these steps:

1. **Click the Compose button on the top-left of the Gmail window.**

   A New Message window appears in the bottom-right corner of your window.

2. **Locate the More Options button in the bottom-right corner of the Email Editor (next to the little trash can) window and click it.**

   A menu appears, revealing several options.

3. **Click Default to full screen.**

   The menu disappears, and the Email Editor window remains the same size. New emails created from this point forward will automatically appear in Full Screen mode.

You can also set the default view of your New Message window to partial screen by following the preceding steps and unchecking the Default to full screen item.

## Creating an email signature

Every good letter deserves a great closing. As you write emails, you may find that your sign-off is the same for each email. Or you may find it helpful to include some contact details at the bottom of each email, such as your email address or phone number. With Gmail, you can create a standard email *signature* so that every email you write contains a standardized closing. To create an email signature, follow these steps:

1.  **With Gmail open, click the Settings icon (which looks like a little gear) near the top right of your Gmail window.**

    The Settings menu appears, revealing several options. (Refer to Figure 6-3.)

2.  **Click See all settings.**

    The full Gmail Settings window appears.

3.  **To ensure that you're in the General tab, click General at the top left of the Settings window.**

4.  **Scroll down to the Signature section and click the Create new button.**

5.  **Name your new signature by typing text in the name field and clicking Create.**

6.  **Click in the text box to the right, shown in Figure 6-8, and begin typing your signature.**

7.  **Below the signature text block, you'll see the Signature defaults label. Select the signature you named in Step 5 in the For New Emails Use and On Reply/Forward Use fields.**

8.  **Scroll to the bottom of the Settings Editor and click Save Changes.**

Place a line or two of blank space at the top of your email signature to ensure that you have enough space separating your signature from the body of your email. You can test your spacing by composing a new email to view your signature. If it doesn't look quite right, go back and modify your signature. Practice makes perfect!

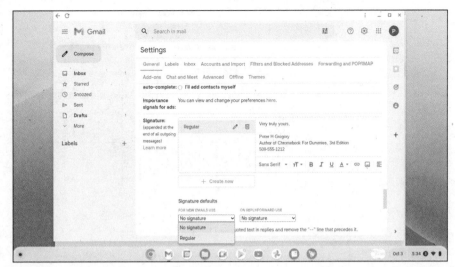

**FIGURE 6-8:** Adding an email signature that will appear at the end of every email message.

# Reading Email

All your incoming email is delivered to your Gmail Inbox. By default, the most current emails appear on top unless you've changed your view to keep all unread emails on the top regardless of the date. Your Inbox gives you enough information about the email to decide whether to read it. Each line starts with the name or address of the sender of the email, followed by the subject of the email. Gmail then previews the contents of the email with the remaining available space.

Unread emails appear with the sender's name and subject line in bold. After you read an email, the message appears unbolded in your Inbox, indicating that it has been viewed. To view an email, place your pointer over the email line and click. Gmail opens and shows the email in the main email area, as shown in Figure 6-9.

When you finish reading the email, you can click the Inbox link in your labels list on the left side of the Gmail window to return to the list of messages in your Inbox. You can also click the Older and Newer email buttons located next to the Settings icon in the top-right corner of the Gmail window (they look like "less than" and "greater than" symbols) if you want to read other messages in your Inbox.

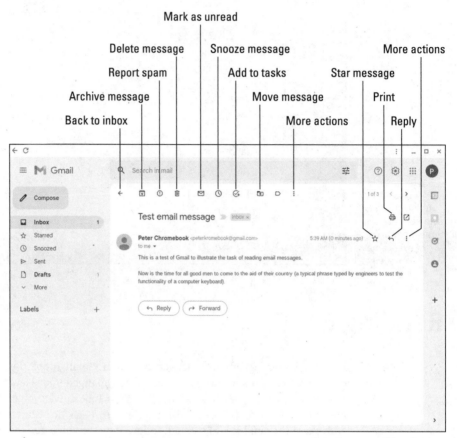

Mark as unread

Delete message          Snooze message                    More actions

Report spam              Add to tasks        Star message

Archive message                Move message          Print

Back to inbox                         More actions          Reply

**FIGURE 6-9:**
Reading an email
message.

# Replying to email

After you read an email, you may want to send a reply message to the sender. You can write a reply email by following these steps:

1.  **While viewing an email in your Inbox, click the Reply button near the upper right corner of the message, or the Reply button at the bottom of the email message. See Figure 6-9.**

    The message you were reading transforms into a window resembling a New Message window containing a flashing cursor, indicating that you can write a reply to an email. The only difference is that you can see the message you are replying to in the upper part of the window.

    **TIP**

    If you're replying to an email sent to multiple recipients, including yourself, you may want to send your reply to every person on the original email. This action is called Reply All. To reply to everyone, click Reply to all in the email message. Reply to all appears after you click More, to the right of the Reply button.

2. **Compose your reply email.**

   Gmail automatically includes the original email message so that you have a history of your email dialogue in one place.

3. **When you're satisfied with your reply, click Send.**

   Your email is sent.

## Organizing your Inbox

Every email you receive is delivered to your Inbox. You can, however, make your Gmail more manageable by placing your emails into groups. Gmail allows you to organize your emails by applying labels.

**REMEMBER**

Gmail uses the term *labels* instead of *folders.* Labels act a lot like folders. However, you can apply multiple labels to an email, thus categorizing it in multiple locations. For instance, you can apply a "family" label to a message sent by a family member, as well as a "vacation" label to a message about your upcoming vacation.

By applying labels to your emails, you can quickly locate emails at a later date. Maybe you want to group all emails from your family members with a label you call Family. Or perhaps you want to group all emails about work with the label Work. Whatever the case, labels are a helpful way to create order in your Inbox. Add a label to an email by following these steps:

1. **With Gmail open, click the Inbox link in the list of labels to ensure that you're in your Inbox.**

   Your Inbox loads into the main email area.

2. **Locate the email you want to label and select the check box to the left of the email.**

   The selected email is highlighted.

3. **Click the Labels icon (which looks like a tag) directly above the main email area.**

   The Label menu appears, as shown in Figure 6-10.

4. **Select the desired labels from the available options or click Create New to create an entirely new label.**

   Clicking Create New opens the New Label pane.

**TIP**

You can also type the name of a label in the Search bar at the top of the Label menu and then click Create New.

5. **Enter the name of the new label.**

6. **(Optional) If you would like to make your label a subcategory of another label, click Nest Label Under and, from the drop-down list, select the label under which you want to create a subcategory.**

7. **Click Create.**

   After you apply a label to your email, that email appears in the associated group in the label list on the left side of the screen.

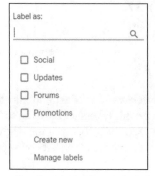

**FIGURE 6-10:**
Placing a label on
an email
message.

**TIP**

With the nested labels feature, you can manage a large volume of incoming email messages into a filing system arranged any way you choose.

## Setting up a vacation responder

When you're ready to go on that monster vacation that you've been planning (or you are planning that *stay*-cation and you want to be offline for a while), you may want to unplug from technology. You don't have to worry about offending your family and coworkers by leaving them wondering and waiting for a reply. You can use the vacation responder to automatically send a message to every person who sends you a message. When you return from your vacation, you can then get to the business of replying to the emails you received while you were away, without needing to explain the delay to everyone who emailed you. To set up your vacation responder, follow these steps:

1. **With Gmail open, click the Settings icon near the top-right corner of the Gmail window.**

   The Settings menu appears.

2. **Click See all settings.**

   The Settings Editor appears in the main email area.

3. **In the General tab, scroll to the bottom of the Settings Editor to the Vacation Responder section. Click the Vacation responder radio button.**

4. **Enter the first day you want your responder to start in the First day field.**

   If you know the last day you want your vacation responder on, enter it.

**WARNING**

   If you don't set the last day for your vacation responder, you need to turn your vacation responder off manually. Otherwise, Gmail will continue to automatically send your message to each email you receive until someone reminds you that your vacation three months ago has probably ended.

5. **Enter the subject in the subject field and body in the body field for your vacation responder email.**

6. **Don't forget to scroll down to the end and click the Save Changes button.**

   Anyone who sends you an email will receive an auto-response at least once while you're away.

**TIP**

Gmail reminds you that your vacation message has been set by displaying a yellow band with a reminder message across the top of your Gmail window. The reminder includes a link where you can change your vacation responder settings.

# Using Google Calendar

I have a calendar hanging in my office. Not to keep track of important dates, but because I like the pictures. For years, I've kept important dates in my Google Calendar, from reminders for garbage and recycling day to important birthdates and anniversaries, and reminders to perform household tasks like changing water filters.

Google Calendar is a part of your Google Account. The easiest way to start Google Calendar is to open a new browser tab and type **calendar.google.com** in the Omnibox. If you're already logged in to Google, you can click the Google Apps button near the upper-right corner (next to your profile photo) and then click Calendar. See Figure 6-11 to view the features of Google Calendar.

**TIP**

Curiously, Google doesn't provide a shortcut for Google Calendar on a Chromebook Shelf. However, you can make one by following these steps:

1. **Open your Gmail window.**

2. **Click the Google Apps icon near the upper-right corner of the Gmail window (it looks like a little tic-tac-toe board) and click Calendar.**

If you see a message that reads, "Open with Google Calendar," go ahead and click Open.

3. **On the Shelf, find the Google Calendar icon. Right-click or Alt-click the Google Calendar icon. A small menu will appear.**

4. **Click Pin.**

Google Calendar is now permanently on the Shelf.

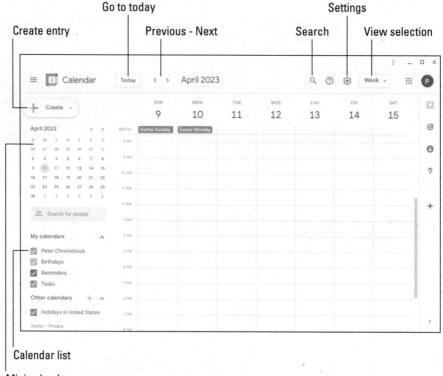

FIGURE 6-11:
Google Calendar.

*Illustration courtesy of Peter H. Gregory*

Your Calendar workspace has a few key areas: the left sidebar, controls at the top, and a calendar view taking most of the window. The left sidebar contains a mini-calendar that defaults to the current month. Below the mini-calendar is a collapsible list of all your calendars. Below your calendars is another collapsible list of calendars that have been shared with you. The top Settings bar contains buttons for changing your view, navigating through your calendar in the current view, and a Settings icon that can display several options for customizing and controlling your calendar.

The main calendar area is a grid of days and hours. The columns are the days of the week or month, and the rows are the hours of the day. Each cell in your calendar grid is a moment in time that can contain one event or multiple events.

## Customizing your calendar view

Your calendar default shows a seven-day week from Sunday to Saturday. Your calendar lets you know the day of the week by highlighting the day in your calendar with a light gray background. Calendar gives you the option to customize the number of days you view. In the Settings toolbar, located above the calendar area, you can change the view by clicking one of the buttons as follows:

» **Day:** Your view shows the current day's calendar from midnight to midnight. Day view is pictured in Figure 6-12.

» **Week:** This is the default view for Google calendar. Sunday to Saturday is shown.

» **Month**: The full month view looks like a traditional calendar. Events are indicated, but little additional information is provided due to space limitations. The Month view is shown in Figure 6-13.

» **Schedule:** The Schedule view gives you a list of events across all days in your calendar. Find events by scrolling.

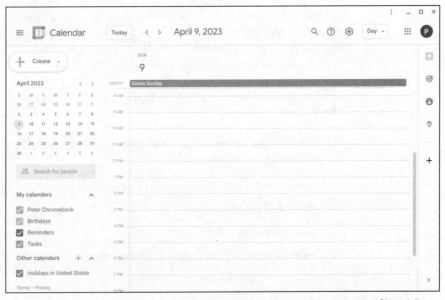

**FIGURE 6-12:**
Google Calendar in Day view.

*Illustration courtesy of Peter H. Gregory*

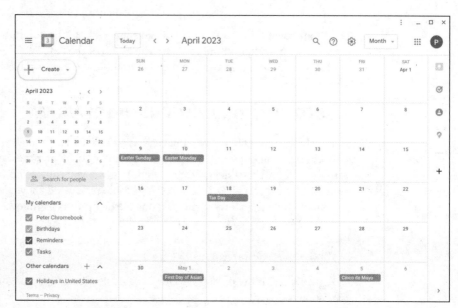

Illustration courtesy of Peter H. Gregory

**FIGURE 6-13:**
Google Calendar
in Month view.

## Creating additional calendars

Google Calendar gives you the option to have multiple calendars so that you can organize your events into groups. Use multiple calendars to separate your work, play, and other activities. If you're a parent trying to manage the activity schedules for each of your children, create a calendar for your children or a calendar for each child. You may want to keep the birthdays of your friends and family organized on a calendar so that those reminders don't clutter up your other calendars. With Google Calendar, you can organize the business of life any way you see fit, with as much simplicity or complexity as you want.

You can add another calendar to your Google Calendar account by following these steps:

1. **With Google Calendar open, click the + (plus sign) to the right of Other Calendars in the left sidebar.**

   A menu of options appears.

2. **Choose Create New Calendar.**

   The Create New Calendar page opens.

3. **In the Name text box, name your calendar.**

   Keep the name short and to the point.

4. **Enter a description for your calendar in the Description text box.**

5. **Choose a time zone for your calendar from the Now Select a Time Zone drop-down list.**

WARNING

The time zone for your calendar is important because Google Calendar will schedule all of your events in this time zone. When you travel to different time zones, Google maintains your calendar based on the default time zone of your calendar events.

6. **Scroll to the bottom of the screen and click Create Calendar.**

Calendar view reappears, and your newly created calendar appears in the My Calendars collapsible menu.

## Creating a calendar event

Your Calendar is an organized collection of activities called events. Each event you create contains the following information that describes the event:

>> Event name

>> Date

>> Start and stop time

>> Time zone

>> Event location

>> Event description

>> Reminders

>> Event guests

Aside from the date, you can create events with as little or as much of the remaining information outlined in the preceding list as you want. However, the more information you include, your calendar becomes more helpful.

Creating a new calendar entry in Google Calendar is simple. You have at least two ways to do it:

>> Click the Create button near the upper-left corner of the Calendar window, then click Event.

>> Click anywhere on the day you want to create an entry.

In either case, a window looks like Figure 6-14. Just fill in the title, time, and click on any other options.

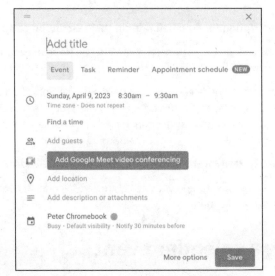

**FIGURE 6-14:**
Adding a new
event to your
calendar.

*Illustration courtesy of Peter H. Gregory*

To see a full list of things you can do in a calendar entry, click More Options; then, a window that looks like Figure 6-15 will appear.

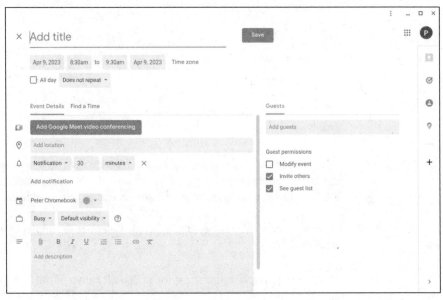

**FIGURE 6-15:**
Adding more
details to a new
event in Google
Calendar.

*Illustration courtesy of Peter H. Gregory*

The items you can add to a calendar entry include the following:

>> **Title:** This is the name of the event; for example, Bobby's Birthday.

>> **Date:** You can put in a single date or a date range; if you're going on a five-day trip, your dates may read August 7, 2023 to August 12, 2023.

>> **All Day:** Select this box if this is an all-day event. If you deselect this, you can put in the time.

>> **Time:** The time of day of the event.

>> **Repeat:** This can be a one-time event, or one that repeats daily, weekly, monthly, or annually. Never forget an anniversary again!

>> **Location:** Put in the address or other information that will help you remember.

>> **Add Conferencing:** This can be a Google Meet video conference.

>> **Notification:** You can set up a reminder that will pop up a notification on your Chromebook before the start of your event.

>> **Email:** You can have Google Calendar send you a reminder email at a set time before the start of the event.

>> **Calendar:** You can specify which calendar to put the event in. This appears only if you have multiple calendars.

>> **Free/Busy:** You can specify whether this event should block time on your calendar. This is handy if you are sharing your calendar with others and you want them to be able to see your busy and free times on your schedule.

>> **Guests:** You can enter the email address of one or more guests. Doing so causes an invitation to be sent to their email.

>> **Guest Permissions:** This item determines whether you will permit guests (people you invite) to be able to modify your calendar entry, invite others, or see the list of guests.

>> **Attachment:** You can add an attachment to the event. Doing so causes the attachment to be emailed to any guests you list.

>> **Save:** This item creates a permanent record of your event in Google Calendar. Don't worry if you don't know all the details for your event now; you can always edit the entry and add more details later.

# Updating and deleting an event

After an event is created, you may need to edit the event to add more notes, change the date or time, and so on. You can edit your events by following these steps:

1. **In your Calendar, click the event you want to edit.**

   A window appears, as shown in Figure 6-16, showing the basic information about the event.

2. **Click the little pencil icon to edit the Event.**

   The Event Details page appears where you can edit the selected event.

**TIP**

   You can quickly remove events from your calendar by clicking Delete instead of Edit Event. The selected event is removed from your calendar.

   Make sure you want to delete an event before you click Delete. There's no undo feature in Calendar, so you must manually re-add any deleted events.

**WARNING**

3. **When you've made your desired changes, click the Save button.**

**FIGURE 6-16:** Editing an event in Google Calendar.

*Illustration courtesy of Peter H. Gregory*

# Inviting others to your event

Events often involve other people. By adding those participants to your Calendar event, you can ensure that other event participants don't forget about your scheduled events. When you add someone to an event, Google Calendar sends each participant an invitation to the event via email. The email invitation contains a calendar entry so your invitees can also add the event to their calendars.

**TIP**

You can invite others to your events when you create a new event. Sometimes, though, you may want to complete the creation of your event first so you can be sure it contains all the necessary details, and then go back and add invitees to the event. Your invitees receive updates every time you modify the event, which can become annoying. To invite participants to a calendar event, follow these steps:

1. **Click the calendar entry to which you would like to add invitees.**

   A window containing the event appears.

2. **Click on the pencil icon to edit the event.**

   The Event Details page loads, with the Add Guests text box on the right.

3. **Enter the email address of an event invitee in the Add Guests text box and click Add.**

4. **Repeat Step 3 for each invitee.**

   The invitee appears below the Add Guests field.

5. **Click the Save button at the top of the page.**

   Upon saving, Google Calendar sends an event invitation to each invitee.

Later, if you need to add or change event details, or cancel the event, all the invitees will be notified.

One cool feature of Google Calendar and other calendar tools is having some standard protocols at work under the surface. For example, you can invite others to your calendar event without knowing whether they use Google Calendar or a different tool such as Microsoft Outlook, Apple Calendar, or something else. Most of the time, people will be able to accept your invites, which places events on their calendar whether they use Google Calendar or something else.

## Sharing calendars

Whether your calendar is for work, home, or family, sharing a calendar can alleviate the need to constantly communicate your availability with others. Share one of your calendars with your coworkers or spouse so they can see your events and even add them directly to your calendars. Share one of your calendars by following these steps:

1. **In the left sidebar, open the My Calendars collapsible menu.**

   All of your calendars appear.

2. **Move your pointer over the desired calendar.**

   An Options icon appears to the right of the calendar name. It looks like three little vertical dots.

3. **Click the Options icon.**

   A menu appears, revealing multiple options.

4. **Click Settings and sharing.**

   The settings menu appears.

5. **Click Share with specific people.**

6. **Click + Add people.**

7. **Enter the email address of the person with whom you want to share your calendar in the Share with Specific People section. (See Figure 6-17.)**

8. **Open the Permission drop-down list.**

   The following options are revealed:

   - **See only free/busy (hide details):** Allows others to see only your events and whether you're free or busy, but does not reveal any other event details.

   - **See all event details:** Allows others to see your events but not make changes.

   - **Make changes to events:** Allows others to view and make changes to your events only.

   - **Make changes and manage sharing:** Allows others to make changes to your calendar and invites others to access your calendar.

9. **Select the desired permission setting and click Send.**

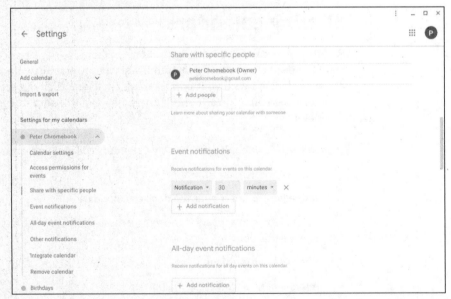

**FIGURE 6-17:** Sharing your calendar with specific people.

*Illustration courtesy of Peter H. Gregory*

You can un-share your calendars by following the preceding Steps 1 through 7 and then clicking the X to the right of the person you want to delete.

If you have a calendar that you would like to make public — that is, so that the *entire world* can view it — follow these steps:

1.  **In the left sidebar, open the My Calendars collapsible menu.**

    All of your calendars are displayed.

2.  **Move your pointer over the desired calendar.**

    A Options icon (three little vertical dots) appears to the right of the calendar name.

3.  **Click the Options icon.**

    A menu appears, revealing multiple options.

4.  **Click Settings and sharing.**

    The Calendar settings details load.

5.  **Click Access permissions for events.**

6.  **Select the Make available to public check box.**

    Your calendar is publicly accessible and completely visible in Google Search.

You can also link people to your calendar so that they can navigate to it and bookmark it. Locate the link by following these steps:

1.  **In the left sidebar, open the My Calendars collapsible menu.**

    All of your calendars appear.

2.  **Move your pointer over the desired calendar.**

    An Options icon (three little vertical dots) appears to the right of the calendar name.

3.  **Click the Options icon.**

    A menu appears, revealing multiple options.

4.  **Click Settings and sharing.**

    The Calendar settings details load.

5.  **Click Access permissions.**

6. **Click the Get shareable link.**

   A shareable link window, as shown in Figure 6-18, contains your calendar's web address (URL). Click on Copy Link and paste it wherever you want to share it — for example, in an email message or a blog post.

---

**Shareable link to your calendar**

With this link, only people you allow can access your calendar.

https://calendar.google.com/calendar/u/0?cid=cGV0ZXJcm9tZWJvb... 

Cancel    Copy link

---

*Illustration courtesy of Peter H. Gregory*

# Chapter **7**

# Working with Files and Google Drive

While your Chromebook typically uses the cloud for storage, there may be times when you want to use local storage space. For instance, you may want to download a file attachment from an email, take a screenshot, or capture some video footage or stills with your Chromebook's camera. You may also want to view photos you took on your smartphone on your larger Chromebook screen. You need local storage space for these files and a way to access them.

To find your files on a Chromebook, you use an app called Files. In this chapter, you find out how to navigate your Chromebook file system, add and use external storage, and set up and use Google Drive. Although you can consider the Chrome browser the gateway to the world of the internet, Files is the gateway to your content, wherever it may be on your Chromebook or "in the cloud" in Google Drive.

## Finding Files with the Files App

To launch Files, follow these steps:

1.  **Click the Launcher icon in the bottom-left corner of your screen.**

    The Launcher opens.

2. **Locate the app icon for Files and click it.**

   Files opens in a new window. Note that the Files app runs separately from your Chrome browser. You'll see a separate icon on the Shelf just for Files.

TIP

If you think you'll be accessing local storage or Google Drive frequently, you can pin the Files app to your shelf.

## Navigating Files

Figure 7-1 shows the open Files app window. On the left side of the window is a listing of storage locations. At first, you'll only have two options here:

>> **Downloads:** Your Downloads folder is your hard drive (also referred to as *local storage*).

>> **Google Drive:** This is internet-based storage (also referred to as *cloud storage*). I discuss Google Drive in the section "Working with Google Drive" later in this chapter.

The toolbar spans the top of the Files app window. In the toolbar, you find the following:

>> Open button (if you have clicked on a file or directory)

>> Share (if you have clicked on a file or directory)

>> Trash can (if you have clicked on a file or directory)

>> Search

>> View button

>> Sort button

>> Settings button

>> Window controls

Click Settings to open the rest of the File toolbar, as shown in Figure 7-1.

In this toolbar, you have the option to launch another Files window, create a new subfolder within the open folder, select all the files currently shown (presumably for some subsequent action), show hidden files, show Google Play files, get help, send feedback to Google, and add a new service.

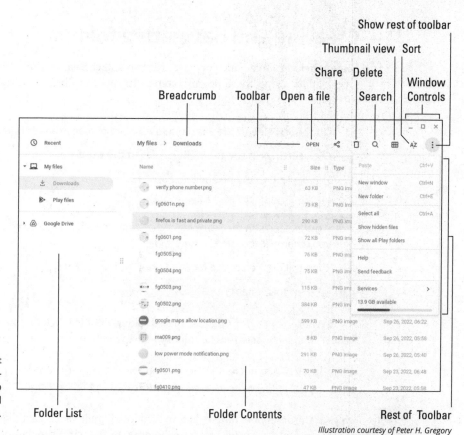

Show rest of toolbar

Thumbnail view  Sort

Share  Delete

Window
Controls

Breadcrumb  Toolbar  Open a file  Search

Folder List          Folder Contents          Rest of Toolbar

*Illustration courtesy of Peter H. Gregory*

**FIGURE 7-1:**
Use the Chrome-
book Files app to
access and
manage files.

REMEMBER

A meter shows your available storage at the bottom of the Settings menu. This information is critical because your Chromebook does not offer much storage, so you want to periodically check to make sure you don't run out. Pictures, screen-shots, music, downloads, and the like add up the more you use your Chromebook, so beware! You can see the storage meter at the bottom of Figure 7-2. Never fear: You'll be storing most of your content in Google Drive, which I discuss later in this chapter, in "Working with Google Drive."

TIP

If your Chromebook runs out of local storage space, ChromeOS might automati-cally (and permanently) delete files in the Downloaded folder, browsing data, browser cache, or files associated with any unused user accounts on your Chrome-book. For this reason, anything worth saving should be saved in Google Drive!

Beneath the Files toolbar is the file browser. This is where you can view, edit, move, or otherwise interact with your files.

# Creating and navigating folders

Folders help organize and sort your files so you can easily find them later. Create a new folder using the following steps. (In this example, you create a subfolder within the Downloads folder.)

1. **On the left side of the Files window, select the Downloads folder.**

2. **Click Settings in the top-right corner of the window.**

   The File Settings menu appears.

3. **Click New Folder.**

   A new folder with the name highlighted indicates that it can be edited. Until you rename it, its name is "New folder."

4. **Type the desired name for the folder and press Enter.**

   The new folder name is saved.

If you want to open your newly created folder, double-click or double-tap the new folder icon. A window for the folder opens, which at first will be empty.

While in your newly created folder, look at the top of the Files app window. You can see your *path*, or *breadcrumbs*, as indicated in Figure 7-1.

On your Chromebook, folders are divided into *parent folders* and *child folders.* A parent folder contains a child folder or folders. In the path, the parent folder appears to the left of a child folder.

Click the parent folder's name in the path to return to the parent folder. In this case, doing so would take you back to the Downloads folder, which is the parent folder.

You can also click the folder name in the breadcrumbs to go to a folder.

Constantly clicking on Settings can get tedious if you need to make several folders. To create a folder quickly, you can type Ctrl+E. You can also rename a folder by following these steps:

1. **Click the desired folder.**

2. **Press Ctrl+E.**

   The folder name becomes editable.

3. **Type the newly desired name and press Enter.**

# Moving files and folders

Use Files to move and otherwise organize your files. Creating several folders to group your files together and keep things in order is useful as you download and store files in your Chromebook's internal storage. You can move files and folders by following these steps:

1. **Click the Launcher icon in the bottom-left corner of your screen.**

   The Launcher appears.

2. **Locate the Files icon and click it.**

   Files opens in a new window.

3. **Click and hold the file you want to move, then drag the file to the desired folder. (See Figure 7-2.)**

**TIP**

   When using the touchpad, after clicking and holding the file, use another finger to drag the file to the desired folder.

   Hovering the file over the folder highlights the folder.

   You know you are dragging a file when you see a little fist next to the filename as you move it while holding the touchpad.

4. **Release to drop the file into the target folder.**

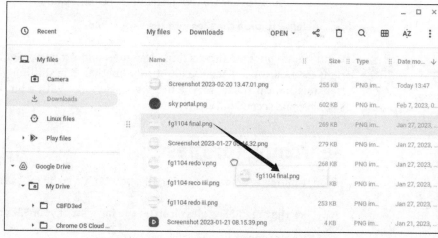

**FIGURE 7-2:**
Dragging a file to
a new location.

*Illustration courtesy of Peter H. Gregory*

To move multiple files and folders at one time, you can do so using the following steps:

1. **From within the Files application window, hold the Ctrl key and click the desired files.**

   The files you click on are all highlighted. Each selected file's icon is replaced by a check mark, indicating that it has been selected. You can Ctrl+click a file again to deselect it.

2. **Click and hold any part of your selection; then, without releasing, drag the selection to the desired location.**

   Hovering the files over the destination folder highlights the folder.

3. **Release to drop the files into the target folder.**

To select an entire collection of files, follow these steps:

1. **Hold down the Shift key and then click with one finger or your thumb and move the pointer with another finger to highlight several consecutive files at one time.**

2. **Click any part of your selection; then, without releasing, drag the selection to the desired location.**

   Holding the files over the destination folder highlights the folder, indicating that it is okay to release your finger from the touchpad.

3. **Release to drop the files into the target folder.**

Don't be discouraged if selecting, dragging, and dropping doesn't work exactly right the first time. It takes a bit of coordination, like shifting gears on a manual transmission car (okay, maybe not *that* tricky). But with a bit of practice, it will soon become second nature.

## Searching for files

If you want to search for a specific file, you can do so by following these steps:

1. **Click the magnifying glass icon on the far right of your Files toolbar.**

   A cursor appears in the Search bar.

2. **Type in the word or words that are in the name of the file you desire.**

   As you type, Chrome displays all files that fit your search term.

# Deleting files and folders

Deleting files and folders can be accomplished with the following steps:

1. **Click the Launcher icon in the bottom-left corner.**

   The Launcher appears.

2. **Locate the Files icon and click it.**

   Files opens in a new window.

3. **Select the file you want to delete by clicking or tapping the file once.**

4. **Click the trash can icon located in the toolbar of the Files app window.**

5. **When Chrome asks, "Are you sure that you want to delete...?" click Delete to delete the file or Cancel if you've changed your mind.**

**WARNING**

Make sure you *really* don't need a file any longer before you delete it, as Chromebooks don't have a "recover from trash" feature. When you delete an item, it evaporates into the ether. Forever.

You can delete multiple files and folders: First, select them by holding down the Ctrl key and clicking the files (or tapping the files with your touchpad). Then press the trash can icon near the upper-right corner of the Files app window to delete all the selected files at one time. If your files are all in a row, you can select them more easily by pressing Shift+click and then moving the cursor to select the desired files.

# Adding and Using External Storage

External storage in the form of a thumb drive (also known as a USB stick or jump drive), an external hard drive, or an SD card can easily be used on a Chromebook. You may have several reasons for using external storage, including to

» Transfer pictures or video from a smartphone, dashcam, GoPro, or digital camera

» Copy pictures to a thumb drive or external hard drive to share with someone else

» Back up data to an external hard drive that you don't want to save to the cloud

If your jump drive or external hard drive has a USB connection, simply plug it into one of your available USB ports on your Chromebook. If your Chromebook has an available SD card slot, insert your card. Chromebook automatically detects your storage devices and makes them available to browse within Files, as shown in Figure 7-3.

Eject Button                    Notification of removable storage device

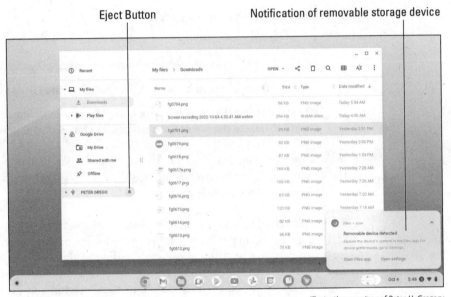

**FIGURE 7-3:**
Accessing external storage.

*Illustration courtesy of Peter H. Gregory*

To navigate to your external storage, select it on the left side of the Files window and follow the directions outlined in the section "Creating and navigating folders" earlier in this chapter. Click and drag files or folders to the desired location. If you want to move them to your Chromebook hard drive, just drag them to the Downloads folder that appears under Files on the left side of the Files window. Hover over the Downloads folder long enough to open the folder and then drop the files or folders on the right side of the Files window.

To remove your external storage devices, you should first click the Eject button, which is next to the device name on the left side of the Files window. After you've clicked the Eject button, the device vanishes from your Files window, indicating that it is safe to remove from your Chromebook.

When dragging and dropping files to or from removable storage, your Chromebook makes a *copy* of the file(s), instead of *moving* them when you drag files from one folder to another.

TIP

**WARNING**

Make sure you have finished downloading or copying everything to or from your external storage device before ejecting it, or else you could lose some or all of the data on the storage device.

# Working with Google Drive

Google Drive (or just *Drive*) is Google's cloud-based storage service. *Cloud-based storage* is really just a fancy way of saying "your hard drive on the internet." Users can create a Drive account at no cost and receive 15GB of storage space. Drive comes with every Chromebook, but you can also install the Google Drive app on your smartphone or another computer like a Mac or a Windows PC. You can also access Google Drive from any web browser where you can add, change, or remove any of your files. Anything you put in your Drive folder is synced across all your devices. Pretty awesome, right?

As a Google Account user, Google gives you access to Google Drive. Google has had a long-standing record of offering additional space on Google Drive at little or no cost. As of late 2022, Google was providing new Chromebook owners with a free one-year membership to Google One, which includes 100GB of free storage space for a year. That's a great value, because other companies charge a few dollars each month for that much storage. To take advantage of that discount, you must first set up your Google Drive account. Read on.

## Starting Google Drive

When you created your Google Account in Chapter 1, Google set up your Google Drive for you, and only you can access it. You don't have to register to gain access to Google Drive from your Chromebook; instead, click the Launcher icon and click on the Google Drive icon to open it.

**TIP**

You may want to take advantage of any free Google Drive upgrades or other offers that are made available to new Chromebook users. Open your browser and go to www.google.com/chromebook/offers, where you can learn about and redeem offers. Make sure you understand and agree to any terms and conditions.

## Using Google Drive

You have a few different ways to use Google Drive. Google Drive has a web interface you can access from any internet-enabled device like a smartphone, tablet,

PC, or Mac. To access the Drive web interface from your Chromebook, follow these steps:

1. **Click the Launcher icon on the lower-left side of your screen.**

   The Launcher appears.

2. **Locate the Chrome web browser icon and click it.**

   The Chrome web browser launches.

3. **In the Omnibox, enter the web address `drive.google.com` and press Enter.**

   Thanks to Chromebook, you are directed to your Drive web interface, where you're already logged in.

As you can see in Figure 7-4, the Google Drive web interface and Files on your Chromebook are somewhat dissimilar in appearance but similar in function.

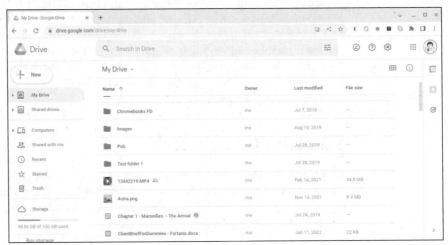

**FIGURE 7-4:**
The Google Drive web interface.

*Illustration courtesy of Peter H. Gregory*

On the left side of the Drive interface, you have several options:

» **My Drive:** This is your main Drive folder where you store all your files.

» **Shared drives:** These are directories in Google Drive that someone else has shared with you. If no one has shared a Google Drive with you, this will be empty or not appear at all.

» **Computers:** This is a list of computers syncing their contents to Google Drive. This will be empty if you have not set up any computers to sync with Google Drive.

>> **Shared with me:** This folder contains all files and folders shared with you by other Drive users. Google Drive is a great tool for collaboration because it simplifies sharing documents and managing versions of documents. When you work on a document, Drive updates the document for everyone who can access it.

>> **Recent:** This folder allows you to quickly access files and documents that you frequently use and can help you get back on track quickly.

>> **Starred:** You can "star" documents and folders in Drive to indicate they're important. Starred files and folders show up in the Starred folder.

>> **Trash:** Whenever you delete a file (or when a file is deleted automatically), that file is stored in the Trash folder before being removed permanently.

>> **Storage:** Beneath the options, you see a little graph showing the total amount of storage available and how much you have used. Figure 7-5 shows that I have used 38GB out of the 100GB of available storage. I took that screenshot after taking advantage of the free upgrade to 100GB that I discuss earlier in this section.

The right side of the Google Drive web interface is broken into two key parts. The top portion of the screen contains a Search bar that you can use to search for files by keyword. Next to the Search bar is the Settings area, which contains some buttons for customizing the appearance of your Drive, as well as a widget for accessing your Drive settings. You also find a button to launch Google apps, and your profile photo appears here, too, which gives you a quick link to your Google profile and your Google Account.

Directly below the Search bar, the My Drive label has a built-in menu that lets you create a folder, upload files, upload a folder, and open any of several Google apps (you need to click on the little down-arrow to see the menu). To the right of this menu, you can change how your files and folders are displayed. To the right, a lowercase letter *i* in a circle lets you view details about your contents.

Directly below the My Drive bar is your main work area. As you add files and folders, they populate this space.

# Uploading files to Google Drive

Transitioning from a Mac or PC to your new Chromebook requires you to migrate your files to Google Drive. Use Google Drive for your file storage to quickly access those files on your Chromebook anywhere you have an internet connection. You have a few different ways to upload files to your Google Drive. Use the steps in the following sections to upload your files from your Mac, PC, or Linux system to your Google Drive.

# Uploading files to Google Drive from a Mac, PC, or Linux system

If you are transitioning to a Chromebook from a Mac, PC, or Linux system, you can use the browser to upload your files. To use your browser, follow these steps:

1.  **Launch your web browser on your Mac, PC, or Linux system.**

2.  **In the navigation bar, enter the URL below and enter:** `drive.google.com`.

    Google Drive's website loads.

3.  **Login using your Google username and password — the same that you use to log in to your Chromebook.**

    You are taken to your Google Drive.

4.  **Click the Upload button on the left side of the screen.**

    The Upload button is located next to the Create button.

    A menu appears, giving you the ability to select files for upload. (See Figure 7-5.)

    You can also drag and drop files onto Google Drive from your computer's Files app.

    TIP

5.  **Select the files you want to upload to Drive and click Open.**

    Drive begins uploading the files immediately. When uploading has completed, you can access your files from your Chromebook or any other device when you log in to Google Drive.

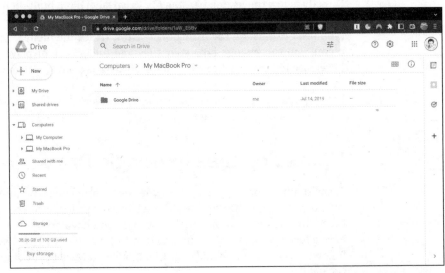

**FIGURE 7-5:**
Uploading files to
Google Drive
from a Mac using
a browser.

*Illustration courtesy of Peter H. Gregory*

# Using Google Drive with Your Smartphone or Tablet

Google Drive is available on Android and Apple smartphones and tablets. For Android, go to the Google Play store and install Google Drive if it's not already installed. For Apple devices, go to the App Store and install Google Drive.

On either platform, you can access all the files you've stored there after you log in to Google Drive. But it goes beyond access: You can create directories, add files, and even update files. Figure 7-6 shows Google Drive on an Apple iPhone 13 Pro.

**FIGURE 7-6:**
Google Drive on an Apple iPhone 13 Pro.

*Illustration courtesy of Peter H. Gregory*

# Collaborating with Drive

Google Drive makes sharing your work with others easy so that you can collaborate. Drive manages changes and controls versions so your team always works on the most current version of documents and worksheets. Before you can collaborate, you need a document, slide, or spreadsheet in your Drive folder. If you do not have one of these file types in your Drive folder, create a sample Docs file by fol-lowing these steps:

1.  **Click the Launcher icon in the bottom-left corner of your screen.**

    The Launcher appears.

2.  **Click the Docs icon.**

    Google Docs loads in a Chrome browser window.

3.  **Click the colorful + (plus sign) in the lower-right corner of the Docs window to create a new document.**

    A new, blank document appears.

4.  **Type some text in the document and then close the window.**

    The file now appears in your Drive folder as Untitled Document.

Now you can share your document with others by following these steps:

1.  **Click the Launcher icon in the bottom-left corner of your screen.**

    The Launcher appears.

2.  **Click the Files app icon.**

    Files load in a window.

3.  **On the left side of the Files window, click Google Drive.**

4.  **Locate the document (in this example, Untitled Document) that you want to share and click it once to select it.**

    The document is highlighted, indicating that it is selected.

5.  **Click the Share button in the toolbar at the top middle of the Files window.**

    The Share pane opens.

6.  **Click Share with others.**

    The Share pane opens in the Docs app.

7.  **Enter the email address of each person you want to invite for collabora-tion. (See Figure 7-7.)**

8.  **Click Done.**

    Everyone you invited receives an email with an invitation to collaborate. Each collaborator can access your file in their Drive folder upon clicking the link. Any changes made by collaborators will be immediately reflected in everyone's Drive folders.

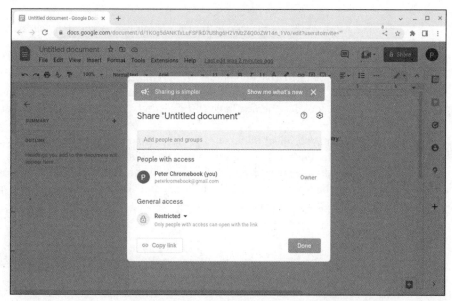

Illustration courtesy of Peter H. Gregory

FIGURE 7-7:
Sharing a
document in
Google Drive.

# Using Google Drive offline

Even though a Chromebook is designed for internet access, you can't be online all the time. If you want, you can tag a file or a directory to be available even when you are not connected to the internet. To configure a folder or file for offline use, right-click or Alt-click the folder or file and change the Available Offline selector. Figure 7-8 shows this selector.

Offline Access enabled for this file

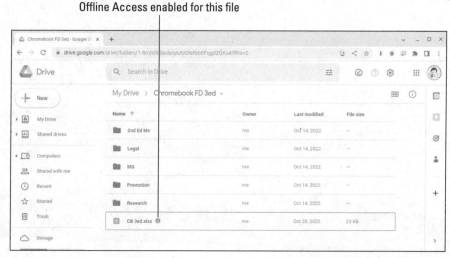

FIGURE 7-8:
Marking files or
folders in Google
Drive for offline
use.

Illustration courtesy of Peter H. Gregory

After you have marked a file for offline use, a small check mark icon appears in Google Drive to the right of the file name.

TIP

The Google Drive app shows which files are available offline with the little Available Offline check mark. To see which files are available offline using the Files app, look for the Available Offline icon to the right of the file name.

When you select folders or files for offline use, you access them with the Files app. In the Files app, navigate to Google Drive and then to the file(s) or folder(s) you selected, as described previously. You can edit these files while offline. When you are back online, your changes are synched with Google Drive and are available from all your devices.

# 2
# Harnessing Business Power with the Chromebook

**IN THIS PART . . .**

Create and edit documents with Google Docs.

Manage tabular data with Google Sheets.

Supercharge your presentations with Google Slides.

Use Microsoft 365 and Adobe Reader.

# Chapter **8**

# Writing with Word Processing

A Chromebook is not just for fun and games. It's a powerful tool for students and business users alike — even published authors! However, what makes the Chromebook powerful is not the hardware; it's the unrestricted access to — and complete integration with — the Google platform.

One key component of the Google platform is its web-based office tools. The name often used to describe the entire suite of these tools, however informally, is *Google Docs.* However, this name can be confusing: *Docs* is also the official name of Google's web-based word processing tool within that suite. For this book, then, when I refer to Google Docs, I'm referring to Google's word processor.

Docs is a powerful word processor that offers an extensive amount of functionality. The goal of this chapter is not to dive into every nook and cranny of the Docs application — which would fill an entire book. Instead, I just cover the basics. By the end of this chapter, you should be able to open and create documents; write, format, and otherwise manipulate text; and save, export, and share your documents with anyone across the web for collaboration. This chapter describes the steps used to create documents such as resumes, recipes, and flyers. If this capability is interesting to you, read on!

# Navigating Google Docs

*Docs* is Google's answer to Microsoft Word. You'll find the interface quite similar if you've had any experience working with Word on a Mac or PC. If you're using a word processor for the first time, don't worry: Docs is highly intuitive. To get started, launch Google Docs by clicking the Docs icon in the Launcher. The Docs application opens in a Chrome browser window, where you can create a new document from one of many templates, or open a document you have edited before. Have a look at Figure 8-1.

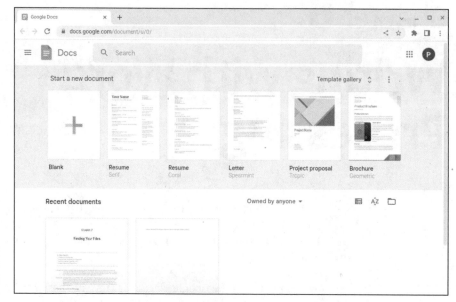

FIGURE 8-1:
Google Docs
typical starting
page.

*Illustration courtesy of Peter H. Gregory*

TECHNICAL
STUFF

*Docs* also shows you a list of documents you have worked on before. When this is the case, and you want to start on a new document, press the + (plus sign) button.

## Surveying the Docs user interface

The Docs user interface is broken into two main areas: The menu area and the document area. The menu area, by default, is composed of the Applications menu and the Edit toolbar, as shown in Figure 8-2.

The Applications menu contains a standard set of application-specific control options, including

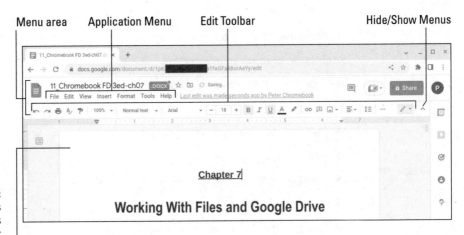

Menu area   Application Menu   Edit Toolbar   Hide/Show Menus

Document area

FIGURE 8-2:
The Docs
Applications
menu and Edit
toolbars.

>> **File:** File-specific options and controls for creating, saving, exporting, printing, setting up your page, and otherwise managing your documents at the file level.

>> **Edit:** Copy, paste, delete, and otherwise move and manipulate text. Also used to find specific text in your document.

>> **View:** Modify your Docs view by adding and removing toolbars or changing the layout of the main document area.

>> **Insert:** Add files, images, symbols, charts, headers, footers, links, and more.

>> **Format:** Manipulate the appearance of your text, including font, size, and features like underline, bold, and strikethrough, as well as the format of paragraphs (indentation, spacing, and so on).

>> **Tools:** Spell-check, translate, determine word count, or define specific text.

>> **Extensions:** get add-ons or run an apps script.

>> **Help:** Get help with Docs, search for menu options, and more.

The Edit toolbar serves as a shortcut bar to several of the common Edit, File, and Format features contained within the Applications menu. With the Edit toolbar, you can quickly

>> Undo and redo recent changes you've made in your document

>> Print your document

>> Spell-check

>> Apply the format of text or a paragraph to another part of your document

>> Zoom in or out of your document

>> Change the font face of your text

>> Change font size

>> Bold, italicize, and underline your text

>> Add hyperlinks

>> Insert images into your document

>> Align text

>> Change line spacing

>> Add and edit bullets and numbering

>> Set indentations

>> Adjust paragraph styles

>> Change basic edit modes (edit, suggesting changes, or read-only)

## Changing your view

Before you begin to type your document, you may find changing your view in Google Docs helpful. One way you can change your view is to hide the Applications menu. Just click the little up arrow at the far-right side of the toolbar. (When you hover over that arrow, it reads "Hide the menus.") When you click the up arrow, the Applications menu disappears.

To restore the Applications menu, click the icon that looks like a *V* on the far-right side of the Edit toolbar.

**TIP**

You can also use the keyboard shortcut Shift+Ctrl+F to hide and reveal the Applications menu.

If you're the type of person who likes to remove clutter from sight before you begin working, you may want to hide the ruler, and maybe even put Docs into Full screen mode. Full screen mode hides everything but the main document area. You can turn on Full screen mode by following these steps:

1. **Click View in the Applications menu.**

2. **In the View menu that appears, click Show Ruler.**

   The check mark next to Show Ruler disappears, and the View menu closes.

3. **Again, click View to open the View menu.**

4. **Click Full screen.**

   Docs goes into Full screen mode.

5. **Exit Full screen mode by pressing Esc.**

**TIP**

If you want to eliminate all distractions, put your browser into Full screen mode by pressing the Full screen key located four keys to the right of Esc. (See Figure 8-3.) This key also maximizes the size of the Docs window if it wasn't already maximized.

**FIGURE 8-3:**
The Full screen key on your keyboard.

*Illustration courtesy of Peter H. Gregory*

# Working with Text

By default, when you open Docs, your cursor is placed in the main document area. This placement is helpful if you want to begin typing text immediately because you don't have to click in the workspace to begin. The blinking cursor (the small vertical line flashing off and on) indicates that you are ready to type. If you do not have a blinking cursor in the main document area, move your pointer anywhere over the main document area and click.

Begin typing a couple of sentences or a paragraph of text. As you type, the cursor moves to the right, leaving characters to the left of the cursor. Google Docs is, by default, *left-justified,* meaning all text is aligned to the left. As you approach the end of a line, the cursor automatically moves to the following line. If you are typing a word that does not fit on the line, Docs automatically moves the word to the following line.

When you are finished typing a paragraph, press Enter to start a new paragraph.

# Moving around your document

As you write your document, you may want to make edits to your text. You can move around your document in several different ways. To start, take a look at the arrow keys, which are at or near the lower right corner of your keyboard. (See Figure 8-4.)

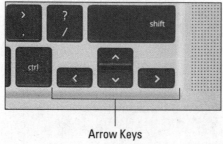

**FIGURE 8-4:**
The arrow keys
on your
keyboard.

Arrow Keys

*Illustration courtesy of Peter H. Gregory*

You can move your cursor by using the arrow keys to navigate to different places in your document. Press and hold the left arrow key to move the cursor leftward until it reaches the left end (left margin) of your line. After you've hit the beginning of the line on the left side, keep pressing the left arrow key, and you will notice your cursor go to the right side of the line above. Conversely, pressing the right arrow key moves the cursor rightward along the line. As you approach the right margin of the line, keep pressing the arrow key to go to the left margin of the next line down. You can also move around the document using the up and down arrow keys to quickly move to lines above or below the current line, respectively.

You can also navigate your document using your touchpad or mouse to move the cursor directly to the desired location. Click once to move the cursor, and then begin editing using your keyboard. If you have several pages of text, you can quickly navigate to various pages by following these steps:

1. **Place two fingers on your touchpad and swipe up or down.**

   If your touchpad is configured to traditionally scroll, swiping up scrolls the document up so you can see previous pages. Swiping down scrolls you down in the document to later pages.

   If your touchpad is configured to reverse scrolling (discussed in Chapter 4), swiping up scrolls your document down to later pages. Conversely, swiping down scrolls your document up to earlier pages.

   Using your touchpad with a two-finger swipe scrolls you to the page containing the text you want to edit.

2. **Using one finger on your touchpad, relocate the pointer to the location of the word or words you would like to edit.**

3. **Click your touchpad.**

   Your cursor appears in the text nearest the location of your pointer.

If you have a touchscreen Chromebook, move around by following these steps:

1. **Place your finger on the screen on the middle of the page and then scroll up and down by holding your finger on the screen and moving it up and down.**

2. **Tap your finger any place in the text in your document.**

   Tapping moves the cursor to this location. If you begin typing, your text will appear here.

You can alternatively use the touchscreen and the arrow keys to move around in the document.

**TIP**

To delete text, move your cursor to the right of the text so you can easily remove it by pressing the Backspace key. To insert text, position your cursor where you want the inserted text and begin typing.

## Looking for text in your document

You can also use a feature called Find and replace to find a specific piece of text within your document. To find text using the Find and replace feature, follow these steps:

1. **Click Edit in the Applications menu.**

2. **In the Edit menu that appears, choose Find and replace.**

   The Find and replace window appears, containing multiple inputs:

   - **Find:** Enter the text you want to find.

   - **Replace:** If you want to replace the text for which you are searching, simply enter the replacement text in this text box.

   - **Match Case:** Select this check box to search for text with the same capitalization as you typed in the Find box.

3. **Enter the text you want to locate in the Find text box.**

   As you type text in the Find text box, Docs highlights words in your document that match your search entry.

You can also quickly find text in your document by typing Ctrl+F. Doing so opens the search bar, where you can search for text in your document. Similarly, you can invoke Find and replace by typing Ctrl+H.

Google Docs treats blank spaces as characters. If you're looking for a particular word that's not immediately followed by punctuation, place a space after your search term to reduce the number of unneeded results. For example, if you want to find the word *pass* and your search shows you other words like *password,* type **pass** followed by a space.

4. **Sort through search results by clicking the Next or Previous buttons near the bottom right of the Find and replace window.**

   As you navigate to the matched words in your document, Docs changes the color of the highlighted word to indicate where you are in the document.

5. **When you successfully locate the word or words in your document, close the Find and replace window by clicking the X in the top-right corner (not the main browser window!).**

   The Find and replace window disappears, leaving your desired word highlighted and ready to be deleted or otherwise edited.

## Copying and pasting text

As you create documents, you can avoid typing repetitive text by using the Copy and Paste functions. You can copy and paste in several ways — on the keyboard, with the touchpad, and with menu commands.

Larger documents that contain several thousand words over numerous pages may be too large to effectively navigate with just your keyboard. Your touchpad comes in handy with these documents because you can quickly locate, select, copy, and paste text.

To copy and paste text, follow these steps:

1. **Using your touchpad, move your cursor to the text you want to copy.**

   You may need to scroll to a different page. To do so, you can

   - Place two fingers on your touchpad and swipe up or down to scroll to a different page within your document.

   - Place one finger on the scroll bar and move your pointer to the vertical scroll bar on the screen's right side. Click anywhere on the bar to quickly scroll to a different page. Or, on the bar itself, click and drag your cursor up or down to scroll to different pages.

2. **Click and drag your cursor over the section of text you want to copy. When all the desired text is selected, release the click.**

A highlighter follows your pointer as you drag it across the text.

You can select text using the keyboard with the arrow keys while holding the Shift key. Go character by character by using the left or right arrow keys. Select entire lines by using the up and right arrow keys at the same time.

3. **In the Docs menu, click Edit and then click Copy.**

   Alternatively, press and hold the Alt key and click the highlighted text. A menu appears where you can choose Copy, as shown in Figure 8-5.

   The selected text is copied to your Clipboard.

The Clipboard is a temporary place where text you copy resides. When you copy or cut, that text resides in the clipboard. When you paste, text in the Clipboard is inserted into your document. The Clipboard works across all applications: You can copy text on a web page you are viewing with the Chrome browser and paste it into a document.

4. **Using your touchpad, scroll to where you want to place your text and click to place your cursor there.**

5. **Open the Edit menu again and select Paste.**

   The copied text is pasted into the document at the location of your cursor.

   You can paste the contents of your Clipboard as many times as you like. If you need to place the text in numerous locations, simply move to each location and paste the text by repeating Steps 4 and 5.

**FIGURE 8-5:**
Open an editing menu by Alt-clicking selected text.

*Illustration courtesy of Peter H. Gregory*

You can also use handy keyboard shortcuts to copy and paste text. After you select the desired text, pressing Ctrl+C copies the text to your Clipboard. After you move the cursor to the place in your document where you want the text to appear, press Ctrl+V to paste the text from your Clipboard into the document.

**TIP**

You can paste text over and over. Pasting text from the Clipboard does not empty the Clipboard; instead, the Clipboard will contain your selected text until you perform the next copy. At that point, you replace the prior contents of the Clipboard with the new content.

## Moving text by cutting and pasting

When you want to replicate text, copying and pasting is the mode of operation you should use. When you want to *move* text but *not* replicate it, however, instead of using Copy, you want to use Cut. To move text in your document using the cut-and-paste method, follow these steps:

1. **Using your touchpad, click and drag your pointer across the text you want to move; then, release your click.**

   The selected text is highlighted.

2. **Alt+click the highlighted text.**

   A menu appears, revealing several options.

3. **Select Cut from the menu.**

   The selected text disappears from the screen. Don't worry; it's sitting in your Clipboard waiting to be pasted.

**WARNING**

When you cut text from your document, the text vanishes, perhaps giving you the impression that you have deleted it. You haven't deleted the text, though — it has just been moved to your Clipboard. However, that text *will* be deleted if you cut or copy additional text before pasting the already-cut text. The Clipboard always and only holds *one* copied item.

4. **Using the touchpad, navigate to the location where you want to paste your text.**

5. **Alt-click in the location where you want to paste your text. In the menu, select Paste.**

   The copied text is pasted in the location of your cursor.

**REMEMBER**

You can paste text as many times as you like. However, when you copy or cut a new selection of text, the previously cut text is replaced with the newly cut text.

**TIP**

Instead of using Alt+Click menus for cutting and pasting, you can press Ctrl+X to cut text (remove from the document and copy to the Clipboard), and Ctrl+V to paste text.

# Formatting Text

Before you can start formatting text, you need to become familiar with a few terms that describe the different characteristics of your text:

>> **Font:** Also known in some circles as *font face,* the *font* is the typeface style. By default, the name of the font used in Docs is Arial.

>> **Font size:** The size of your text is often used to indicate hierarchical structure, writing format, or style. By default, the size of your text is 11 points. This is about the normal text size on an ordinary printed page.

>> **Font weight:** *Weight* refers to the thickness or boldness of the letters in a font. A *heavy* font weight means the text is bold, or very thick and dark.

>> **Font slope:** *Slope* indicates how much your text leans, and in what direction. For example, *italicizing* letters means adding a left-to-right slope.

The formatting of your text is important not only for style but also to adequately communicate your message. Font weight, slope, and size are all used to convey meaning, emphasis, and more. Font face can also help establish a personality, tone, and brand. Google Docs allows you to modify all these characteristics of your text so that your documents look great and say what you want them to say.

## Changing fonts

With Docs, you can change the font of any text contained in your document. Creatively speaking, having many different fonts from different font families in a single document isn't recommended. Still, you might wish to use a couple of different fonts in your document. Google Docs comes preloaded with more than 20 fonts, including these:

>> Arial

>> Comic Sans MS

>> Courier New

>> **Impact**

» Times New Roman

» Verdana

To change your font, follow these steps:

1. **Using your touchpad, click and drag your cursor across the text you want to select.**

   Docs highlights the selected text.

2. **Using the Edit toolbar, click to open the Font menu.**

   The Font menu is located directly to the left of the Font Size menu. The Font menu shows the name of the font currently in use. (See Figure 8-6.)

TIP

   In the Edit toolbar, the Font menu appears with the font name for the selected body of text. By default, all text uses the Arial font.

3. **Select one of the fonts listed.**

   Your highlighted text is changed to the selected font.

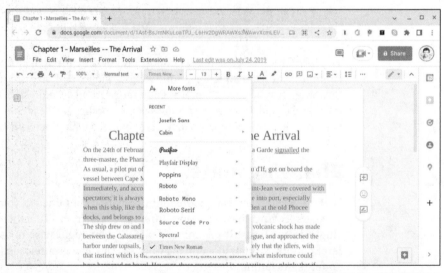

**FIGURE 8-6:**
Selecting a font in Google Docs.

*Illustration courtesy of Peter H. Gregory*

If no text was highlighted when you changed the font, the new font will apply only to new text. Any text typed from the cursor's current location will appear with the font face of the selected font.

# Adding new fonts

Google Docs gives you around twenty fonts to work with. You can add other fonts to your Docs from an extensive collection of over nine-hundred fonts. Follow these steps:

1. **Click the Font menu in the Edit toolbar.**

2. **Select More Fonts.**

   The Font selection window, shown in Figure 8-7, gives you a long list of new fonts from which to choose. Scroll down through the list to reveal more fonts.

   The fonts you already have are highlighted in blue with a check mark and listed to the right under the My fonts list.

3. **Select the desired fonts by clicking each one.**

   Each selected font is highlighted in blue and given a check mark.

4. **Click OK to finish adding the fonts to your Font menu and exit.**

   When you are ready to change the font of your text, you can choose from a list containing your original fonts plus your newly selected fonts from the Font menu.

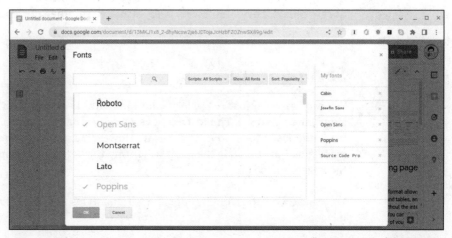

**FIGURE 8-7:**
Adding new fonts to Google Docs.

*Illustration courtesy of Peter H. Gregory*

# Removing fonts from the Font menu

The more fonts you add, the more fonts you will have to rifle through when deciding to change the font of your text. The time may come when you want to remove fonts that you added to your list. Think of it as decluttering or spring cleaning. To remove fonts from Docs, take these steps:

1. **Open the Font menu in the Edit toolbar.**

2. **Select More Fonts.**

   The Font window appears. On the left of the window, a list of new fonts appears; on the right is a list of fonts currently in use by your Docs account.

3. **Scroll through the list of fonts on the right side of the window under My Fonts and locate the font or fonts you want to remove. Then, to remove a font, click the X to the right of that font's name.**

   The font vanishes from the list of available fonts.

4. **Click OK.**

**TIP**

Removing a font from your list of fonts doesn't affect your documents, even if they contain a font you removed from the menu. Further, after you use a font in your document, you can change more text to use that font even if you removed it from your Font menu. (However, a removed font won't be available in any *new* documents or existing documents that don't contain the font.)

**TIP**

Adding fonts to Google Docs makes these fonts available for Google Sheets and Google Slides. They aren't, however, available in other Chromebook apps, such as Text.

## Styling fonts

You can easily confuse the *style* of your font with the *face* of your font. Font face is simply the font itself. Think of a font as a designer pair of jeans. A fashion designer made the jeans look a particular way. However, no matter how the jeans were made, you can still style the jeans by cuffing the bottoms, cutting the jeans off at the knees, and so on.

You can accentuate a font by applying various styles to the font itself. Those styles include

>> **Size:** Makes your text bigger or smaller, depending on where it fits in a hierarchy.

>> **Bold:** Makes the text become visibly heavier. This is why a **bold** font is said to have a *heavy font weight*.

>> **Italics:** Makes the font slant to the right. A slanted font is often referred to as *italic*.

>> **Underline:** Places a line under your text (for example, to indicate <u>importance</u>).

>> **Strikethrough:** Places a line through the middle of your text, ~~like this~~. Useful in communicating a change in your text or simply to illustrate a point.

>> **Superscript:** Lifts the text above the line and reduces its size. You may remember this from high school algebra, like the 2 in $X^2$.

>> **Subscript:** Moves the text slightly lower and reduces its size. This is like the 2 in the chemical formula for water, $H_2O$.

>> **Color:** Tracks changes, distinguishes individual users in collaboration, or simply adds style to your text by changing the color of the text itself or by adding a permanent color highlight.

## Text size

You can change the size of your text by following these steps:

**1.** **Using your touchpad, click and drag your cursor across the text you want to change; then, when you've selected the desired text, release your click.**

The selected text is highlighted.

**2.** **Open the Font Size menu in the Edit toolbar.**

It's the number found between the Font menu and the Bold button. (See Figure 8-8.)

TECHNICAL
STUFF

The size of a font is called the *point size*. The *point* is the smallest whole unit of measure in typography. In the industrial era, *typesetting* was the process of manually setting letters into a printing press to print entire sheets of text. The original point varied in actual size between 0.18mm and 0.4mm. In the modern era, the point (abbreviated *pt.*) size doesn't necessarily correspond directly to an actual size on the printed page. Today, a *desktop publishing point* is 1/72 of an *international inch*, or about 0.353mm.

**3.** **Select the desired font size.**

Your selected text becomes the chosen size.

TIP

You can quickly make selected text bold by clicking the Bold button (which displays a capital B) in the middle of the Edit toolbar. You can also bold your selected text by pressing Ctrl+B.

Font size selector

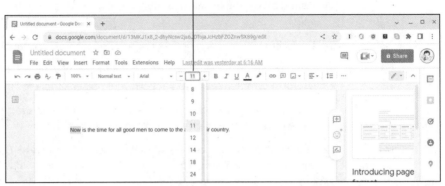

**FIGURE 8-8:**
Selecting different text sizes in Google Docs.

*Illustration courtesy of Peter H. Gregory*

## Applying bold, italics, underline, or strikethrough

To style a specific selection of text with bold, italics, underline, or strikethrough, follow these steps:

1.  **Using your touchpad, click and drag your cursor across the text you want to change; then, when you've selected the desired text, release your click.**

    The selected text is highlighted.

2.  **Open the Format menu in the edit toolbar.**

3.  **Select Bold, Italic, Underline, or Strikethrough.**

    Your selected text changes accordingly.

**TIP**

As a quick alternative, you can style selected text just by clicking the appropriate button in the middle of the Edit toolbar. Click the B button for bold, the I button for italic, or the U button for underline. (No button exists for strikethrough on the standard Edit toolbar.) Similarly, you can apply styles by pressing Ctrl+B (bold), Ctrl+I (italic), Ctrl+U (underline), or Alt+Shift+5 (strikethrough). Pressing again undoes the same style.

## Coloring your text

Google Docs allows you to change the color of your text or the highlighting you want to apply to your text. Change the color of your text by using these steps:

1.  **Using your touchpad, click and drag your cursor across the text you want to change; then, when you've selected the desired text, release your click.**

    The selected text is highlighted.

2. **Click the Text Color menu in the Edit toolbar.**

   It's the heavily underlined "A" found to the right of the Underline button.

3. **Select your desired color.**

   Your selected text now appears in the selected color.

To apply a highlight to your text, you can do so by following these steps:

1. **Using your touchpad, click and drag your cursor across the text you want to change; then, when you've selected everything, release your click.**

   The selected text is highlighted.

2. **Open the Highlight Color menu in the Edit toolbar.**

   It's to the right of the Text Color button and looks like a tiny, slanted highlighter.

3. **Select your desired color.**

   Your selected text now appears highlighted in the selected color.

# Aligning your text

The *alignment* of your text determines the orientation of the edges of lines, paragraphs, or pages in your document. Google Docs gives you several options for changing the alignment, including:

» **Left alignment:** This is the default alignment for new documents in Docs. The text is flush with the left margin of your document.

» **Right alignment:** The text is flush with the right margin of your document.

» **Center:** The middle of your document is the halfway point between the left and the right margins. With centered alignment, all text is centered on this midway point, regardless of the relation between document margins and document dimensions.

» **Justified:** *Justifying* your text aligns the text evenly along both the left and right margins. To ensure that your text's left and right sides are flush with the left and right margins, Docs introduces additional spaces between each word. The highlighted paragraph in Figure 8-9 is formatted in Justified alignment; see how the left and right edges line up neatly?

You can change the alignment of text in your document by the line, paragraph, or page by following these steps:

1. **Using your touchpad, select the text you want to realign.**

   The selected text is highlighted.

2. **Click the align button in the Edit toolbar.**

   The alignment buttons appear.

3. **Click the desired alignment button.**

   The selected text is realigned. Alignment buttons are shown in Figure 8-9.

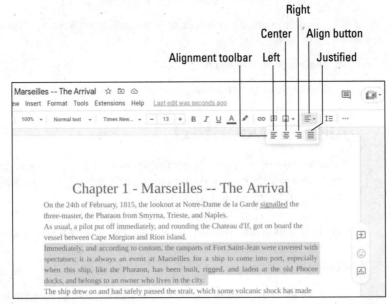

**FIGURE 8-9:**
Left, Right,
Center, and
Justified
alignment
buttons in Google
Docs.

*Illustration courtesy of Peter H. Gregory*

TIP

You don't have to select the entire paragraph to change its alignment. You need only to place the cursor anyplace in the paragraph before changing its alignment.

## Clearing formatting

Sometimes you need to start with a blank slate. You may be given a document that requires editing, or maybe you got too enthusiastic about the formatting tools that Google Docs provides. Docs makes it incredibly easy to wipe out all formatting in a section of text or a complete document. To clear your formatting, follow these steps:

1. **Select the formatted text.**

   The selected text is highlighted.

   TIP

   To clear the formatting of an entire document, press Ctrl+A instead of selecting a section of text. Pressing Ctrl+A selects the entire document.

2. **Open the Format menu in the Applications menu.**

3. **Select Clear Formatting. This is the last item in the Formatting list, and you may need to scroll down in the list to see it.**

   The selected text is reset to defaults: left-aligned text with all style elements — including color, underline, strikethrough, italics, bold, and so on — removed. Font sizes are not affected by Clear Formatting.

# Saving Documents

One of the many reasons to use Google Docs is the symbiosis between Docs and Google Drive. Google Drive is Google's cloud-based storage solution that allows you to safely store your files and access them from any device with an internet connection. Every document you create with Docs is saved to your Drive folder so that you can access it at home, on the road, at work, or anywhere else you may need it, using any device with a browser.

When you create a new document with Docs, Docs automatically saves the document to your Drive. As you edit your document, Docs continuously saves each change to Drive, so you have almost no risk of losing your information. For this very reason, Docs has no manual Save feature: You may forget to save your document, but Docs won't.

Rest assured; your work is safe with Google.

## Naming your document

When you open a new document with Docs, the default name for the document is Untitled Document. However, you won't want to leave your document named this way. Drive doesn't have a problem storing multiple files with the same name, but such naming may easily confuse you. It's best to immediately give your document a more intuitive name. To name your document, follow these steps:

1. **Open a new document.**

   The easiest way to do this is to launch Docs from the Launcher.

   A Chrome web browser opens and loads Docs.

2. **If Docs shows you a list of documents you have previously edited, click the colorful + (plus sign) button in the lower-left corner of the Google Docs page to start a new document.**

3. **Click File from the menu at the top of the Google Docs window.**

4. **Click Rename.**

   The cursor moves to the document name at the top of the Google Docs window, as shown in Figure 8-10.

5. **Type the new name for your document in the Name field and press Enter.**

   The name Untitled Document in the top-left corner has been replaced with the new name you entered.

Renaming a document

FIGURE 8-10: Changing the name of a Google Docs document.

*Illustration courtesy of Peter H. Gregory*

Your document now appears in Google Drive with the new name. As you edit the document, those changes will be updated and saved in real-time.

> **TIP**
>
> You can also rename a document by clicking on the document's name and typing the new name.

## Exporting documents

Unfortunately for you, the entire world does not use the Google platform exclusively. Therefore, you may need to export your documents to formats others may be comfortable with. Docs presently allows you to export documents to a few standard formats, including

- » Microsoft Word (.docx)
- » OpenDocument (.odt)
- » Rich Text (.rtf)
- » PDF (.pdf)
- » Plain Text (.txt)
- » Web Page (.html, Zipped)

**WARNING**

Exporting documents to different file types may change or remove some or all of the formatting within your document. The Plain Text format, for instance, is as the name says: plain text. No formatting is carried through when you export your document to Plain Text. Before sending your exported documents, review them to ensure everything is as it should be.

You can export your documents by following these steps:

1. **Open the File menu in the Docs Applications menu.**

2. **In the File menu, hover your cursor over Download.**

   A submenu appears, revealing the document types available for export. (See Figure 8-11.)

3. **Select the desired file type.**

4. **Click Save.**

   Your Docs file is exported in the desired file type and is automatically downloaded to your Chromebook's Downloads folder.

   If you want your newly exported document to be saved in Google Drive, you can move the document from the Downloads folder on your Chromebook to your Google Drive. To do so, open the Files app, find your Downloads folder and the new exported document, and copy it to Google Drive. I cover this procedure in Chapter 7.

**TIP**

Your original document is unaffected when you export your document to a new format. Your original document is still there, and you can continue making changes.

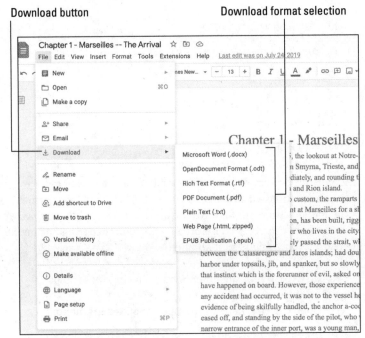

**Download button**

**Download format selection**

Chapter 1 - Marseilles -- The Arrival ☆ ⊡ ☁

File  Edit  View  Insert  Format  Tools  Extensions  Help   Last edit was on July 24 2019

↶ ↷    目    nes New... ▾   −   13   +   **B** *I* U̲   A   ✎   co ⊡ 🖾

目 New ▸
🗁 Open      ⌘O
⎙ Make a copy

   Chapter 1 - Marseilles

   i, the lookout at Notre-

&⁺ Share ▸
✉ Email ▸
⤓ Download ▸

Microsoft Word (.docx)
OpenDocument Format (.odt)
Rich Text Format (.rtf)
PDF Document (.pdf)
Plain Text (.txt)
Web Page (.html, zipped)
EPUB Publication (.epub)

n Smyrna, Trieste, and
diately, and rounding t
l and Rion island.
o custom, the ramparts
nt at Marseilles for a sh
on, has been built, rigg
er who lives in the city
cly passed the strait, wh

✎ Rename
⤴ Move
&#8682; Add shortcut to Drive
🗑 Move to trash

⟲ Version history ▸
⊘ Make available offline

between the Catasareigne and Jaros islands; had dou
harbor under topsails, jib, and spanker, but so slowly
that instinct which is the forerunner of evil, asked or
have happened on board. However, those experience
any accident had occurred, it was not to the vessel he
evidence of being skilfully handled, the anchor a-co
eased off, and standing by the side of the pilot, who
narrow entrance of the inner port, was a young man,

ⓘ Details
🌐 Language ▸
🗎 Page setup
🖶 Print      ⌘P

**FIGURE 8-11:**
Exporting your
document to a
new format with
the Download
submenu.

*Illustration courtesy of Peter H. Gregory*

# Collaborating in Docs

By default, Docs and Drive make your files inaccessible to anyone other than yourself. You can, however, change the visibility settings on your files and invite specific people, or even the entire world, to comment, view, or edit your documents.
To share a document with specific people, follow these steps:

**1.** **Open your document with Docs.**

**2.** **Click the blue Share button in the top-right corner of your Docs window.**

A window appears, giving you several options for sharing your document. (See
Figure 8-12.)

**3.** **In the Add people and groups text box in the pane, enter the email
address of each person with whom you want to share your file.**

Be sure to separate multiple email addresses with commas.

**REMEMBER**

If the email address is in your address book, Docs will try to auto-fill the
information.

4. **If you want to set the permissions of the collaborators, click the Editor drop-down menu to the right of the person you're sharing with.**

5. **To change the permissions for each user, click the link directly to the right of the invitee's name.**

   A drop-down menu with three options appears:

   - **Viewer:** Allows users to only view the document. They cannot make changes.

   - **Commenter:** Allows users to view and comment on the document but not change any content or security settings.

   - **Editor:** Allows users to view, comment on, and edit the document and change permissions.

   This is shown in Figure 8-13.

6. **Select from the menu the permission setting you want to apply to this collaborator.**

   You may select additional collaborators and specify a different sharing mode (view, edit, comment) for each.

7. **Select the Notify People box below the name(s) to notify the specified collaborators by email that you have shared a document with them.**

8. **Click Send.**

   Your document is made available to the collaborators immediately.

**FIGURE 8-12:**
The Share window lets you share documents with others.

*Illustration courtesy of Peter H. Gregory*

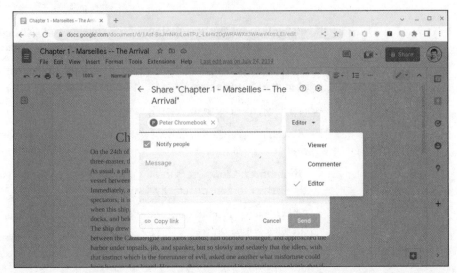

**FIGURE 8-13:**
Advanced
settings let you
specify editing
rights for each
person.

**TIP**

The collaborators invited to view, edit, or comment on your document will have to log in to Google Docs using the email address with which you shared the document. If your collaborators don't have a Google Account under the email address that you used, you'll see a warning saying that the document can be edited by anyone who has the email invitation.

# Tracking Document Revisions

Keeping track of revisions is very important when creating and working with documents, especially when multiple collaborators are working with them. Luckily, Google Docs handles version control masterfully. As you and your collaborators make changes to your documents, Docs time-and-date stamps those changes so that you can view previous versions of your document and even revert to an earlier version if you need to.

Revision tracking is a default feature of Docs. To view your revision history, follow these steps:

1.  **Open a document with Docs.**

2.  **Open the File menu in the Docs Applications menu.**

3. **Select Version history and then See version history.**

   A Version history pane appears on the right portion of your screen. (See Figure 8-14.) The box contains the various versions of your document, in order from most recent to oldest.

4. **Click a revision date in the Version history box.**

   A preview of the revision you chose appears in the main document area. Changes that occurred between versions appear in green. When you hover over each change, the name of the person who made the change is shown.

5. **To make a copy of a previous version of the document, click the menu button (three dots) to the right of the revision and then click Make a copy.**

   You now have a new document with the original name, including the date the version was saved. Your current document remains unchanged.

6. **To restore your document to an older version, click the Restore this version button from the More actions drop-down menu.**

   The restored version becomes the current version.

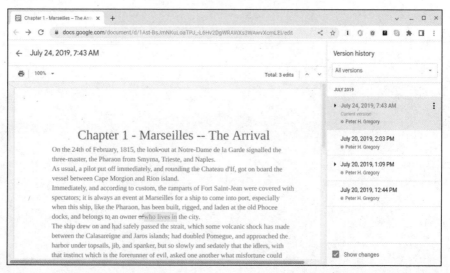

**FIGURE 8-14:** The Version History box.

*Illustration courtesy of Peter H. Gregory*

# Using Docs Offline

Google Docs is an online, web-based word processor, meaning you must have an internet connection to access all its features. However, an offline version of Docs is available if you find yourself without a connection to the internet.

To use Google Docs offline, follow the steps at the end of Chapter 7 to mark the files or folders you want to use offline. Then, you'll be able to edit those marked documents.

While offline, you won't be able to access some of the features available to Docs users connected to the internet. You will, however, be able to create documents and save them. Later, when you connect to the internet, Google Drive uploads the saved documents and enables all internet-only features.

# Chapter **9**

# Summarizing Spreadsheets

B efore the era of computers, accounting and other business finance–related mathematical computations were performed with good old paper and pencil. Today, calculating power goes far beyond what was possible in even the most sophisticated hardcopy workbooks.

Personal computers have revolutionized how businesses and finance profession-als conduct business. Digital spreadsheets make it easier to enter data and auto-matically calculate results. Pencil erasers and white-out are no longer needed!

In this chapter, you take an introductory look at Google's spreadsheet tool that is known as Sheets: You can explore the Sheets interface and find out how to enter data into a cell, edit data, and perform basic calculations. Collaboration is also important with Sheets, so you discover how to save and export your data and share it with others.

This chapter also describes the steps to create worksheets in which you can create lists of things like budget items, business records, expenses, and the like.

# Navigating Google Sheets

Google Sheets is Google's functional equivalent to Microsoft Excel. If you've had any experience working with Excel, you'll find the Sheets interface quite similar. If this is your first time using a spreadsheet tool, you'll find that Sheets is highly intuitive.

To get started, launch Google Sheets by opening the Launcher and clicking the Sheets icon. The Sheets application opens in a Chrome browser window and creates a new, untitled spreadsheet, shown in Figure 9-1. If you have used any worksheets in the past in your Google account, you will see a list of those spreadsheets. Click the + (plus sign) button at the lower-right corner of the window to create a new, blank spreadsheet.

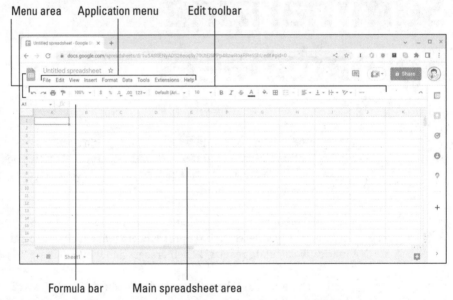

**FIGURE 9-1:** The Sheets Application menu, Formula bar, and Edit toolbar.

## Surveying the Sheets menu area

The Sheets work area is broken into two key areas: the menu area and the main document area, which is the actual spreadsheet. The menu area comprises the Applications menu, Edit toolbar, and Formula bar.

The Applications menu in Google Sheets is located at the top of the menu area and is home to several application-specific controls and options, including

- **File:** Create, save, export, print, and otherwise manage your document on the file level.

- **Edit:** Copy, paste, delete, and otherwise move and manipulate data.

- **View:** Modify your view by adding and removing toolbars or change the spreadsheet's appearance and layout by adding or removing gridlines, freezing columns and rows, and more.

- **Insert:** Insert rows, columns, cells, worksheets, charts, images, and more.

- **Format:** Manipulate the appearance of your data, auto-format number data, align cell contents, and otherwise edit the appearance of your cells.

- **Data:** Sort and filter your data.

- **Tools:** Spell-check, protect the sheet to ensure that data isn't overwritten, or create a form to gather data.

- **Extensions:** Add features and functions such as add-ons and macros to Google Sheets. This is a more advanced feature that I don't discuss further in this book.

- **Help:** Get help with Sheets, search for menu options, and more.

The Edit toolbar, located directly under the Applications menu, contains several shortcuts to features included in the Applications menu. The Edit toolbar makes the performance of routine tasks faster and easier. With the Edit toolbar, you can quickly perform these tasks on one or more cells in your worksheet:

- Print your worksheet, undo, or redo prior edits

- Zoom in or out

- Format number data as currency or percentages

- Display values with more or fewer decimal points

- Change fonts and font size

- Bold, italicize, or strikethrough your text

- Color your text

- Fill a cell or cells with color

- Add, edit, or remove cell borders

- Merge multiple cells into a single cell

- Edit the horizontal and vertical alignment of the contents of a cell

- Allow text in a cell to wrap into multiple lines

>> Rotate text in a cell

>> Add hyperlinks, comments, or charts, and perform common calculations such as sums and averages

The Formula bar is located directly under the Edit toolbar. You use the Formula bar to insert data into cells and to type formulas for performing calculations.

## Working with the spreadsheet area

The spreadsheet area of your Sheets workspace is directly under the Formula bar. The spreadsheet is made up of a grid of columns and rows. The top of the columns is the column header, and the left side of the rows is the row header. Columns are referenced by letters (A, B, C, and so on), and rows are referenced by numbers (1, 2, 3, and so on). Permanent scroll bars are located at the right and bottom of your spreadsheet so that you can quickly scroll left and right, and up and down, through your spreadsheet.

At the bottom of the spreadsheet area, a *tab* labeled Sheet1 appears. The name of your current worksheet is Sheet1. You can, however, have multiple worksheets — represented by tabs — in one Sheets workbook.

Row numbers and column letters are imperative for precisely communicating locations within a spreadsheet. A cell's coordinates are always expressed first with the column letter and then with the row number. For example, A8 means the cell in column A, row 8.

In Sheets, you refer to a range of cells in a single row or column by specifying the starting and ending cell coordinates separated by a colon. For example:

A8:A20

This example references a range of cells starting in the A column at row 8 and ending at row 20. Figure 9-2 illustrates what this range looks like.

To reference a *matrix* of cells (meaning a range of cells spanning multiple rows and columns), you specify the coordinates of the top-left corner and the bottom-right corner of the matrix separated by a colon. For example:

A8:C20

Figure 9-3 illustrates what this range looks like in the spreadsheet when selected.

*Illustration courtesy of Peter H. Gregory*

*Illustration courtesy of Peter H. Gregory*

# Customizing your view

Before you dive into your first spreadsheet, you may find it helpful to change your view in Google Sheets.

If you prefer to hide the Applications menu, along with the Edit toolbar, you can do so by opening the View menu and choosing Full screen. When you select Full screen, the Applications menu and Edit toolbar vanish. To exit Full screen mode, simply press the Esc key.

If you prefer to have nothing but cells on your screen, you can remove the Applications menu, Edit toolbar, and Formula bar by following these steps:

1. **Click View in the Applications menu.**

2. **In the resulting View menu, uncheck Formula bar.**

   The Formula bar vanishes.

3. **Open the View menu again and choose Full screen.**

   The Applications menu and Edit toolbar disappear, as shown in Figure 9-4.

**FIGURE 9-4:**
Google Sheets in Full screen mode with no Formula bar.

*Illustration courtesy of Peter H. Gregory*

In your spreadsheet, each cell is outlined with thin gray lines called *gridlines*. Gridlines are not borders; they are imaginary boundaries for reference only and won't appear when you print your worksheet. If you want to work without gridlines, you can hide them by opening the View menu and clicking Gridlines. Give it a try — you might like the cleaner look.

**REMEMBER**

To turn gridlines back on, open the View menu and choose Gridlines.

# Working with Data

Spreadsheet software was developed to give you the ability to manipulate numeric data with great ease. That doesn't mean, however, that the only data that can go into a spreadsheet is numeric. You can type text and characters, or even add pictures and graphs.

Open a new Google Sheets spreadsheet. Cell A1 is highlighted with a blue border. This blue border indicates the active cell in your spreadsheet. Also, notice that the A in the column heading is a darker gray than other columns, and that the 1 row heading on the left side is darker gray. If you click the left, right, up, and down arrows on your keyboard, notice that the blue cell outline moves, and the gray row and column indicators move as well. Clicking these arrows is the method for moving around in a worksheet. You can also move the cursor with your mouse or touchpad and click on a cell. On a touchscreen, simply touch the cell.

To enter data into a cell, make sure that the blue border is around a cell and begin typing. As you type, your entries appear in the highlighted cell and the Formula bar, as shown in Figure 9-5.

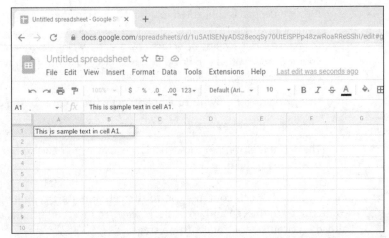

**FIGURE 9-5:**
Data entered appears in the selected cell and the Formula bar.

*Illustration courtesy of Peter H. Gregory*

When you finish typing, press Enter to save what you've typed in the cell. Pressing Enter also moves the highlight bar to the next cell down. If the text you entered is larger than the cell, your text will hang over into adjacent cells until you resize the column width or row height. (I tell you about resizing cells in the section "Resizing columns and rows" later in this chapter.)

# Moving around in a spreadsheet

As you enter more and more data into your spreadsheet, you may need to hop around to different cells to update your entries. You can move to other cells in a number of ways with Sheets. To start, take a look at the arrow keys on your keyboard.

Google Sheets can contain as many as 10 *million* cells with a maximum of 18,278 columns. You don't have to create the cells to use them; you can simply navigate to them by using your directional arrows. Move one cell up, down, left, or right by pressing the corresponding directional arrow key once. If you want to quickly move several cells in any particular direction, press and hold the corresponding directional arrow.

You can also navigate your spreadsheet by using your touchpad or mouse. Click the desired cell once to move the cursor, and then begin typing using your keyboard. If you need to get to a section of your sheet that is several rows down or columns over, you can quickly navigate there by following these steps:

1.  **Place two fingers on your touchpad and move them in your desired direction.**

    If your touchpad is configured to traditionally scroll, swiping up scrolls up, and swiping down scrolls down. On the other hand, if your touchpad is configured to reverse scroll, swiping up scrolls down, and swiping down scrolls up. Using your touchpad with a two-finger swipe scrolls you to the general area of the cell or cells you want to edit.

2.  **Using one finger on your touchpad, move the pointer to the desired cell.**

3.  **Click your touchpad.**

    The desired cell is now active, enabling you to insert new text or change text that's already there.

TIP

To overwrite the cell contents, go to the cell and start typing. To delete the cell contents, go to the cell and press Backspace. To insert additional data in a cell that already contains data, follow these steps:

1.  **Click the desired cell once.**

    The selected cell is highlighted with a blue border.

2.  **Click anywhere in the Formula bar.**

    A blinking cursor appears in the Formula bar, indicating that you can add, edit, or delete text using your keyboard.

3.  **Add, edit, change, and remove text as you like; then press Enter.**

You can also use a feature called Find and replace to find a specific piece of data within your spreadsheet, as shown in Figure 9-6. To find data using the Find and replace feature, follow these steps:

1. **Open the Edit menu and choose Find and replace.**

   You can also use the keyboard shortcut Ctrl+H.

   The Find and replace window appears. In this window, you can specify what you want to search for and what you want the search string replaced with, among other options.

   You can move the window around on the screen if it's covering cells you're working with.

2. **Fill in the information you want to use for your search.**

   You can specify any of the following options:

   - **Find:** The text or data you want to find.

   - **Replace:** To replace the data you're searching for, simply enter new data here.

   - **Search:** In this section, you can specify the scope of the search in a drop-down menu, including every sheet in your document, the current sheet, or a specific range of cells. You can also select boxes to match case or entire contents of a cell, or to search formulas and formula expressions.

**FIGURE 9-6:**
Find and replace content in Google Sheets.

*Illustration courtesy of Peter H. Gregory*

- **Match case:** Select this box to search for text exactly as you type it (regarding any use of upper- or lowercase, or any combination) in the Find box.

- **Match entire cell contents:** The complete cell must match your search query.

- **Search using regular expressions:** Search for a particular character pattern.

- **Also search within formulas:** Search formulas, in addition to the contents of cells.

- **Also search within links:** Search hyperlinks, in addition to the contents of cells.

Use the provided checkboxes to fine-tune your search and reduce potentially inaccurate search results.

**TIP**

3. **Click Find.**

If you are confident that the values you typed into the Find and replace fields are accurate, you can click Replace all to make all changes immediately.

**TIP**

4. **Sort through search results by clicking the Find button at the bottom-right of the Find and replace pane.**

As you navigate through the search results in your document, Sheets changes the highlight color on the cell to indicate where you are in the spreadsheet.

5. **When you successfully locate and replace the word or words in your spreadsheet, click the _X_ in the top-right corner of the Find and replace pane to close that pane.**

The pane disappears, but the text you searched for remains highlighted and ready to be deleted or edited.

## Copying and pasting data

As you enter data into your spreadsheet, you can avoid typing repetitive text using the Copy and Paste functions. Copying and pasting can be done in a couple of ways — on the keyboard, with the touchpad, or a combination of both. To copy and paste a single cell, follow these steps:

1. **Select the cell that you want to copy.**

To copy and paste a range of cells, select the first cell in the range, hold the Shift key, and then select the last cell in the range.

**TIP**

The selection area is highlighted in blue.

2. **Open the Edit menu and choose Copy.**

   The selected cell's contents are copied and stored in the Clipboard.

   The Clipboard can remember *only one thing* at a time. If you copy a selection of text and then copy another selection of text without pasting the first selection of text, Sheets forgets the first selection.

3. **Navigate to the cell where you want to paste the copied data.**

4. **Once again, open the Edit menu. This time, choose Paste.**

   The data copied to the Clipboard is now pasted into the selected cell.

TIP

When copying and pasting large data areas, you can easily underestimate the amount of space needed for the paste and inadvertently overwrite meaningful data. However, you can undo any past action by clicking the Undo button in the Edit toolbar. The Undo button looks like an arrow in the shape of a half-circle pointing to the left (counterclockwise). If you keep clicking Undo, your edits are undone, one at a time.

You may find that navigating through your spreadsheet with the keyboard is too slow for pasting the contents of one cell into a cell that's several rows or columns away. Your touchpad offers a fast and convenient option to copy and paste quickly. To copy and paste a cell by using your touchpad, use the following steps:

1. **Using your touchpad, move your cursor to the cell you want to copy.**

2. **Tap the desired cell once to select it.**

TIP

   To select a range of cells, tap the first cell in the range and, without releasing your finger, move to the other end of the range you want to copy, and then release.

3. **Open the Edit menu and select Copy.**

   The selected cell is copied to the Clipboard.

4. **Using your touchpad, scroll to the desired location, and tap the selected cell.**

   To paste a range of cells, select the cell you want to be the top-left corner of your pasted range.

5. **Open the Edit menu and choose Paste.**

   The copied selection is pasted in.

TIP

You can use shortcut keys to copy and paste cells to save time. Press Ctrl+C to copy a cell or cells, and press Ctrl+V to paste the copied cells. You can also quickly undo a paste (or many other actions) by pressing Ctrl+Z.

**TIP**

Alt-click your selection to reveal a menu of actions, including Copy and Paste. (See Figure 9-7.) You may need to scroll through the menu to reveal all actions.

| Format | Data | Tools | Extensions | Help | Last edit was 11 minutes ago |
|---|---|---|---|---|---|

$ % .0 .00 123 ▾

mmies

| | | | | G |
|---|---|---|---|---|

✂ Cut     Ctrl+X

ojects

🗐 Copy     Ctrl+C

📋 Paste     Ctrl+V    :00

📋 Paste special     ▸    3860

| ub Dat | Title | | | | ge: |
|---|---|---|---|---|---|
| 2000 | Solaris Securi | + Insert 1 row above | | | 290 |
| 2000 | Solaris Securi | | | | |
| 2000 | Solaris Securi | + Insert 1 column left | | | |
| 2001 | Sun Certified | + Insert cells ▸ | | | 448 |
| 2003 | Enterprise Inf | | | | 168 |
| 2003 | Enterprise Inf | 🗑 Delete row | | | |
| 2002 | CISSP For Dur | | | | 136 |
| 2003 | Security+ Cer | 🗑 Delete column | | | 136 |
| 2004 | Computer Vir | 🗑 Delete cells ▸ | | | 292 |
| 2005 | Blocking Spar | | | | 190 |
| 2006 | SIP Communi | 🕓 Show edit history | | | 72 |
| 2006 | VoIP Security | | | | 68 |
| 2007 | Converged Ne | 🔗 Insert link | | | 52 |
| 2007 | IP Multimedi: | 💬 Comment   Ctrl+Alt+M | | | 32 |
| 2007 | Midsized Busi | | | | 52 |
| | | 🗒 Insert note | | | |
| | | ⓔ Convert to people chip | | | |

**FIGURE 9-7:** Actions that you can carry out on a cell or selection of cells in Google Sheets.

*Illustration courtesy of Peter H. Gregory*

## Moving data with Cut and Paste

When you want to replicate data, Copy and Paste is the mode of operation you should use. When you want to *move* data but not replicate it, use Cut and Paste. To move data in your sheet using the Cut and Paste method, follow these steps:

1. **Using your touchpad, click to select the cell whose contents you want to move (or click and drag your cursor across all the cells whose contents you want to move) and then release.**

   The cell(s) are highlighted.

2. **Alt-click the highlighted cell(s).**

   A pop-up menu appears, revealing several options.

3. **Select Cut from the menu.**

   A dashed border surrounds your selection, indicating that the enclosed data has been cut.

4. **Using the touchpad, navigate where you want to paste your data.**

5. **Alt-click the cell where you want to paste your data.**

   A pop-up menu appears.

6. **Select Paste.**

   The data is moved accordingly.

You can paste data you've cut as many times as you like. However, when you copy or cut a *new* selection of text, the previously cut text is replaced with the newly cut text.

## Using Autofill to save time

The Autofill feature in Sheets makes it easy to copy and paste a particular pattern of data or expand a series of data without manually entering the data or using the Copy and Paste feature repeatedly. To use Autofill to expand a series of data, follow these steps:

1. **In cell A1, type July 28.**

2. **In cell A2, type July 29.**

3. **In cell A3, type July 30.**

4. **Click cell A1 and select these cells by dragging your cursor down to cell A3.**

   Notice that a tiny blue square appears in the bottom-right corner of your selection, as pictured in Figure 9-8. This blue square is called the Autofill square and has magical power.

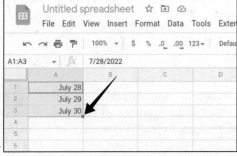

**FIGURE 9-8:**
The Autofill square in Google Sheets.

*Illustration courtesy of Peter H. Gregory*

5. **Click the blue Autofill square and drag your selection down to Cell A10.**

6. **Release your click.**

   Sheets automatically fills your selection with the identified date sequence, as shown in Figure 9-9.

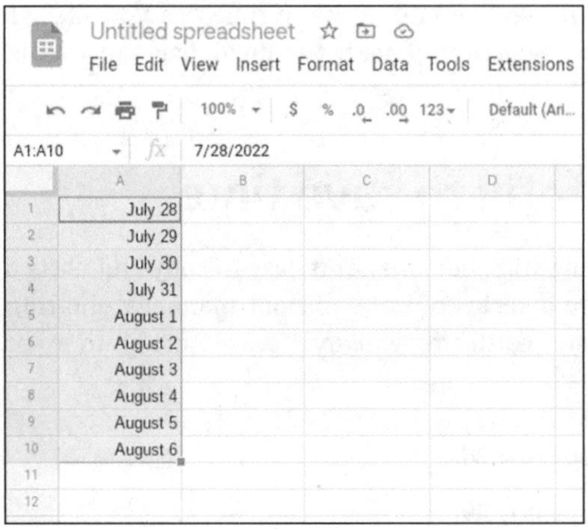

FIGURE 9-9: Sheets completes the sequence of dates with Autofill.

*Illustration courtesy of Peter H. Gregory*

You can use Autofill to complete most sequences as long as you give Autofill enough information to guess what your sequence is. If Autofill can't identify your sequence, it simply replicates your data as a pattern.

**TIP** It takes a bit of practice to use the Autofill square, partly because it is very small on the screen. Note how the cursor changes when you hover over it correctly — the pointer changes to a small "crosshairs" pattern.

# Formatting Data

Google Sheets gives you great control over the appearance of the content in your spreadsheet. You can change the formatting of a complete spreadsheet, rows, columns, or single cells. You can, in some instances, apply multiple style changes to the contents within a cell. For instance, you can apply different types of formatting, such as bold or italics, within one cell. On the other hand, you can't mix font sizes within a single cell.

Google Sheets allows you to style your sheet in many different ways, including the following:

>> **Font formatting:** *Font* means the style of typeface. With Sheets, you can change fonts; change the size or color of a font; or apply new styles like bold, italics, underline, or strikethrough to a font.

>> **Cell formatting:** You can put borders around a cell or group of cells, or apply a background color. You can also auto-format numbers in a cell to take on a particular format. For example, you may want to auto-format currencies, percentages, dates, and times, to name a few.

>> **Alignment:** You can change the horizontal alignment of the text within a cell to be left-, center-, or right-aligned, or change the vertical alignment so that your text appears at the top, middle, or bottom of the cell. You can even style text so that it wraps to another line in your cell; this feature allows a cell with a lot of content to occupy multiple lines of text.

TIP

If you read Chapter 8 before reading this chapter, by now, you should be noticing numerous similarities with the operation of Docs and Sheets, including formatting, copying and pasting, and more. These similarities make all of the Google tools easier to learn and use.

## Working with fonts

With Sheets, you can change the font of any data in your spreadsheet. The options are potentially limitless, but for clarity, it's better to limit the number of fonts in one spreadsheet. Google Sheets comes preloaded with over 20 fonts, and you can add more fonts if you need more. Your initial font options include

>> Arial

>> Courier New

>> **Impact**

>> Times New Roman

>> Verdana

To change your font, follow these steps:

1.  **Using your touchpad, select the cells you want to change by clicking and dragging your cursor.**

    Sheets highlights the selected cells.

2. **Open the Format menu; then open the Font submenu.**

The Font submenu reveals available font choices.

The Font submenu is titled with the font name for the selected body of text. By default, all text appears in Arial font.

3. **Select any one of the fonts listed.**

The contents of the highlighted cells are changed to the selected font.

If the selected cells contain no data, the new font will apply to new text you add later.

## Adding new fonts

The Google Sheets default list of fonts is a brief list of eight. Other spreadsheet programs, such as Microsoft Excel, have extensive lists of fonts by default. Google provides users with an initial list of the most globally popular fonts to keep things simple at first. You can, however, add fonts to your spreadsheets. To do so, follow these steps:

1. **Click the Font menu in the Edit toolbar.**

2. **Select More Fonts to add fonts.**

The Font selection window, shown in Figure 8-6 in Chapter 8, gives you a robust list of new fonts from which to choose. Scroll down through the list to reveal more fonts.

3. **Select the desired fonts by clicking each one you want.**

Each selected font is highlighted in blue and given a check mark.

4. **Click OK to finish adding the fonts to your Font menu and exit.**

When you are ready to change the font of your text, you can choose from a list containing your original fonts plus your newly selected fonts from the Font menu.

Adding fonts to Google Sheets makes these fonts available for Google Docs and Google Slides.

## Removing fonts from the Font menu

The more fonts you add, the more fonts you will have to rifle through when deciding to change the font of your text. Sometime in the future, you may decide that you have too many fonts and it's time for some decluttering. To remove fonts from Sheets, take these steps:

1. **Open the Font menu in the Edit toolbar.**

2. **Select More Fonts.**

   The Font window appears. A list of new fonts appears on the left of the window; on the right, a list of fonts currently in use by your Sheets account appears.

3. **Scroll through the list of fonts on the right side of the window under My Fonts and locate the font or fonts you want to remove. Then, to remove a font, click the X to the right of that font's name.**

   The font disappears from the list of available fonts.

4. **Click OK.**

TIP

Removing a font from your list of fonts does not affect your spreadsheets, even if they contain a font you removed from the menu. After you use a font in your spreadsheet, you can change more text to use that font, even if you removed it from your Font menu. (A removed font, however, will not be available in any new spreadsheets or existing spreadsheets not containing the font.)

## Styling your data

You can accentuate a font by applying various styles to the font itself, including

>> **Size:** Make your content bigger or smaller as you see fit.

>> **Bold:** Make content bold. Making the text Bold font is sometimes referred to as having a *heavy weight*.

>> **Italics:** Make the content italicized, or slanted to the right.

>> **Underline:** Place a line under your content to indicate importance.

>> **Strikethrough:** Place a line through the middle of your content. This is useful in communicating a change in your text or illustrating a point.

>> **Color:** Track changes, distinguish individual users in collaboration, or add style to your content by changing the color.

## Changing font size

You can change the size of your content by following these steps:

1. **Using your touchpad, select the cells you want to change by clicking and dragging your cursor.**

   The selected text is highlighted.

2. **Open the Font Size menu in the Edit toolbar.**

It's the number found to the left of the Bold button in the Edit toolbar. When you click it, a menu appears, revealing several font sizes (in points) to choose from.

3. **Select the desired font size.**

Your selected data is now the chosen size.

## Applying bold, italics, underline, or strikethrough to your content

To apply formatting to a specific selection of cells, follow these steps:

1. **Using your touchpad, select the cells you want to change by clicking and dragging your cursor.**

The selected cells are highlighted.

2. **Apply bold, italics, underline, or strikethrough, as needed.**

You can use either of the following methods:

- **To add bold, italics, or strikethrough:** Click the appropriate button in the Edit toolbar — the **B** button for bold, the *I* button for italic, or the S button for strikethrough. (No button exists for the underline on the standard Edit toolbar.)

- **To add an underline:** Open the Format menu in the application menu and select Underline.

Your selection changes appropriately.

TIP

You can quickly apply styles to your data by using hotkeys. Just press Ctrl+B (for bold), Ctrl+I (italic), Ctrl+U (underline), or Alt+Shift+5 (strikethrough).

## Coloring your content

Google Sheets allows you to change the color of your data to group your data visually, indicate important information, or just give your spreadsheet a little pizazz! To change the color of your data, follow these steps:

1. **Using your touchpad, select the cells you want to change by clicking and dragging your cursor.**

The selected cells are highlighted.

2. **Open the Color menu in the Edit toolbar.**

   It's the **A** button found to the right of the **S** button.

   A Color menu appears, revealing several color options, as shown in Figure 9-10.

3. **Select your desired color.**

   The data in the selected cells now appears in the selected color.

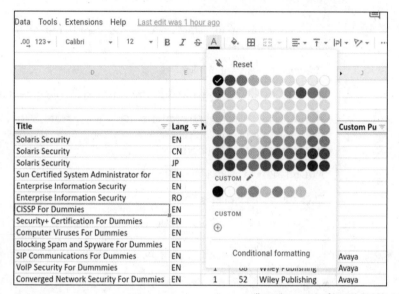

Illustration courtesy of Peter H. Gregory

FIGURE 9-10:
Selecting
colors for text in
Google Sheets.

**TIP**

You can change the color of text in a cell as well as the color of the cell itself. I discuss cell color later in this chapter.

## Changing alignment

Google Sheets gives you several options for changing your data's horizontal and vertical alignment. Horizontal alignment options include

» Left

» Right

» Center

Vertical alignment options include

» Top
» Middle
» Bottom

To adjust the alignment of your data, follow these steps:

1. **Using your touchpad, select the cells you want to realign by clicking and dragging your cursor.**

   The selected cells are highlighted.

2. **In the Edit toolbar, find and click the appropriate Alignment button.**

   The Horizontal Alignment button is located a few buttons to the right of the text color button. The Vertical Alignment button is located to the right of the Horizontal Alignment button.

   A menu with the alignment options appears.

3. **Click the desired alignment.**

   The selected cells of data are realigned accordingly.

**REMEMBER**

You can hover over the alignment buttons to see their function, as shown in Figure 9-11.

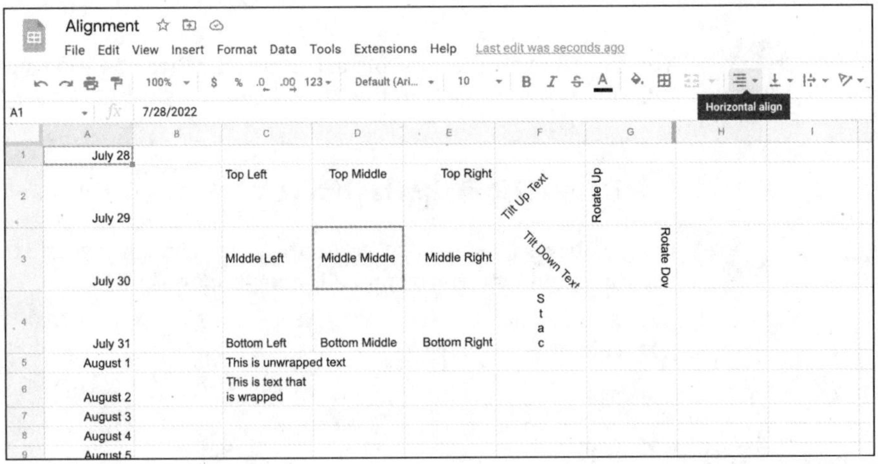

FIGURE 9-11:
Hovering over alignment buttons reveals their purpose.

*Illustration courtesy of Peter H. Gregory*

# Wrapping text in a cell

By default, when you enter text into a cell, the text appears on a single line, so to show all the entered text, you may have to adjust the width of your cell. However, Sheets has a feature called *wrap text* that causes text to go to the next line after it reaches the maximum width of your cell. With this feature, you can set text to wrap in one cell or every cell in a sheet. To activate wrap text, follow these steps:

1. **Use your touchpad to select the desired cells by clicking and dragging your cursor.**

   The selected cells are highlighted.

2. **Open the Format menu.**

3. **Choose Wrap text.**

   Text that extends beyond the boundaries of your cell walls will be wrapped to another line. Here, the text in cell C5 is too long for the cell, spilling over the cells to the right. The text in cell C6 is set for wrap text, so all the text stays in the cell, which takes multiple lines.

# Clearing formatting

Sometimes you just need to start over. The good news is that Sheets makes it easy to wipe out all formatting in a section of cells or your complete spreadsheet. To clear your formatting, follow these steps:

1. **Select the formatted cells you want to clear.**

   The selected cells are highlighted.

2. **Open the Format menu in the Applications menu.**

3. **Select Clear formatting.**

   The selected data is reset to defaults: left-aligned, with all style elements — including color, underline, strikethrough, italics, bold, and so on — removed.

   You can also use the Clear formatting shortcut, which is Ctrl+\.

**TIP**

To clear the formatting of an entire document, press Ctrl+A instead of selecting cells. Pressing Ctrl+A selects the entire worksheet. (If your workbook has multiple worksheets or tabs, pressing Ctrl+A clears formatting only in the worksheet you are viewing.)

# Customizing Your Spreadsheet

When you open Sheets for the first time (and when you click the + [plus sign] button to create a new spreadsheet), you're presented with a blank canvas of empty, uniform cells organized in a neat grid pattern. Sheets allows you to customize this grid of information so that it looks and works exactly how you like. In addition to all the text formatting discussed earlier, you can

>> Add and remove columns and rows

>> Change the height of rows and the width of individual (or all) columns

>> Hide rows and columns

>> Merge multiple cells into one cell

>> Change how numbers are displayed

>> Add borders to individual cells and groups of cells

>> Customize the background color of cells

## Adding and deleting rows and columns

Adding rows or columns makes it easier to insert data into areas already populated with data. Instead of cutting and pasting data to make room, you can simply add an empty row or column.

The same goes for removing rows or columns. Deleting a column or row is a fast way to remove extraneous cells from your spreadsheet. When you get into formulas (see the section "Performing Calculations with Formulas" later in this chapter), you will find that adding and deleting rows and columns keeps your formulas and formatting intact.

### Adding a new row or column

You can add a new row or column by following these steps:

1. **Using your touchpad, move your cursor to the row or column header next to which you want to insert a new row or column, and Alt-click the row or column header.**

**REMEMBER**

Column headers are indicated by a letter. Row headers are indicated by a number.

A menu appears, revealing several options. The menu for rows is shown in Figure 9-12.

**2.** **Insert a new row by choosing Insert 1 row above or Insert 1 row below, or insert a new column by choosing Insert 1 column left or Insert 1 column right.**

A new row or column is inserted accordingly.

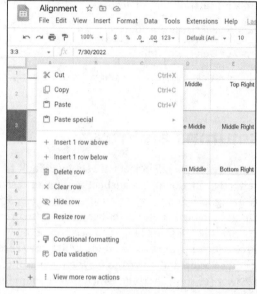

**FIGURE 9-12:**
The Alt-click
menu for rows in
Google Sheets.

*Illustration courtesy of Peter H. Gregory*

You can see from the menu that you can do other things with a row or column, including:

» Delete a row or column

» Clear a row or column

» Hide a row or column

» Resize a row or column (meaning, its width or height)

» Merge all cells in a row or column into a single cell

**TIP**

Don't worry about making your spreadsheet too big. Size is never a problem. The largest spreadsheet you can make with Sheets can have up to 10 *million* cells and as many as 18,278 columns. (I'm having trouble imagining a real-world reason why anyone would have a spreadsheet so large — maybe a huge mailing list?)

## Deleting a row or column

You can delete a row or column by following these steps:

1. **Using your touchpad, move your cursor to the header of the row or column you want to delete.**

2. **Alt-click the row number or column letter.**

   A menu appears, revealing several options.

3. **Click Delete row or Delete column.**

   The row or column is deleted. The remaining rows or columns move together to fill the gap.

# Resizing columns and rows

The row and column sizes in Google Sheets are set by default to an arbitrary size. You can build a perfectly functional spreadsheet and never resize any columns or rows. However, resizing is a great way to ensure that your data is viewable and useful. If a text string is too big for the current column width or row height, Sheets lets you quickly change the width or height to accommodate your needs. Also, if your columns are too wide or your rows too high, which may result in your having to scroll back and forth (or up and down) to view all your content, you can make some columns narrower (or rows shorter), which makes room for more content to appear on your screen.

To resize your column or row, follow these steps:

1. **Using your touchpad, move your pointer to the column or row header you want to resize.**

   Make sure your pointer is over the line on the right side of the column or bottom side of the row that you would like to resize.

   Your pointer turns into a set of arrows, and the border between the two column or row headings turns blue, indicating that Sheets is ready for you to resize.

2. **Click and drag to change the column or row size.**

3. **When you are satisfied with the new size, release your click.**

**TIP**
You can also change the size of multiple rows or columns at the same time. To do so, the columns or rows must be sequential. For example, you can resize columns 1, 2, and 3 simultaneously, but you can't resize columns 1, 2, and 5 at the same time. To resize multiple columns or rows, follow these steps:

1. **Using your touchpad, click the header for the first column or row in the series you want to resize.**

   The selected row or column is highlighted.

2. **Shift-click the header for the last column or row in the series you want to resize.**

   Every row or column in the series is selected.

3. **Relocate your pointer so it rests over the line dividing two rows or columns in your selection.**

   The pointer turns into a set of arrows, and the border between the two column or row headings turns blue.

4. **Click and drag the column or row to resize.**

5. **When you're satisfied, release your click.**

   Each row or column in the series is resized.

## Hiding columns and rows

Hiding rows and columns is handy when you're presenting a spreadsheet and want to hide a row or column of notes, or when some of your data is necessary for calculations but not relevant enough to be shown. Hiding is a great way to keep data in its place but out of sight. To hide a row or column, follow these steps:

1. **Using your touchpad, move your pointer over the header of the row or column you want to hide.**

2. **Alt-click the row or column header.**

   A menu appears, revealing several options.

3. **Select Hide column or Hide row, whichever is appropriate.**

   The associated row or column vanishes, leaving only a set of arrows over the column or row dividing line.

   To restore your hidden column or row, click these arrows.

## Merging cells

Sometimes you want or even need to have a heading over several columns or rows. To do this, you need to merge multiple cells to form a single cell spanning multiple columns or rows. To merge cells, follow these steps:

1. **Shift-click the contiguous cells you want to merge.**

   The selected cells become highlighted.

2. **Click the Merge cells button in the Edit toolbar, located a few buttons to the right of the Bold, Italic, and Strikethrough formatting buttons.**

   The highlighted cells merge.

**WARNING**

   Any data in one or more of the merged cells may be lost. Be sure to have a copy of the cell's contents before merging or be ready to Undo the merge if you experience unintended results.

3. **To unmerge the cells, select the newly merged cell and click the Merge cells button again.**

   The cells that you merged are restored to being individual cells. If you placed content in the merged cell, that content will appear in the first row or column of the previously merged set.

## Formatting numbers

People often use spreadsheets to organize and calculate numeric data. With Google Sheets, you can auto-format your cells to accommodate several numeric data types, including

>> Currency

>> Percentages

>> Decimals

>> Financial notation

>> Scientific notation

>> Dates

>> Times

Formatting cells for these numeric types can be done by following these steps:

1. **Use your touchpad to select the cell or cells you want to format.**

2. **Open the Format menu.**

3. **Move your pointer over Number in the menu.**

   A submenu appears, revealing several formatting options.

4. **Select the desired formatting style, as shown in Figure 9-13.**

   The selected cells now auto-format numeric entries to match the chosen style.

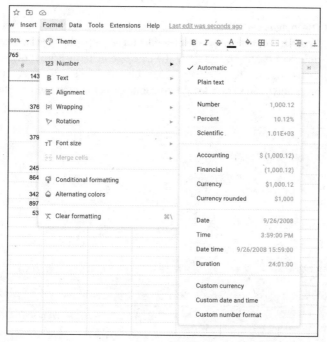

**FIGURE 9-13:**
Applying number
formatting to
selected cells in
Google Sheets.

# Grouping cells with colors and borders

When working with spreadsheets containing large amounts of data, the numbers and letters can begin to blend together. You can distinguish groups of cells with borders or colors to make navigating your spreadsheet easier. Borders and cell shading can also add a nice touch of style to your spreadsheets.

You can add borders to your spreadsheet by following these steps:

1. **Using your touchpad, select the cells you want to style by clicking and dragging your cursor.**

   The selected cells are highlighted.

2. **Click the Border button in the Edit toolbar.**

   The Border button, which looks like a little square with four squares inside, is a few buttons to the right of the Bold, Italic, and Strikethrough formatting buttons.

   A menu appears, giving you several options.

3. **To simply place a border around your cells, locate the image that shows a border outline and click it.**

**TIP**

The images in the Border menu, as shown in Figure 9-14, illustrate precisely where the border will go if selected. You can also change the border style to dotted or dashed by selecting the Line option in the Border Style menu, or you can change the color of your border by using the Border Color option, the drop-down menu on the right that looks like an underlined pencil.

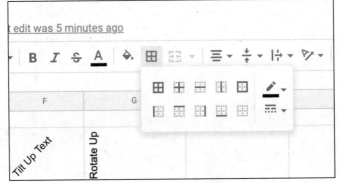

**FIGURE 9-14:**
Adding a border to cells in Google Sheets.

You can also create visual separation in your spreadsheet by incorporating color into your cells. To apply a color background to a cell or group of cells, follow these steps:

1. **Using your touchpad, select the cells you want to color by clicking and dragging your cursor.**

   The selected cells are highlighted.

2. **Click the Background Color button in the Edit toolbar.**

   This button is located just to the right of the Bold, Italic, and Strikethrough buttons and looks like paint being poured out of a can. When you hover over the button, the words *Fill Color* appear.

   A menu appears, giving you several options.

3. **Select a color from the menu.**

   The background of the selected cells is changed to the chosen color.

# Performing Calculations with Formulas

Google Sheets is a powerful spreadsheet tool. With Sheets, you can perform analysis on text and numeric values alike, and incorporate financial, mathematical, and statistical analysis. The following sections serve as an intro to Sheets' basic functions and formulas.

## Using basic mathematical formulas

Sheets can perform mathematical calculations for you. All you have to do is tell Sheets that you want it to perform a calculation on the information contained in cells in your spreadsheet. You must start your equation with an equal sign (=) to do this. Make sheets do basic addition by following these steps:

1. **With Sheets open, select a cell.**

2. **Type the following string of characters precisely:**

   ```
   =50+50
   ```

3. **Press Enter.**

   Sheets solves the equation and displays the answer, 100.

TIP

Although the cell displays 100, if you look at the Formula bar, you see the formula still reads what you typed in: =50+50.

You can use several mathematical operators to perform calculations with Sheets. They include

>> **Addition:** +

>> **Subtraction:** –

>> **Division:** /

>> **Multiplication:** *

Sheets interprets the order of operations according to the standard mathematical order of operations: It performs calculations within parentheses first, followed by multiplication or division (from left to right), and finally, addition or subtraction (from left to right).

To ensure that Sheets always follows the mathematical order of operations you intended, use parentheses to group operations together. For example, in a cell, enter the following equation:

=((5+5)*8)/2

You get the answer 40. When more than one set of parentheses exists, Sheets performs the instructions within the innermost set first and then works its way outward. Without parentheses, the equation becomes

=5+5*8/2

This equation returns the answer 25. Use parentheses to ensure that your operations are performed in the order you intended.

**WARNING**

Building formulas can become complex very quickly. To edit a formula, select the cell that contains the formula and then click in the Formula bar at the top of your Sheets window to edit the formula. Typing in the cell itself overwrites the contents, leaving you to start again!

## Adding formulas to calculate values in cells

Google Sheets was designed for use beyond just standard calculator functions. You can also use Sheets to perform calculations using data in multiple cells within your spreadsheet. Instead of entering numbers into your equations, you can enter cell coordinates. To see how this works, you first have to have numbers in some cells, so this example walks you through adding some data and then entering the formula for Sheets to calculate:

1. **With Sheets open, enter the number 25 into cell A2.**

2. **Enter the number 50 into cell A3.**

3. **Enter the number 75 into cell A4.**

4. **In cell A5, enter the following equation:**

   =A2+A3+A4

5. **Press Enter.**

   Sheets adds cells A2, A3, and A4 together and then displays the answer — 150 — in cell A5.

   Next, try changing the data in cells A2, A3, or A4 and see how the value in cell A5 changes immediately.

**TIP**

Don't forget to put the equals sign (=) before a formula; otherwise, the cell's contents will contain the characters in the formula instead of the result that Sheets would get by performing the calculation.

You can also use Google Sheets to perform a calculation using values in cells along with other values in the formula. Try it yourself with these steps:

1. **With Sheets open, enter the number 25 into cell A2.**

2. **Enter the number 50 into cell A3.**

3. **Enter the number 75 into cell A4.**

4. **In cell A5, enter the following equation:**

   =(A2+A3+A4)*10

5. **Press Enter.**

   Sheets adds cells A2, A3, and A4 together and then multiplies the total by 10. The resulting answer is 1500, displayed in cell A5.

## Working with spreadsheet functions

Sheets has an extensive library of functions that perform various computations. However, the most widely used functions in Sheets are

- **»  SUM:** Adds all the numbers in a range of cells.

- **»  AVERAGE:** Outputs the average of the values in a specific set of cells or a range of cells.

- **»  COUNT:** Counts how many numbers are in a list of cells. You can specify cells or enter a range.

- **»  MAX:** Outputs the largest number in a specific set of cells or a range.

- **»  MIN:** Outputs the smallest number in a specific set of cells or a range.

Functions simplify the process of writing complex formulas and reduce the typing needed to get the desired result. To try using the SUM function, follow these steps:

1. **With Sheets open, enter the number 25 into cell A2.**

2. **Enter the number 50 into cell A3.**

3. **Enter the number 75 into cell A4.**

4. **In cell A6, enter the following equation:**

   =SUM(A2:A4)

5. **Press Enter.**

   The formula tells Sheets that you want to add the values in cells A2 through A4. The output value is 150, which Sheets displays in cell A6.

6. **To use parentheses to set the order in which functions are used in the equation, in cell A6, enter the following equation:**

   =(SUM(A2:A4)*10)

7. **Press Enter.**

   Sheets first calculates the sum of the values in cells A2 through A4 and then multiplies the total by 10, displaying 1500 in cell A6. This is shown in Figure 9-15.

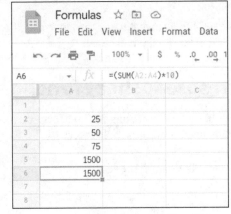

**FIGURE 9-15:** Using functions to add the contents of cells together.

*Illustration courtesy of Peter H. Gregory*

**TIP**

There are hundreds of functions available in Sheets that can be used in formulas. A complete list is available at support.google.com/docs/table/25273.

# Saving Documents

As you work in Google Sheets, Google saves almost every change in real-time to your Google Drive account (remember that Google Drive is the cloud-based storage that allows you to safely store your files and access them from any device with an internet connection). Every file you create with Google Sheets is saved to your Drive folder so that you can access it at home, on the road, at work, or anywhere else you may need to, and from any device you happen to be using at the time. As is the case with Docs, Sheets has no manual Save feature.

# Naming your document

When you open a new spreadsheet with Sheets, the default name for the spreadsheet is Untitled Spreadsheet. You don't, however, want to leave your spreadsheet untitled. Drive doesn't have a problem storing multiple files with the same name. Still, it's best to name your spreadsheet immediately to save yourself a little confusion. To name your spreadsheet, follow these steps:

1. **Open a new spreadsheet.**

   The easiest way to open a new spreadsheet is by launching Sheets from the Launcher.

   A Chrome web browser opens and loads Sheets.

2. **Click the "+" to start a new worksheet.**

   After Sheets is open, the name of your new document, Untitled Spreadsheet, appears in the top-left corner. This works just like renaming a word processing file as shown in Figure 8-10.

3. **Click Untitled Spreadsheet in the top-left corner of your spreadsheet.**

   The cursor is positioned preceding the words Untitled Spreadsheet.

4. **Type the new name for your spreadsheet and press Enter.**

   The name Untitled Spreadsheet is now replaced with your new name.

   The next time you look at Google Drive, you'll see the new filename, which is your renamed spreadsheet. The spreadsheet will be updated and saved in real-time as you continue to make edits.

# Exporting documents

From time to time, you may need to export your spreadsheets to formats that others may be comfortable with. Sheets allows you to export spreadsheets to a few standard formats, including

>> Microsoft Excel (.xlsx)

>> OpenDocument (.ods)

>> PDF (.pdf)

>> Comma-separated values (.csv)

>> Tab-separated values (.tsv)

>> Web page (.html)

Exporting documents to different file types may change the formatting within your document. For example, exporting to the CSV and TSV formats strips out all formatting, such as borders, fonts, and colors. Before sending your spreadsheets after an export, you should review them to ensure everything is as it should be!

You can export your documents by following these steps:

1. **Click File and hover your cursor over Download as.**

   A submenu appears, revealing the file types that are available for export.

2. **Select the desired file type.**

   You see a preview of your exported spreadsheet.

3. **Click the Export button in the upper right of the Sheets window.**

   Google Sheets now asks you to specify the name of the file to create, as well as the location. By default, your file will be located in the Downloads folder. You can, however, click a different folder on the left side of the Save file as pane, including Google Drive or even a folder within Google Drive.

4. **Click the folder you want to save the file in, click the filename, and then click Save.**

   Your spreadsheet is exported to the specified location in the desired file type.

5. **To view the downloaded file, open the Files app, go to the folder you specified in Step 4, and look for the file.**

Exporting a worksheet to a different format works just like the export function in Google Docs that is shown in Figure 8-11.

When you export a spreadsheet, there are several options in the Export window, including whether you want to export just the tab displayed or all tabs, page orientation (portrait or landscape), formatting, margins, and more. Try these to see how your exported spreadsheet appears. (You can always delete these files later using the Files app.)

Exporting a spreadsheet doesn't change the original spreadsheet; instead, it makes a copy of it in the specified format. The original Google Sheets file is still there; you can continue editing it as much as you like.

# Collaboration with Sheets

By default, Google Sheets and Google Drive make your files accessible only to you. You can, however, change the visibility settings on your files and invite specific people, or even the entire world, to comment, view, or edit your spreadsheet! To share your spreadsheet with specific people, follow the same steps you would to share a Google Doc, which is explained in Chapter 8.

**TIP**

The users invited to view, edit, or comment on your spreadsheet have to log in to Google Sheets using the email addresses with which you shared the spreadsheet. If your collaborators don't have a Google Account under the email address that you used, you'll see a warning saying that the document can be edited by anyone who has the email invitation.

# Tracking Versions of Your Spreadsheet

Keeping track of revisions is very important when creating documents with multiple collaborators. Fortunately, Google Sheets handles version control masterfully. As you and your collaborators make changes to your spreadsheets, Sheets stamps those changes with the time and date so that you can view previous versions of your spreadsheet and even revert to an earlier version if you need to.

Version tracking is a default feature of Google Sheets, so you don't need to do anything to take advantage of it. To view your version history, follow these steps:

1.  **Open the File menu, hover over Version history, and tap See version history.**

    A Version history pane appears on the right portion of your screen. The pane contains the various versions of your spreadsheet in order from the most recent to the oldest. If you made multiple changes on any given day, a tiny black arrow appears to the left of the date; click the arrow to see the details for that date. The names of the people who saved the spreadsheet are also shown. (If you are not sharing your spreadsheet, it will always be your name.) This feature works the same way as in Google Docs, shown in Figure 8-14.

2.  **Click a version date in the Version history box.**

    A preview of the version you chose appears in the main document area. Changes that occurred between versions appear in green.

3. **To change versions, click on the three little dots, then Restore this version.**

Google Sheets will ask you to name this version.

The restored version becomes the current version, and the previous version of the application is saved in the Version history, so you can revert to it if needed.

# Using Sheets Offline

Google Sheets is a web-based spreadsheet tool, meaning you must have an internet connection to access all its features. However, an offline version of Sheets is available if you find yourself without a connection to the internet.

To use Google Sheets offline, follow the steps at the end of Chapter 7 to mark one or more spreadsheet files or folders that you want to use offline. Then, you'll be able to edit those marked spreadsheets.

While offline, you can't access some of the features available to Sheets users connected to the internet (such as downloading new fonts). You can, however, create spreadsheets and save them. Later, when you connect to the internet, Drive uploads the saved spreadsheets and enables all internet-only features.

Chapter **10**

# Preparing Presentations

resentations have come a long way in the past 40 years. While slide and overhead projectors were technological marvels years ago, today, they have been replaced with interactive presentations involving text, images, audio, and video. When Microsoft introduced PowerPoint in 1987, it changed presentations forever. Today, it has become so entrenched in business and education that the name is almost used interchangeably to mean presentation, the way people refer to tissues as Kleenex and lip balm as ChapStick. But the market penetration of PowerPoint didn't keep Google from creating a presentation software that could rival it.

Google Slides is a free, web-based presentation software program that allows you to make high-powered, engaging presentations that you can access anywhere in the world, thanks to the Google online platform. This isn't an either/or proposition, however. Slides created with Google Slides can be viewed and edited with PowerPoint, and vice versa.

In this chapter, you discover how to create beautiful presentations with Google Slides. Use existing templates or create your own; add, edit, and style images and text; collaborate with teams around the globe; and export your presentations to multiple formats to share your presentations with colleagues, coworkers, class-mates, and more. Google Slides is a powerful communication tool in any setting.

# Navigating Google Slides

Like the rest of the Google office suite, Slides is easy to use for beginners and experienced presentation makers alike. If you have experience with PowerPoint, the transition will be easy for you. As with other Google tools, Slides can easily read and also create presentations in PowerPoint format that another person using PowerPoint can also use.

 To launch Google Slides from your Chromebook, open the Launcher and click the Slides icon. The Slides application opens in a Chrome browser window and creates a new untitled document resembling what you see in Figure 10-1.

Illustration courtesy of Peter H. Gregory

**FIGURE 10-1:**
The Google Slides startup screen.

## Creating your presentation

To begin creating your presentation, click the colorful + (plus sign) icon near the lower-right corner of the Slides window (the first time you start Slides, it will be shown near the top left, as Figure 10-1 shows). Slides creates the first slide for you — a blank title slide. To the right, Slides shows a list of themes you can select if you like. (See Figure 10-2.) You can scroll through the many different color and style themes. When you see one you want, just click it, and all the slides you create in your presentation will be styled according to the selected theme.

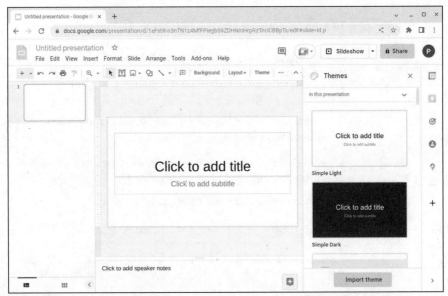

FIGURE 10-2:
Your new Google
Slides presenta-
tion with the
Themes selector.

Note that themes have names. The name of the default theme is Simple Light.

**TIP**

After you select a theme, or to dismiss the list of themes, just click the *X* at the top of the Themes selector. To bring the Themes selector back, click the Theme button on the Slides toolbar.

After selecting a theme, the next order of business is to select the shape of the slides in your presentation. Slides gives you three standard options for screen shapes concerning the aspect ratio of your screen (or the projector that you may plan to use to present your slides):

>> **Standard 4:3:** This was the standard shape of all video captured from the early days of television and motion pictures. It's often referred to as the video format of the 20th century.

>> **Widescreen 16:9:** This is the shape of video shown in cinemas and the standard for widescreen HD televisions and most laptop and computer monitor screens.

>> **Widescreen 16:10:** Also referred to as 8:5, this format is the format of tablet computers, as well as some computer and monitor screens.

If you don't pick the desired aspect ratio for your presentation at this point, Slides defaults to 16:9.

To select the aspect ratio of your presentation, follow these steps:

Changing the aspect ratio of your slides won't distort any images in your slides. You may, however, need to rearrange elements on your slides if you change the aspect ratio.

1. **Click File in the Slides menu and then, in the window that appears, scroll down and select Page setup.**

    A page setup window appears, revealing the three aspect ratio options in the drop-down list, as shown in Figure 10-3.

2. **Choose an option and click Apply.**

    The shape and size of your presentation are set as selected.

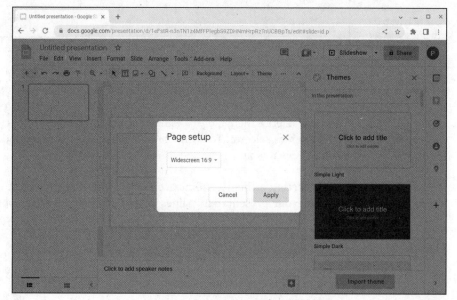

**FIGURE 10-3:**
Selecting an aspect ratio for your Google Slides presentation.

*Illustration courtesy of Peter H. Gregory*

## Surveying the Slides menu area

Google Slides is divided into four main areas: the menu area, the slide navigator, the slide editor, and the speaker notes editor. The menu area can be broken up into two parts: the Applications menu and the Edit toolbar. These areas are all shown in Figure 10-4.

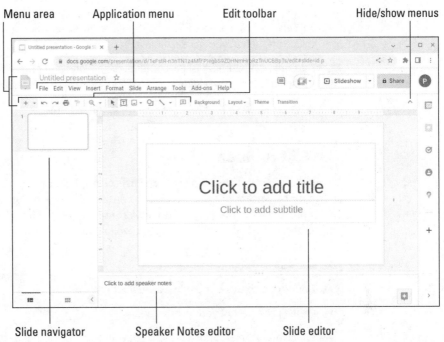

Menu area     Application menu     Edit toolbar     Hide/show menus

FIGURE 10-4:
The Google Slides
main areas.

Slide navigator     Speaker Notes editor     Slide editor

*Illustration courtesy of Peter H. Gregory*

## The Applications menu

The Applications menu features several options:

» **File:** File-specific options and controls for creating, saving, exporting, printing, and managing your presentation overall.

» **Edit:** Copy, paste, delete, and otherwise move and manipulate the contents of your presentation. Also, you can look for content and undo or redo previous changes.

» **View:** Modify your view by adding and removing toolbars, zooming in, showing the ruler or speaker notes, and going into Presentation mode.

» **Insert:** Add images, text boxes, videos, lines, shapes, tables, word art, animation, comments, and other objects.

» **Format:** Manipulate the appearance of your text, apply styles, edit paragraph formats, crop images, and so on.

» **Slide:** Add, edit, duplicate, or delete slides, layouts, themes, or transitions — basically, perform any function that pertains to a particular slide.

» **Arrange:** Arrange objects like text boxes, images, videos, and so on so that they align neatly.

» **Tools:** Spell-check, research information, or define words.

>> **Table:** Insert tables and add, edit, or delete rows and columns. This feature is visible only when you have a table already in your slide.

>> **Add-ons:** (sometimes visible, sometimes not) Find and obtain additional capabilities for Google Slides to make your presentation even better.

>> **Help:** Get help with slides or search for menu options.

## The Edit toolbar

The Edit toolbar, located directly beneath the Applications menu, contains several shortcuts to commonly used features contained in the Applications menu. The Edit toolbar makes the performance of routine tasks faster and easier. With the Edit toolbar, you can quickly perform these tasks:

>> Add slides to your presentation

>> Undo/redo changes you've made to your presentation

>> Print all or a part of your presentation

>> Apply formatting found in one part of your slide to another part of your slide

>> Zoom into and out of your presentation

>> Set your pointer to select objects

>> Add text boxes to your slide

>> Add images to your slide

>> Add or draw shapes

>> Add or draw lines

>> Add comments

>> Change slide backgrounds

>> Select a different layout for your slide

>> Change themes

>> Change slide transitions

## The slide navigator

The slide navigator is located directly under the Applications menu and to the left of the slide editor. Slides you add to your presentation appear in the slide navigator in miniature. Use the slide navigator to rearrange slides, delete slides, hide slides from presentations, and copy and paste slides within the navigator.

Any selected slide has an orange border. When selected, a slide appears in the slide editor to the right of the slide navigator. When you create a new presentation, you have one slide in your presentation, and therefore just one slide in the slide navigator. You can add more slides to your presentation by following these steps:

**1. Click the arrow beside the Add slide button in the Edit toolbar.**

It's the first button on the left side of the toolbar.

A menu appears with several layout options for your new slide, shown in Figure 10-5.

**2. Click any slide layout in the menu to select it.**

Your new slide appears in the slide navigator directly following the active slide.

**TIP**

If you click the + (plus sign) part of the Add slide button, Slides puts a new, blank slide after the slide you are viewing, with the same layout as the slide you are viewing. You can also quickly add slides by pressing Ctrl+M.

**FIGURE 10-5:**
Adding a slide and choosing a layout.

*Illustration courtesy of Peter H. Gregory*

If you add a slide in the wrong place in your presentation, you can rearrange your slides by following these steps:

**1. In the slide navigator, locate the slide you want to move.**

**2. Click and drag the slide up or down your slide navigator to the desired location.**

A location indicator, like the one pictured in Figure 10-6, moves with your selection as you scroll through the slide navigator.

3. **Place the location indicator between the two slides where you would like to relocate your selected slide, and then release the click.**

   The slide is moved to the new location.

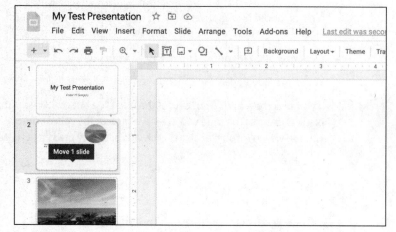

**FIGURE 10-6:**
Moving slides within a presentation.

*Illustration courtesy of Peter H. Gregory*

To delete a slide from your presentation, use the following steps:

1. **Click the slide you want to delete in the slide navigator.**

   The selected slide is highlighted with a blue border.

   You can select multiple slides by Ctrl-clicking each slide.

TIP

2. **Alt-click the selected slide.**

   A menu with several options appears.

3. **Select Delete slide.**

   The selected slide is deleted immediately.

TIP

You can also delete a slide by selecting the slide in the slide navigator and pressing the Backspace or Delete key.

## The slide editor

The slide editor (see Figure 10-4) is the large work area located directly below the menu and directly to the right of the slide navigator. In the slide editor, you can add text, images, video, and other elements. The selected slide in the slide navigator will appear in the slide editor area, thus making it available to be edited.

Below the slide editor is a speaker notes editor, in which you can add notes about the current slide. The notes aren't visible to the audience when you show your presentation, but they can serve as memory cues and talking points so that you aren't simply reading the contents of your slides.

## Customizing your view

Before you dive into your first presentation, you may find it helpful to change your view in Google Slides. You can compact the Applications menu area by clicking the Hide the Menus button, which appears as a tiny up arrow to the far right of the toolbar beneath the Share button. (See Figure 10-4.) When you click this button, the Applications menu compacts and disappears.

To restore the menu, click the Show Menus button at the far right of the Edit toolbar. When the Applications menu is hidden, this button appears as a tiny down arrow.

TIP

You can also use the keyboard shortcut Shift+Ctrl+F to toggle between having the Applications menu displayed or compacted.

If you prefer to completely hide the Applications menu and the Edit toolbar, you can do so by opening the View menu and choosing Full screen. (Figure 10-7 shows Slides, but with the menu and toolbar hidden.) To exit Full screen mode, simply press the Esc key.

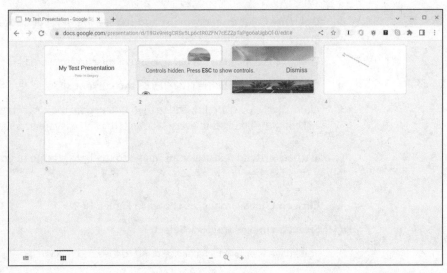

**FIGURE 10-7:**
Google Slides in
Full screen mode.

*Illustration courtesy of Peter H. Gregory*

**TIP**

To hide the speaker notes editor, open the View menu and choose Show Speaker Notes.

# Styling Your Presentation

Google Slides allows you to customize your presentation to have the look and feel you want. You can use any prebuilt theme to apply a predetermined look and feel to your presentation. You can also customize your theme with background colors, textures, or images, and apply different styles to the text in your presentation.

## Changing background color or background image

Each slide in your presentation will have a default background specific to the theme you select for your presentation. If you select the Light theme, for example, your background will be solid white. You can, however, change the color of the background of your slide by following these steps:

1. **Using the slide navigator, select the slide that will receive the new background.**

    The selected slide appears in the slide editor.

2. **Click the Change background in the Slide menu.**

    The Background window appears, as shown in Figure 10-8.

3. **Open the Color drop-down list and choose the new color for the background of your slide.**

    The color is applied to the background of the current slide.

4. **Click Done to apply the changes to the current slide.**

    Alternatively, you can click Add to theme to update the current theme, which will apply the changes to every slide with the same layout in your presentation.

To add a background texture or an image to the background of your slide or slides, follow these steps:

1. **Click on Choose image, as shown in Figure 10-8.**

2. **Select an image and click Select.**

    The image is applied as a background to the current slide.

3. **Click Done to apply the changes to the current slide.**

   Or you can click Add to theme to update your theme, which will apply the changes to every slide of the same layout in your presentation.

FIGURE 10-8:
The Background
feature in Google
Slides.

*Illustration courtesy of Peter H. Gregory*

If you decide that you want to clear the color or the image of a slide, you can easily reset a single slide or every slide in your presentation to your theme's default by following these steps:

1. **Using the slide navigator, select the slide you want to reset.**

   The slide appears in the slide editor.

2. **Click the Background button in the Edit toolbar.**

   The Background window appears.

3. **Click Reset.**

   The background for the selected slide is reset to the theme's default.

4. **Click Done to apply the changes to the current slide.**

   Alternatively, click Add to theme to update your theme, which will apply the changes to every slide with the same layout in your presentation.

## Applying a different theme

The good news is that if you change your mind about a theme, you can change it, even long after you've begun building your presentation. To change your theme, follow these steps:

1. **Click the Theme button in the Edit toolbar.**

   The Theme gallery appears to the right of the slide editor.

2. **Scroll through the list of available themes to view available options.**

3. **Click a theme's thumbnail to select it.**

   The theme is highlighted, indicating your selection.

4. **Click OK.**

   The selected theme is applied to all of the slides in your presentation.

TIP

You can import a presentation theme by clicking Theme in the Edit toolbar, find a theme you want to import, then select Import theme.

# Working with Text

In Slides, each piece of content you add to a slide is treated as an *object*, including images, tables, charts, videos, and even text blocks. You can then arrange and organize objects on the slides to fit each slide's desired look and feel.

To simplify things and provide consistency within your presentation, your theme has several predefined slide layouts. These are particularly useful in ensuring that text boxes, such as those for slides, appear in the same location from slide to slide. You don't have to use layouts; you can make every slide appear as you want by adding and deleting objects at will. The benefit of this approach is that it gives you a blank canvas on which to create the exact look you like. Using default slide layouts ensures that your text is in the same place from slide to slide, however, so avoiding layouts can produce slides that appear sloppy or out of sync.

To apply a defined layout to a slide, follow these steps:

1. **Create a new slide by pressing Ctrl+M or clicking the New slide button on the left end of the toolbar.**

   A new slide appears in the slide navigator with a default layout applied.

2. **Using the slide navigator, select the newly created slide.**

   A yellow highlight appears on the selected slide.

3. **Click the Layout button on the Edit toolbar.**

   A menu appears, revealing multiple options.

4. **Select the layout you want to apply to your selected slide.**

   The layout is applied to the slide.

You can explore the different layouts available in your current theme by changing the layout of your slide and then looking at the new layout on your slide. Depending on your selected theme, you may see one or more text boxes and possibly other graphics features, such as colors, patterns, or images.

## Adding and deleting text boxes

New layouts primarily involve placing text boxes, containers for the text on your slides. When you want to add text to a slide, you must first add a text box, and then you can begin adding text within the text box.

You can add a text box to any slide, regardless of that slide's layout. The following steps show you how. (To minimize confusion, in this example, you add a text box to a blank slide.) Follow these steps to add a text box:

1. **Create a new slide by pressing Ctrl+M.**

   A new slide appears in the slide navigator with a default layout applied.

2. **Using the slide navigator, select the newly created slide.**

   A yellow highlight appears on the selected slide.

3. **Click the Layout button in the Edit toolbar.**

   A menu appears, revealing multiple options.

4. **Select the Blank layout.**

   Nearly every theme has a slide layout called Blank with no text boxes at all, and very little else, in most cases.

5. **Click the Text box button in the Edit toolbar.**

   The Text box button is on the menu bar and shows a capital T with a box around it.

   After you click the Text box button, your pointer turns into crosshairs.

6. **In the slide editor, move your pointer to where you would like to draw your text box.**

7. **Click and drag your pointer across the slide.**

   A rectangular box appears that can be resized depending on the movement of your pointer.

8. **When you're satisfied with the shape and size of your text box, release the click.**

   Your text box is created and active, as shown in Figure 10-9.

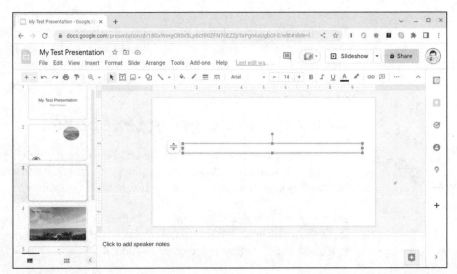

FIGURE 10-9:
A newly created
text box in
Google Slides.

*Illustration courtesy of Peter H. Gregory*

You can delete a text box almost as easily as you created it by following these steps:

1. **Ensure that your pointer tool is selected by clicking the Select button in your Edit toolbar or pressing Esc.**

   Your pointer should look like an arrow.

2. **Click the edge of the text box you want to delete.**

   The text box becomes highlighted with a blue border. The cursor no longer appears in the text box.

3. **Using your keyboard, press the Backspace or Delete key to delete your text box.**

   Alternatively, click Edit on the menu bar and then click Delete.

   The text box vanishes.

## Resizing, moving, and rotating a text box

After you create a text box, you may need to adjust its placement on your slide by moving the text box, resizing the box to adjust its shape and size, or rotating the text box, which rotates the contents accordingly. This section shows you how to make these adjustments.

## Resizing

To resize a text box, follow these steps:

**1.** **Ensure that your pointer tool is selected by clicking the arrow button in your Edit toolbar.**

Your pointer should look like an arrow.

**2.** **Click your text box.**

If your text box doesn't contain any text, click within the general area of the text box.

The text box becomes highlighted, and resize points appear in the corners and the middle of each side of the box.

**3.** **Move your pointer over one of the resize points on your text box.**

Your mouse pointer changes shape to a double-sided arrow. See how the double arrow changes as you hover over different resize points? The arrow changes orientation. This change is a clue that shows you how you can use each resize point to change the shape of the text box.

**4.** **Click and drag the resizing point to shrink or enlarge the text box.**

The box resizes with the movement of your pointer.

**5.** **Release the click when you are satisfied with the new size of your text box.**

## Moving

You can move your text box by following these steps:

**1.** **Ensure that your pointer tool is selected by clicking the arrow button in your Edit toolbar.**

Your pointer should look like an arrow.

**2.** **Click your text box.**

If your text box doesn't contain any text, click in the general area of the text box.

The text box becomes highlighted.

**3.** **Move your pointer over the text box.**

Your mouse pointer changes into four arrows, one pointing in each cardinal direction.

4. **Click and drag the text box to a new location on the slide.**

   The box moves with the movement of your pointer.

5. **Release the click when you are satisfied with the new location of your text box.**

TIP

You can also use the arrow keys to move a text box (or any object on the slide). Each arrow key click moves the object a tiny amount, so you may need to click the arrow key a lot (or hold it down).

## Rotating

Google Slides also allows you to rotate your text box at will. This feature comes in handy when you want to create a vertical text label or add styling to your slide. To rotate your text box, follow these steps:

1. **Ensure that your pointer tool is selected by clicking the arrow button in your Edit toolbar.**

   Your pointer should look like an arrow.

2. **Click your text box.**

   If your text box doesn't contain any text, click in the general area of the text box.

   The text box becomes highlighted, indicating your selection.

3. **Move your pointer over the alignment handle (the tiny circular dot that extends above the top center of your text box).**

   Your mouse pointer changes into crosshairs.

4. **Click and drag the crosshairs left to rotate the box counterclockwise, or right to rotate the box clockwise.**

   The box rotates in the direction and angle of your pointer movement. Your pointer indicates the degree of the angle as you rotate.

5. **Release the click when you're satisfied with the new angle of your text box.**

   Figure 10-10 shows a slide with a text box rotated to the right.

TIP

You can use the procedure above to rotate any object on a slide. Grab its alignment handle and rotate away!

Alignment handle

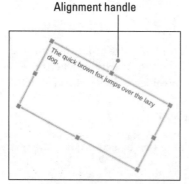

# Copying and pasting text boxes

As you create presentations, you can easily add text boxes using the Copy and Paste functions. To do so, just follow these steps:

1. **Ensure that your pointer tool is selected by clicking the Select button in your Edit toolbar.**

   Your pointer should look like an arrow.

2. **Click the text box you want to copy.**

   If your text box doesn't contain any text, click in the general area of the text box.

   The text box becomes highlighted, indicating your selection.

3. **Press Ctrl+C.**

   The text box and its contents are copied into memory.

4. **Use the slide navigator to set the slide where you want to paste your text box.**

5. **Press Ctrl+V.**

   The text box is pasted to the new slide. Move and adjust it as needed.

Copying text boxes from one slide to others is a handy way to make a block of text appear on several slides without having to manually retype the text on every slide.

TIP

When you paste a text box onto another slide, it's placed in the same position it occupied on the slide containing the text box you copied.

# Formatting text

With Slides, you can change the font and size of any text in your presentation. The options are potentially limitless, but for clarity, it's better to limit the number of fonts in one presentation. Google Slides comes preloaded with a handful of fonts.

To change your font, follow these steps:

1. **Using your touchpad, click the text box containing the text you want to format.**

   The text box is highlighted in yellow.

   To change only a section of the text in a text box, make your selection by double-clicking the text box and then dragging your pointer over the text you want to change. See Figure 10-11 for an example.

2. **Open the Font menu on the Edit toolbar.**

   The Font menu is located directly to the left of the Font Size menu.

   The Font menu displays the name of the font for the selected body of text. By default, all text is written with the Arial font.

3. **Select one of the fonts listed.**

   All the selected text is formatted with your newly selected font.

**FIGURE 10-11:**
Selecting text in a text box.

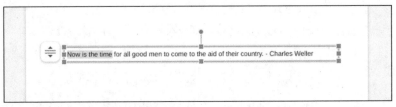

Now is the time for all good men to come to the aid of their country. - Charles Weller

*Illustration courtesy of Peter H. Gregory*

## Adding and removing new fonts

Google Slides provides users with an initial list of the most globally popular fonts to keep things simple. You can, however, add fonts to your Slides font list. Follow these steps:

1. **Select some text in a text box on a slide in your presentation.**

2. **Open the Font menu in the toolbar.**

   The text on the Font button is the name of the font currently used for your selected text.

3. **Choose More fonts.**

The Fonts window appears (see Figure 8-6 in Chapter 8), giving you a robust list of new fonts. Scroll down through the list to reveal more fonts.

4. **Select the desired fonts by clicking them.**

Each selected font is highlighted in blue and given a check mark.

5. **Click OK to finish adding the fonts to your Font menu and close the Fonts pane.**

When you're ready to change the font of your text, you can choose one of your newly selected fonts from the Font menu.

Fonts you add in Slides are available in Docs and Sheets, and vice versa.

The more fonts you add, the more fonts you have to rifle through when deciding on a change. To remove fonts that you added to your list, take these steps:

1. **Open the Font menu in the toolbar.**

2. **Click More fonts.**

The Fonts pane appears, displaying a list of fonts. On the right, the My Fonts list shows the fonts currently in use by your Slides account.

3. **Scroll through the My fonts list to locate the font or fonts you want to remove. To remove fonts, click the X to the right of each font.**

The selected fonts vanish from the list of accessible fonts.

4. **Click OK.**

## Changing text size

You can change the size of your text by following these steps:

1. **Using your touchpad, double-click the text box that contains the text you want to format.**

The text box is highlighted in blue. A blinking cursor appears.

2. **Click and drag your pointer to select the text whose size you want to change.**

The selected text is highlighted.

3. **Click the Font size menu.**

It's the number located to the left of the B (Bold) button in the Edit toolbar.

**4.** Select any desired font size.

Your selected text becomes the chosen size, as shown in Figure 10-12.

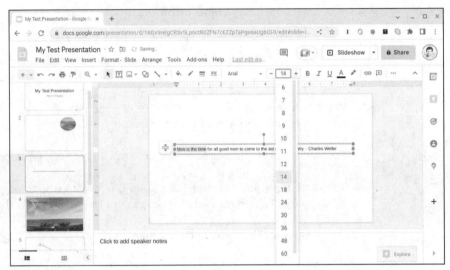

**FIGURE 10-12:**
Changing the size
of selected text in
Google Slides.

## Applying boldface, italics, underline, or strikethrough

To make a specific selection of text bold, italic, underlined, or strikethrough, follow these steps:

**1.** Using your touchpad, double-click the text box that contains the text you
want to format.

The text box is highlighted in yellow. A blinking cursor appears in the text box.

**2.** Select the text you want to change by clicking and dragging.

The selected text is highlighted.

**3.** Apply boldface, italics, underline, or strikethrough as needed.

To apply formatting, use one of the following methods:

- **To add boldface, italics, or strikethrough:** Click the appropriate button
  in the middle of the Edit toolbar — the B button for bold, the I button for
  italic, or the U button for underline. (No button exists for strikethrough on
  the standard Edit toolbar.)

- **To add strikethrough:** Open the Format menu, click Text, and select Strikethrough.

Your selection changes appropriately.

TIP

You can quickly apply styles to your data by using hotkeys. Just press Ctrl+B (for bold), Ctrl+I (italic), Ctrl+U (underline), or Alt+Shift+5 (strikethrough).

## Coloring your text

Slides allow you to change the color of your text or the color of the background behind your text (that is, to add a highlight). You change the color of your text by following these steps:

1. **Using your touchpad, double-click the text box that contains the text you want to color.**

2. **Select text by clicking and dragging.**

   The selected text is highlighted.

3. **Click the Text color button in the toolbar.**

   It's the underlined *A* found to the right of the Underline button.

   The color palette appears, similar to Figure 9-10 in the spreadsheet chapter.

4. **Select the desired color.**

   Your selected text now appears in the selected color.

To apply a highlight to your text, follow these steps:

1. **Using your touchpad, double-click the text box that contains the text you want to format.**

2. **Select text by clicking and dragging.**

   The selected text is highlighted.

3. **Click the Highlight color button in the toolbar.**

   This button looks like a highlighter pen and appears at the right of the Text color button. The Highlight color palette appears.

4. **Select your desired color.**

   Your selected text now appears highlighted in the selected color.

# Aligning your text

The *alignment* of your text determines the orientation of the edges of lines or paragraphs in a text box. Slides gives you several options for changing the alignment. Horizontal alignment choices include

>> **Left:** This is the default alignment for new text boxes in Slides. The text is flush with the left side of the text box.

>> **Right:** The text is flush with the right side of the text box.

>> **Center:** The middle of your text box is the halfway point between the left and the right sides. With centered alignment, all text is centered on this midway point.

>> **Justified:** *Justifying* your text aligns the text evenly along both the left and right sides. To ensure that the left and right sides of your text are flush with the left and right sides of the text box, Slides introduces additional spaces between each word.

Vertical alignment options include

>> Top

>> Middle

>> Bottom

You can change the alignment of text in a text box by the line, paragraph, or page by following these steps:

1. **Using your touchpad, double-click the text box that contains the text you want to realign.**

2. **Select the text you want to realign by clicking and dragging.**

    The selected text is highlighted.

3. **Click the Align button in the Edit toolbar.**

    The Alignment tool opens, as shown in Figure 10-13. You can select left, center, right, and justified alignment and top, middle, and bottom alignment.

4. **Click the desired alignment.**

    The selected text is realigned.

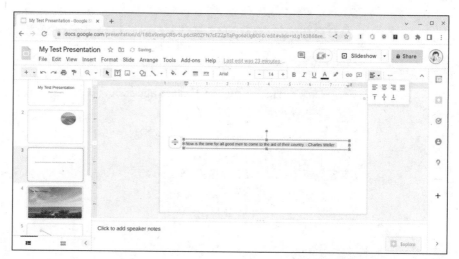

FIGURE 10-13:
Changing the
alignment of text
in Google Slides.

*Illustration courtesy of Peter H. Gregory*

## Clearing formatting

Google Slides offers a feature that makes it easy to clear the formatting you applied to a body of text. This feature can save you quite a bit of time if you intend to clear the formatting from several text boxes. To clear formatting, follow these steps:

1.  **Use your touchpad to click once on the text box you want to select.**

    The selected text box is highlighted.

2.  **Click Format and then click Clear formatting in the menu bar.**

    The alignment of the selected text is reset to left alignment, and all style elements are removed, including color, underline, strikethrough, italics, bold, and so on.

# Working with Images

Presentations need more than just text boxes and a colored background to make them interesting. Images can help tell your story. The good news is that you can add images of all types to your presentation. Slides also gives you the ability to apply basic tweaks to your images so that you can make them look just right. With Slides, you can add images from files or use your device's camera to take pictures. You can rotate, resize, relocate, add borders, and even apply shapes to your pictures.

# Adding images to your presentation

You can add an image to your presentation in a few quick steps:

1. **Click the Image button, located about nine buttons from the left on the Edit toolbar.**

   A small menu appears, as shown in Figure 10-14.

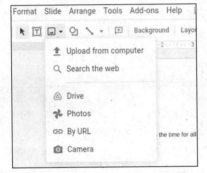

*Illustration courtesy of Peter H. Gregory*

**FIGURE 10-14:**
The Image
selector menu.

2. **Select the source for the image you want to insert into your slide.**

   The options for the source for your image are as follows:

   - **Upload from computer:** Any image you previously created or downloaded that is stored in your Chromebook

   - **Search the web:** A Google Images search to find an image on the internet

   - **Drive:** An image you previously stored in your Google Drive

   - **Photos:** An image you uploaded to Google Photos

   - **By URL:** An image whose URL you happen to know

   - **Camera:** A picture you take using the camera on your Chromebook

3. **Choose the desired option for obtaining an image for your presentation.**

   The image is added to your slide.

You can also add an image from the internet by following these steps:

1. **Click the Image button on the toolbar.**

   The Insert Image window appears.

2. **Click By URL.**

A text box appears where you can paste the URL to the image you want to add from the internet.

3. **Type or paste the URL for the image you want to add to your slide.**

   If the URL works, Slides shows you a preview of the image.

4. **To insert the image, click Insert.**

   The image appears on your slide.

# Resizing, rotating, and relocating images

After you add an image, you may need to adjust its placement on your slide. You can do so by moving the image, resizing the image, or rotating the image. This section shows you how to perform each of these actions.

## Resizing

To resize an image, follow these steps:

1. **Ensure that your pointer tool is selected by clicking the Select button in the toolbar.**

   Your pointer should look like an arrow.

2. **Click your image to select it.**

   The selected image is highlighted. Resize points appear in the corners and the middle of each side of the image.

3. **Move your pointer over one of the corners of the image.**

   Your mouse pointer changes shape to a double-sided arrow.

4. **Click and drag the corner to shrink or enlarge the image.**

   The image resizes proportionately.

   Resizing your image using the points located in the middle of the sides of your image stretches the image without respect for the image's original proportion.

5. **When you're satisfied with the new size, release the click.**

WARNING

If you resize an image using the points on the sides of an image instead of on the corners, you'll end up stretching or squishing your image, distorting it from its original view.

# Moving

You can also move your image to a different place on your slide by following these steps:

1. **Ensure that your pointer tool is selected by clicking the Select button in the toolbar.**

   Your pointer should look like an arrow.

2. **Click your image to select it.**

   The selected image is highlighted.

3. **Move your pointer over the middle of the image.**

   Your mouse pointer changes into four arrows, one pointing in each cardinal direction.

4. **Click and drag the image to a new location on the slide.**

   The image moves with the movement of your pointer.

5. **When you're satisfied with the new location of your image, release the click.**

# Rotating

Google Slides also gives you the ability to rotate your images. This feature comes in handy if you need to reorient an image in line with your slide. To rotate your image, follow these steps:

1. **Ensure that your pointer tool is selected by clicking the Select button in the toolbar.**

   Your pointer should look like an arrow.

2. **Click your image to select it.**

   The selected image is highlighted.

3. **Move the pointer over the circular dot that extends above the top center of the image.**

   Your mouse pointer changes into crosshairs.

4. **Click and drag the image left or right toward the angle you desire.**

   The image rotates in the direction and angle of your pointer movement. Your pointer indicates the degree of the angle as you rotate, as shown earlier in this chapter about rotating a text box in Figure 10-10.

5. **When you're satisfied with the new angle of your image, release the click.**

**TIP**

Advanced image editing features are available, such as changing color saturation and contrast. Click on an image, then Alt+click, then click Format options. The Format options menu will appear, showing several available operations.

## Cropping images

In Google Slides, you can crop your images. *Cropping* means cutting off portions of an image to retain only the desired area. If you have a smartphone and have taken pictures using fun applications like Instagram, you may be familiar with cropping images. Figure 10-15 illustrates what the Slides Crop tool looks like.

**FIGURE 10-15:**
Cropping an image in Google Slides.

*Illustration courtesy of Peter H. Gregory*

To crop an image, follow these steps:

1.  **Select the image you want to crop.**

    The selected image is highlighted.

2.  **Click the Crop image button on the right portion of the Edit toolbar.**

    Alternatively, you can Alt+click the image and select Crop.

    Crop marks appear on the corners and sides of the image, indicating that you've enabled cropping.

3.  **Using the touchpad, move the pointer over one of the black crop marks.**

    The pointer changes to arrows pointing in two directions, indicating where to drag the crop mark.

4. **Click and drag the crop marks to the desired size.**

   The portion of your image that falls outside the crop margins appears grayed out.

5. **Click the Crop image button in the Edit toolbar again, or just click outside the image.**

   Your crop settings are applied to the image.

TIP

After you have cropped your image, if you decide that you removed too much from your image, just click the Crop image button again. You'll be shown your original image and the current cropping. You can readjust cropping as needed. Click the Crop image button when you're done.

TIP

While in cropping mode, you can still resize and move an image.

Google Slides also comes with an image-masking option. *Masking* essentially places your image into a shaped container. The only parts of the image shown are the portions not *masked* by the mask filter. Figure 10-16 shows an image with a shape mask applied.

FIGURE 10-16:
Masking an image
in Google Slides
with an oval.

*Illustration courtesy of Peter H. Gregory*

To mask an image, follow these steps:

1. **Select the image you want to mask.**

   The selected image is highlighted.

2. **Click the Mask image button on the toolbar.**

   The Mask image button is the down-pointing arrow on the right portion of the Crop image button.

   A menu appears, revealing several shapes.

3. **Using the touchpad, navigate the menu and select the shape you want to apply to the image.**

   The image is now masked according to the shape you selected.

If you decide that you do not like the crop or image mask that you applied to your image, you can remove it by following these steps:

1. **Double-click the image.**

   The original image is revealed, along with the cropping indicators.

2. **Click the Reset image button in the toolbar.**

   The crop marks are removed from the image, and it's restored to its uncropped or unmasked state.

**TIP**

Sometimes you must try cropping or masking a few times until you get it right. You can also undo your masking or cropping by clicking the Undo button that is near the left end of the toolbar.

# Viewing Presentations in Presentation Mode

You can launch Presentation mode when ready to make a presentation with Google Slides. Presentation mode shows nothing but your finished slides, so you can navigate through them while you present. To launch Presentation mode, follow these steps:

1. **Using your slide navigator, click the first slide in your presentation.**

   Slide 1 becomes highlighted. When you launch Presentation mode, the presentation commences at the active slide in your navigator. If you want to start from the beginning, ensure that you've selected your first slide.

2. **Click the Slideshow button in the top-right portion of your screen.**

   The Slideshow button is next to the Share button.

Your presentation launches into full-screen Presentation mode, taking up the entire screen.

Near the top of the screen, the message "Press Esc to exit full screen" appears for a few moments.

A presentation menu appears near the bottom of the screen; after several seconds, the menu disappears. You can make it reappear by moving the pointer near the bottom of the screen.

3. **To exit Presentation mode, press the Esc key.**

Your presentation closes, and the slide editor reappears.

While in Presentation mode, you can navigate between slides in some different ways. To move forward in your presentation, press the down- or right-arrow key, or the spacebar. To move backward in your presentation, press the left- or up-arrow keys.

## Presenting on additional displays

Running Presentation mode on your Chromebook is a great way to test your presentation before you present it to an audience. When you're ready to present, you'll likely be presenting using a projector or flat-screen television. To launch your presentations on a display device, you can connect your Chromebook to a projector, monitor, or TV, or cast to a smart TV. (If you don't know how to cast to a smart TV, go to Chapter 14. To connect an additional display to your Chromebook, flip to Chapter 17.) After your additional display is connected to and recognized by your Chromebook, launch your presentation using these steps:

1. **Using your slide navigator, click the first slide in your presentation.**

Slide 1 is highlighted.

2. **Click the arrow on the right side of the Slideshow button in the top-right portion of your screen.**

A menu with three options appears:

- Presenter view
- Present from the beginning
- Present on another screen

3. **Select Presenter view.**

Presentation mode commences without going into Full screen mode, and the Presenter view appears in a separate window shown in Figure 10-17.

4. **Click and drag the presentation window to the display you're using to present and leave the Presenter view window on the display your audience won't see.**

5. **In your presentation window, click the three vertical dots on the Navigation pane near the lower-left corner of the window, then click the Enter full screen, as shown in Figure 10-18.**

   Your presentation goes into Full screen mode, ready for you to present.

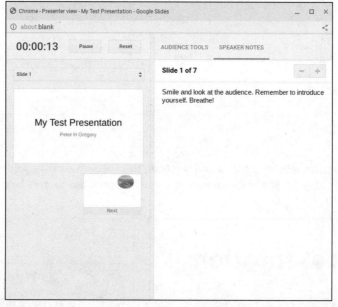

*Illustration courtesy of Peter H. Gregory*

**FIGURE 10-17:** The Presenter view in Google Slides.

# Using Presenter view

When you launch a presentation in Presenter view, a window launches that contains all your slide notes, as well as some navigation tools and a timer so that you can keep track of how much time you're using in your presentation.

The window is broken into two main areas. The left side of the window contains your presentation controls. The right side of the window contains any and all notes written for the current slide. Navigate through your presentation by clicking the slide subtitled Next. Navigate backward by clicking the slide subtitled Previous. You can also skip to slides by clicking Slide # and selecting a slide from the drop-down list that appears. You can also pause the timer by clicking Pause, and resume it by clicking Resume. If you click Reset, the timer starts back at zero.

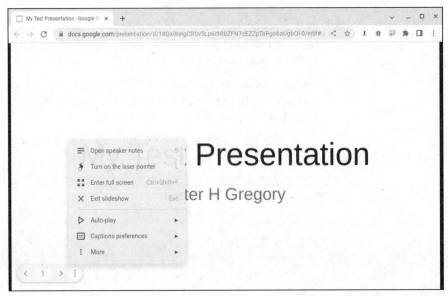

Illustration courtesy of Peter H. Gregory

**FIGURE 10-18:** The Presenter toolbar.

**TIP**

Don't read your notes aloud; instead, use them as talking points or cues for presenting. Present to your audience and let the slides merely be props that support your presentation.

# Saving Presentations

As you work in Google Slides, Google saves almost every change in real-time to your Google Drive account. Drive is Google's cloud-based storage solution that allows you to safely store your files and access them from any device with an internet connection. Every file you create with Presentation is saved to your Drive folder so you can access it at home, on the road, at work, or anywhere else you may need to. If you never name your presentation, it will be called "Untitled presentation." As with Docs and Sheets, Slides has no manual Save feature.

## Naming your presentation

When you open a new presentation with Slides, the default name is Untitled presentation. You don't, however, want to leave your presentation untitled forever. Drive doesn't have a problem storing multiple files with the same name, so it's best if you name your presentation to save yourself a little later confusion. To name your presentation, follow these steps:

1. **Open a new or existing presentation.**

   The easiest way to open a presentation is simply to launch Slides from the Launcher.

   A Chrome web browser opens and loads Slides — and automatically opens a new presentation.

   After Slides is open, the top-left corner of the screen displays your presentation's name: Untitled presentation, as shown earlier in this chapter in Figure 10-2.

2. **Click Untitled presentation.**

   The appearance of the name Untitled presentation changes so that you can type in a new name.

3. **Type a new name for your presentation and press Enter.**

   The new name that you chose to replace Untitled presentation appears.

Your newly named presentation now appears in Google Drive. The file is updated and saved in real-time as you continue to make edits to the presentation.

## Exporting your presentation

From time to time, you may need to export your presentation to formats that others may be comfortable with. Google Slides presently allows you to export to a few standard formats:

>> Microsoft PowerPoint (.pptx)

>> ODP document (.odp)

>> PDF document (.pdf)

>> Plain text (.txt)

>> JPEG image (.jpg)

>> PNG image (.png)

>> Scalable Vector Graphics (.svg)

You can export your presentation by following these steps:

1. **Open the Files menu in the Applications menu within Slides.**

2. **Hover over Download As to reveal a submenu containing file types available for export.**

3. **Select the desired file type.**

   Your Slides file is exported to the desired file type and automatically down-loaded to your Chromebook.

4. **Choose a name for the exported file and then click Save.**

5. **To view the file on your Chromebook, open the Files app and navigate to the folder in which you saved the exported file.**

6. **Double-click the filename to launch an app to display the presentation.**

Exporting your presentation makes a copy and does not alter your original presentation file.

# Collaborating in Slides

By default, Slides and Drive make your files inaccessible to everyone else. You can, however, change the visibility settings on your files and invite specific people, or even the entire world, to comment on, view, or edit your presentation. To share your presentation with specific people, follow the steps to share a Google Doc, which is explained in Chapter 8.

A user who is invited to view, edit, or comment on your presentation has to log into Google using the email address with which you shared the presentation. If your collaborators don't have a Google Account under the email address that you used, you'll see a warning saying that the document can be edited by anyone who has the email invitation.

# Tracking Revisions

Keeping track of revisions is very important when creating documents with multiple collaborators. Luckily, Google Slides handles version control masterfully. The Version history tool, however, is not intended to be used as a Track Changes tool in Google Docs. As you and your collaborators create changes to your presentation, Slides will time-and-date stamp those changes so that you can view previous versions and even revert to an earlier version if you need to.

Version tracking is a default feature of Slides, so to view your version history, follow these steps:

1. **Open the File menu in the Applications menu within Slides.**

2. **Choose Version history and then choose See version history.**

   The Version history pane appears in the right portion of your Slides window. The pane contains the various versions of your presentation, from most recent to oldest.

3. **Click a revision date in the Version history box.**

   A preview of the revision appears in the presentation area. Changes appear in green. Figure 10-19 shows a presentation with two available versions.

4. **To change the current version to the version you're viewing, click Restore this version.**

   The restored version becomes the current version, and the previous version of the application is saved in the version history so that you can revert to it at any point, if needed.

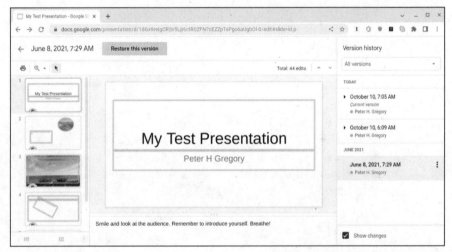

**FIGURE 10-19:** Viewing available versions of a Google Slides presentation.

*Illustration courtesy of Peter H. Gregory*

# Using Slides Offline

Google Slides is a web-based presentation tool, meaning you must have an internet connection to access it and all its features. However, an offline version of Slides is available if you find yourself without a connection to the internet.

To use Google Slides to work on your presentations offline, follow the steps at the end of Chapter 7 to mark the presentations and folders you want to use offline. Then, you'll be able to edit those marked presentations when offline.

Offline, you can't access some of the features available to Slides users connected to the internet, such as downloading new fonts or searching the internet for images to insert into your presentation. You can, however, create presentations and save them. When you connect to the internet, Google Drive uploads the presentations and enables all internet-accessible features.

Chapter **11**

# Using Other Office Tools

G oogle has made tremendous headway with its suite of office products: Gmail for email, Docs for word processing, Sheets for spreadsheets, and Slides for presentations. They are popular both in business as well as with home users. And, as previous chapters note, they all work great on Chromebooks. That said, you may have your reasons for considering and using alternatives.

The undisputed leader in office software around the world in business, schools, and homes is Microsoft 365. Its powerhouse programs include Outlook for email, calendar, and contacts; Word for word processing; Excel for spreadsheets; Power-Point for slide presentations; OneNote for note-taking; and OneDrive for storing data in the cloud. These tools are all available in the Microsoft 365 suite. Not only are they available for Windows PCs and Macs, but they also work great on Chromebooks.

For the average user, it's fair to say that Microsoft 365 and Google's suite of tools are roughly equivalent in terms of features and functions. *How* you get things done varies a bit between the two. But if you are reasonably good at Google Docs, for instance, it'll take you no time at all to be productive with Microsoft Word. The same can be said of Sheets versus Excel and Slides versus PowerPoint. Only a professional user is likely to spot the differences, but for everyone else, Google versus Microsoft is a bit like Coke versus Pepsi, Ford versus Chevy, or the Yankees versus the Mets. They're all good, and they get the job done.

In this chapter, you dive into the Microsoft 365 world, including installing and using all the tools. I don't go into as much detail on the Microsoft 365 tools as I do the Google tools (Gmail, Docs, Sheets, Slides, and Drive) in other chapters, but I show you enough to get started. If you want to use Microsoft tools on your Chromebook, I recommend you pick up a copy of *Microsoft Office 2021 All-in-One For Dummies* by Peter Weverka or the latest edition of *Microsoft Office 365 All-In-One For Dummies* by Peter Weverka and Matt Wade (both published by Wiley).

This chapter also takes a quick look at working with PDFs.

# Getting Started with Microsoft 365

To get started with Microsoft 365, also known as Microsoft Office or just Office, make sure you're logged into your Chromebook. Open your Chrome browser and go to www.office.com.

As with Google's suite of tools, you can use the basic version of Microsoft 365 for free. Microsoft 365 includes 5GB of free storage in OneDrive and versions of Word, Excel, PowerPoint, and other apps. The information offered in this chapter deals mainly with the use of a free account.

If you don't have a Microsoft 365 account, this is the time to create one. You need an account to use the free or paid versions of Microsoft 365. Go to www.office.com and click Sign up for the free version of Microsoft 365 or Get Microsoft 365 to set up a monthly paid subscription. Then, find the link to create an account. Your email address will be your user ID (even if it's a Gmail address), and you'll need to create a password and answer other questions. After your account is set up, go back to www.office.com and sign in. After signing in with your new account, you see the Microsoft 365 home page, shown in Figure 11-1.

WARNING

If you want a separate outlook.com email address, click Get a new email address and type a username in the Create Account field when signing up with Microsoft 365. If you input your full Gmail email address, Outlook email will send your email as though it was sent from Gmail (email sent *to* your Gmail address will still appear in Gmail, and only in Gmail).

TIP

As any good for-profit company would, Microsoft will try to convince you to go with one of the paid versions of Microsoft 365 instead of the free version. Getting a paid account isn't necessary unless you know for sure that you require features that are available *only* with the paid versions.

If you use Microsoft 365, bookmark the landing page because this page is where you begin. You can access all the free Microsoft 365 tools on the landing page, which I briefly explore in this section.

## Verifying your Microsoft 365 account

You may be asked to verify your account as soon as you begin some operation in Microsoft 365 (sending your first email, for example). Microsoft 365 asks for your email address to send you a code to enter. This safeguard helps prove that you are logging in to your Microsoft 365 account rather than some hacker who luckily guessed your user ID and password (or obtained them in another way). Figure 11-2 shows an example of a verification email.

## OneDrive File Storage

OneDrive is the Microsoft app you use to store your data in the cloud. If you know the basics about Google Drive, you already understand OneDrive: You have folders and files that you can upload and download; you can also create and edit them using word processing, spreadsheet, and presentation tools.

From the Microsoft 365 main page, click OneDrive. Your list of files and folders appears. The first time you use OneDrive, you see a Welcome page with an offer to show you around. I suggest that you take a minute for the nickel tour.

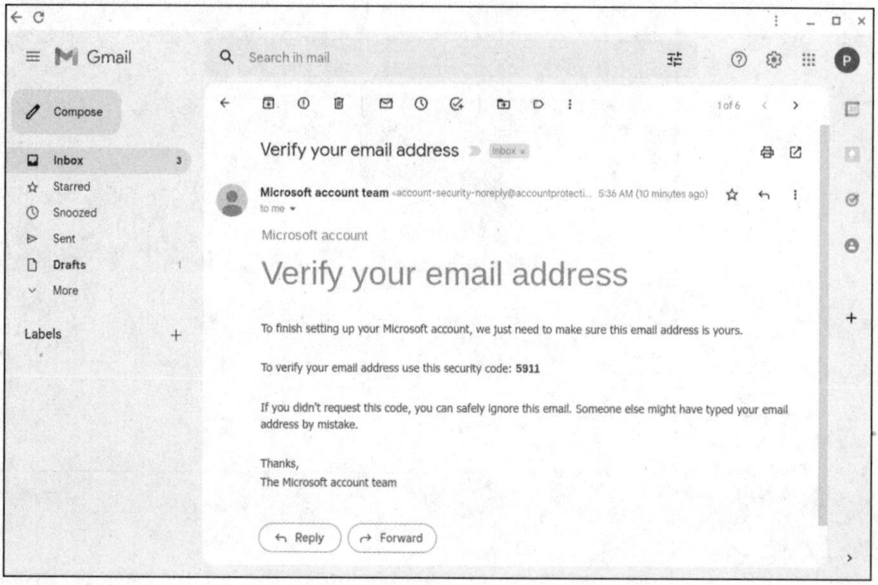


**FIGURE 11-2:** Microsoft 365 uses codes sent via email to verify your identity.

*Illustration courtesy of Peter H. Gregory*

TIP

One nice thing about Microsoft 365 is that apps usually open in new browser tabs, which means that your Microsoft 365 main page is still there on another tab. Sure, you can also get back to it with your browser bookmark or clicking the little Home link near the upper-left corner of the Microsoft 365 window.

The main OneDrive window shows two default folders, Documents and Pictures, and a file called Getting Started With OneDrive. Until you are familiar with OneDrive, I suggest you keep that Getting Started file as a handy reference. Your initial OneDrive page should resemble Figure 11-3.

In OneDrive, you can upload files or directories by following these steps:

1. **Click the Upload button near the top of the OneDrive screen.**

   A small File Upload window appears.

2. **Click Files.**

   The file selector window appears.

3. **Navigate to the file you want to upload to OneDrive. Click on the filename(s).**
4. **Click Open near the lower-right corner of the window.**

   The selector window closes, and your selected files are uploaded to OneDrive.

*Illustration courtesy of Peter H. Gregory*

You can also use a drag-and-drop method to upload files to OneDrive. First, make sure your browser is not in Full-Screen mode. Reduce the window size a little bit until you see a part of the desktop. Then follow these steps to upload files from other folders:

1. **Navigate to your main OneDrive page, which shows your folders and files.**

2. **Open the Files app and position it so that you can see the Files app and your browser.**

3. **Click the Files app and then navigate to the folders or files you want to upload to OneDrive.**

4. **Click and drag the files you want from the Files window to the middle of the OneDrive window in your browser. (See Figure 11-4.)**

**TIP**

As of the writing of this book, Microsoft offers 100 GB of storage for $1.99 per month. This is a real bargain, and it's competitive with Google Drive.

# Outlook Email

Outlook is the Microsoft 365 app used for email and managing calendars and contacts.

To launch Outlook, log in to Microsoft 365, which gets you to the Microsoft 365 main page (refer to Figure 11-1). Click Outlook, which opens that app in a new tab in your browser. The first time you log in, you may see a little Get Started pane asking some questions, including your preferred language and time zone. After you get through any of those one-time formalities, you see the Outlook main page, which includes the display of an initial message welcoming you to your new Outlook.com account. Figure 11-5 should pretty closely resemble what you see.

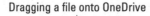
Dragging a file onto OneDrive

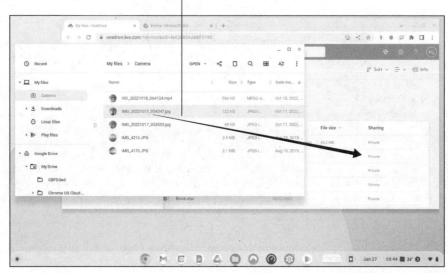

**FIGURE 11-4:**
Dragging and
dropping files
from your
Chromebook or
Google Drive to
OneDrive.

*Illustration courtesy of Peter H. Gregory*

TIP

The first time you start Outlook, Microsoft sends you the welcome email message that now appears.

Outlook is functionally equivalent to the combination of Gmail, Google Calendar, and Google Contacts — all in one app. Along with Figure 11-5, which shows all the different parts of the Outlook main window, here's a brief tour of Outlook so that you can find your way around:

>> **Inbox:** Contains a list of your incoming email messages. By default, it displays the sender's name, subject line, and the first few words of the body of the message.

>> **Message preview:** The body of the message selected in the Inbox. The subject line is at the top; beneath that is the sender's name and email address, followed by the start of the body of the message.

>> **Message body:** More of the message from someone (or some thing). For longer messages, scroll down to read.

>> **New message:** Click this button to compose a new message.

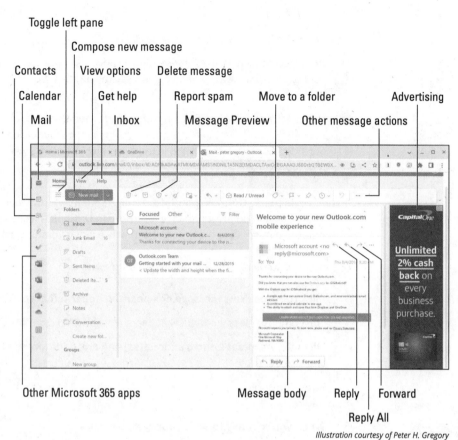

Toggle left pane

Compose new message

Contacts    View options    Delete message

Calendar    Get help    Report spam    Move to a folder    Advertising

Mail    Inbox    Message Preview    Other message actions

**FIGURE 11-5:**
The Outlook main
page with a
welcome
message from
the Outlook
Team.

Other Microsoft 365 apps    Message body    Reply    Forward

Reply All

>> **Toggle left pane:** Shows or hides your folder list. Hiding it provides more space to view the contents of messages.

>> **View Options:** Click here to view and change Outlook options.

>> **Help:** Instructional content on the use of Outlook.

>> **Reply:** Compose a reply to the sender of the message displayed.

>> **Reply All:** Compose a reply to the sender and all other recipients of the message displayed.

>> **Forward:** Forward the message to someone else.

>> **Move to:** Move the message to a folder within Outlook.

>> **Message actions:** Brings up a little menu in which you can mark a message as read, flag the message, print the message, snooze the message, pin the message, or block the message.

>> **Trash:** Delete the message being displayed.

>> **Advertising:** Be aware of banner ads and advertising messages appearing in your Outlook window. Generally, you'll see the tiny "Ad" box inside or near them.

>> **Other Microsoft 365 apps:** Icons for Calendar and Contacts, plus Word, Excel, PowerPoint, and OneDrive. If you click on any of the Outlook icons (Mail, Calendar, Contacts), it will open in the same tab. The others will open in a new tab.

If you decide to use Outlook, you'll find that its main window has a lot of controls like Gmail. You can do pretty much everything in Outlook that you can do in Gmail, although the controls are arranged differently. Chevy versus Ford.

Follow these steps to compose a new email message:

1. **Click the blue, New message box near the upper-left corner.**

   The Compose Message window appears, as shown in Figure 11-6.

2. **Fill in the recipient's email address(es) and any additional people you want to CC.**

3. **Enter the subject in the subject line and your message in the message body.**

4. **When you're ready to send your message, click Send.**

## Outlook Calendar

Like Google Calendar, Outlook has a built-in calendar system that lets you make appointments, set reminders, and invite others to events. To access Outlook Calendar, click the Calendar icon at the left side of the Outlook window; it looks like a tiny calendar. The main calendar is displayed (see Figure 11-7) and contains the following controls:

>> **Add Calendar Item:** Add a new appointment, reminder, or event.

>> **Search:** Look for an event in your calendar.

>> **Go to Today:** Click to instantly view the current day on your calendar. If you are viewing one day at a time, your screen shows you the current day. If you're showing any of the week or month views, the calendar goes to the week or month that includes today.

>> **Next/Previous:** Go to the next month, week, or day, depending upon the view.

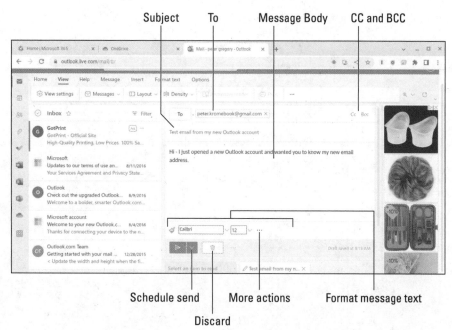

Subject    To    Message Body    CC and BCC

Schedule send    More actions    Format message text

Discard

Illustration courtesy of Peter H. Gregory

**FIGURE 11-6:**
Composing a new message with Outlook.

>> **Selector:** This is the range of days, weeks, or months that can be viewed.

>> **Day/Week/Month view:** Choose whether you want to view one day at a time, a workweek, a whole week, or an entire month.

>> **View/Hide calendar sidebar:** You can show or hide a view of "today" and any appointments, reminders, or events scheduled for today.

>> **Settings:** Change elements of your calendar, like the days of the week and hours of the day you work, reminders, display colors, and shared calendars.

To add an item to your calendar, click the Add Calendar Item button (refer to Figure 11-7). A new pane opens and allows you to fill in some details:

>> **Title:** Describe the event or reminder.

>> **Date and time:** Enter whatever you want for the date plus start and end times.

>> **Location:** Enter an address; the name of a city name, business, or friend; or anything else. Outlook helps you with place names by trying to guess what you are typing (which is sometimes helpful, but also annoying at times).

View/Hide calendar sidebar

Add calendar item

View settings

Go to: Today    Selector

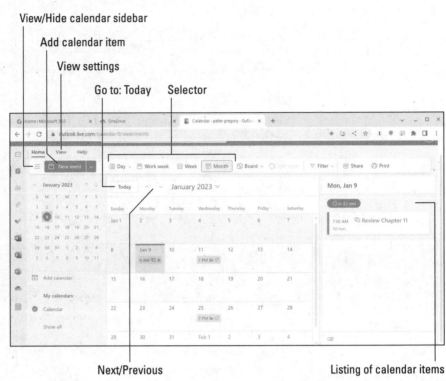

FIGURE 11-7:
The Outlook
Calendar.

Next/Previous                    Listing of calendar items

*Illustration courtesy of Peter H. Gregory*

>> **Repeat:** Outlook asks whether this is a repeating event, such as an anniversary, a weekly chore, or a monthly appointment. If you select this, you have more details to specify, including the frequency of the event and the number of times it should occur (or on what date it should end).

>> **More options:** If you click More options, a larger window will open, where you can fill in more details, such as time zones, attendees to invite, and files to attach to the invite.

When you have filled everything out, click the Save button. The event or item appears on your calendar.

TIP

This section barely scratches the surface of the Microsoft 365 Calendar. It offers so much more, like the ability to invite others to appointments and events, manage multiple calendars, and more.

# Outlook Contacts

Outlook contacts keeps track of the people in your life, work, or both! Like an address book or a Rolodex, Outlook Contacts helps you remember all those details. Google Contacts does this, too, so Outlook Contacts doesn't have any particular advantage here.

To view your contacts, click the People icon on the left edge of the Microsoft 365 window. Microsoft 365 switches to the People view.

You probably have no contacts there if you've just opened a new Outlook account. To add a contact, follow these steps:

1. **Click the familiar New contact button.**

   The Add Contact pane appears.

2. **Enter the contact's name, email, and phone in the appropriate fields.**

3. **Scroll down to also enter other items.**

   These include the name of the contact's company, home and work addresses, multiple phone numbers, nickname, birthday, anniversary, web page, and any notes you may want to include in a free-form notes field.

4. **When you're done, click the Save button.**

   If you change your mind and don't want to add the contact now, click Cancel.

That's all there is to it!

After you have added a contact, you will see the entry in the list to the left. On the right side, several links to other tasks appear, such as setting up a calendar event (which invites the contact) or sending an email. If you sync the contact to your phone, you can call the person if you've filled in a phone number.

You can edit a contact later on by following these steps:

1. **Select the contact from the list of contacts.**

2. **Click the pencil icon near the top of the window.**

3. **Scroll to the fields you want to add or change and enter the information.**

4. **To remove one of the contact's details (such as the phone number), go to that item and use the Delete key to remove the characters one by one.**

5. **Click the Save button.**

   Your changes are saved.

6. **If you change your mind and don't want to keep your changes, click Cancel.**

   Your changes are discarded, and the contact's information is unchanged.

The main power of Outlook Contacts is the ability to send emails to people without having to remember their email addresses. In Outlook email, when composing a message, a nifty feature called *Autocomplete* helps you by filling in the rest of a recipient's email address after you've typed the first few letters of their email address or their name.

# Word

 Microsoft Word is one of Microsoft's flagship software products, going back to 1983. Today, Microsoft Word is the gold standard for business word processing, and it's available on Chromebooks.

Okay, a bit of a disclaimer: The version of Word in Microsoft 365 and on Chromebooks is not quite as full-featured as the versions available for Windows and Macs. But for many users, Word has more capabilities than they will ever need. I'm writing this part of the chapter on my Chromebook using Word, and a part of it using Word Online on my Mac.

To open Word, go to your Microsoft 365 main page (www.office.com) and click Word. Figure 11-8 shows the Word Online main page after you click New Document.

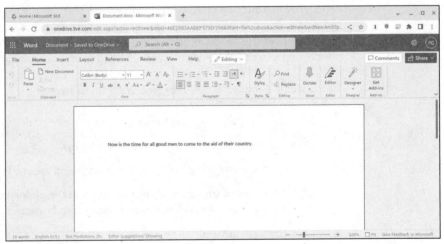

**FIGURE 11-8:** Using Word from Microsoft 365 on a Chromebook.

*Illustration courtesy of Peter H. Gregory*

On the Word main page, you have a lot of options. You can open a new blank document, open a document from one of many templates provided by Word, or upload a file from your Chromebook and edit it with Word. Word employs a toolbar called the Ribbon. If you look again at Figure 11-8, you can see that the Home tab is open. On this tab, you can format your text in many different ways, including your choice of font, font size, bold, underline, text color, and highlight color. You can format paragraphs to be left- or right-justified, centered, or full, and you can add bullets and numbering. If you click the Layout tab on the Ribbon, you see you find ways to control page size and orientation, margins, and more. On the Review tab, you can run the spelling and grammar checkers, insert comments, and count the number of words in your document.

Word and Google Docs are compatible. In other words, you can create and work on a document in Word and then send it to someone else who can work on it using Google Docs. Until you get into some of the very advanced features of Word, such as the use of Word template ".dot" files, you'll never run into a problem.

Word works great on Chromebooks. Entire books have been written about Word, so you can find far more information than I have time and space to show you here.

## Excel

Microsoft Excel is the undisputed king of spreadsheets in the business world. And as you can with Outlook and Word, you can use Excel on your Chromebook. In this section, you dive right in.

To start Excel, log in to your Microsoft 365 account at Office.com and click the Excel button. When Excel starts, you see a start page. You have several choices: You can create a new, blank spreadsheet by clicking any of the several templates shown; you can upload a spreadsheet (called a *workbook*) that is stored on your Chromebook; or you can open a spreadsheet that is stored in your OneDrive. Figure 11-9 shows Excel with the New Blank Workbook template chosen.

As with Google Sheets, a spreadsheet in Excel consists of cells arranged in rows and columns. You can put numbers or other text, such as dates (or just words, phrases, and sentences) in a cell. You can adjust the height of rows and the width of columns. You can put in formulas to calculate things, like the total or average of cells in a column of cells.

Microsoft Excel and Google Sheets are compatible, which means that, for the most part, you can create a spreadsheet in one program and use it in the other.

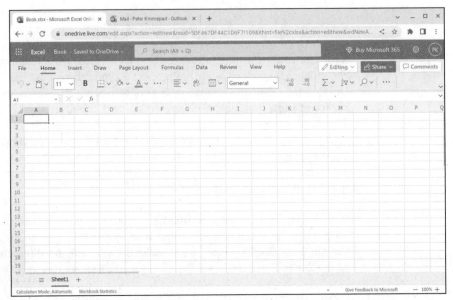

**FIGURE 11-9:**
A new, blank
spreadsheet in
Microsoft Excel.

# PowerPoint

PowerPoint is Microsoft's presentation app, and it's very much like Google Slides. More accurately, Google Slides is a lot like Microsoft PowerPoint. Like other Microsoft 365 applications, PowerPoint is the ruler of presentation applications. Just as you can do with Word and Excel, you can create a presentation in Power-Point that someone else can view and make changes to using Google Slides. This doesn't mean that every minute feature is available and exactly alike, but they do work together pretty well.

To open the PowerPoint program, log in to Microsoft 365 at www.office.com and click the PowerPoint link. PowerPoint starts and shows a screen like those in Word and Excel. When you create your first PowerPoint slide presentation, you start with a blank presentation, as shown in Figure 11-10.

The paradigm for PowerPoint is just the same as that for Google Slides. Each page is called a slide; slides have different layouts; and you can add and arrange text boxes, shapes, and images on each slide. The place for speaker's notes is the same as in Google Slides. You can view your presentation in a presentation mode that allows others to see your big, beautiful slides on a big screen or projector. At the same time, you can sit back and view it in Presenter's view, which lets you read your notes and not forget what you want to say.

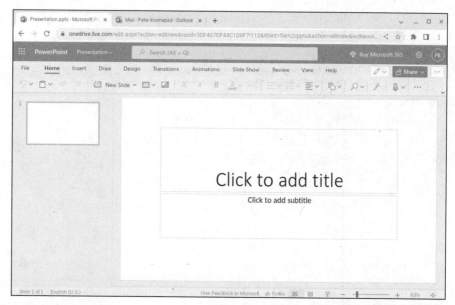

FIGURE 11-10:
A new, blank
presentation in
Microsoft
PowerPoint.

## OneNote

The OneNote app is made for general note-taking and organizing notes according to categories that the user sets up. OneNote is quite popular for busy people who need to organize random bits of information on many different topics.

To start OneNote, log in to Microsoft 365 at www.office.com and click the OneNote icon. If you haven't used OneNote before, a window opens that offers to give you a short tour of OneNote's features. I suggest you take the time to view this — it takes only a minute. The tour asks you a couple of questions about how you may use the program, and it sets up a set of initial categories for storing your notes. I chose the "personal" categories and accepted the defaults. The result was some pre-made categories that you can see in Figure 11-11.

TIP

If your Chromebook's screen is small, you may not see the OneNote icon. If this is the case, click the Apps button near the bottom left of the Microsoft 365 window. The OneNote icon will appear in a small pane that opens, along with other Microsoft 365 apps you can explore.

These are the areas and controls you'll see and use in OneNote.

>> **Sections:** The main categories in which your notes will appear.

>> **Pages:** The individual notes that appear in each category.

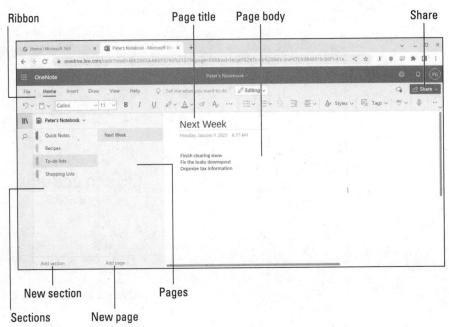

Ribbon     Page title     Page body     Share

**FIGURE 11-11:**
OneNote's initial
screen with
categories chosen
in the tour.

New section

Sections     New page

Pages

*Illustration courtesy of Peter H. Gregory*

>> **Page title:** The name of a note.

>> **Page body:** Where you enter the details of your note, whether it's a shopping list, a recipe, a list of invitees for an event, or notes from an important telephone call.

>> **New Section:** Click this to create a new section for notes.

>> **New Page:** Click this to create a new note.

>> **Ribbon:** Lets you change the appearance of text and paragraphs in your notes.

As with other Google and Microsoft 365 tools, you can share a note by clicking the Share button near the upper-right corner.

# Collaborating in OneDrive

Just as Google Drive allows two or more persons to edit a Docs document, Sheets spreadsheet, or Slides presentation simultaneously, Microsoft's OneDrive allows multiple people to edit a document, spreadsheet, or presentation at the same time.

For two or more people to edit a document simultaneously, the document owner must share the document with others. You click the Share button to share in Excel,

Word, or PowerPoint. Figure 11-12 shows a user in Excel sharing a spreadsheet with another user. When you fill in a user's email address and click Share, the recipient(s) receives an email containing a URL that users can click to open the document and view or edit it.

FIGURE 11-12: Sharing a spreadsheet with another user in Microsoft Excel.

# Working with PDF Documents

PDF, or Portable Document Format, is a widely recognized standard for documents the world over. Although your Chrome browser can read and display PDF documents right in the browser window, you may want — or need — to display PDF documents using the built-in Gallery app, Chromebook's app for reading PDF documents.

If someone emails you a PDF document, or you download one from a website, you can open it right within your Chrome browser. For instance, if someone emails you a PDF as an attachment, clicking on it will open it right in the browser. You can also save the PDF to your Chromebook or your Google Drive.

If you have saved a copy of a PDF, navigate to it with the Files app. When you open the PDF file, ChromeOS opens it with the Gallery app, as shown in Figure 11-13. You can read the document, print it, and even make comments in it.

TIP

Note that some PDFs may be "locked," preventing editing, commenting, and/or printing.

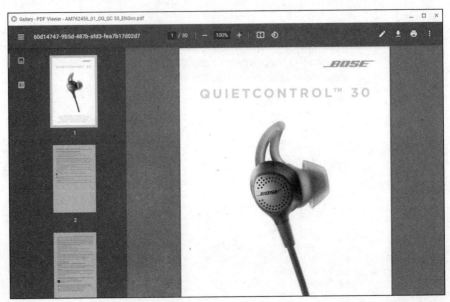

**FIGURE 11-13:**
The Gallery app displays PDF files for reading and annotating.

# 3
# The Chromebook Recreational Vehicle

# Chapter **12**

# Managing Your Music

Before the internet, the primary delivery mechanism for broadcast music was radio and television. Broadcast media effectively dictated what was popular simply because you had no other way to be exposed to new music unless you scoured the record (or CD) bins at the local music store. Or maybe you had friends with cool older siblings who gave out mixtapes to broaden your musical horizons. The internet turned the entire media industry on its head by providing access to anything (everything!), anywhere, anytime.

These days, purchasing physical music media is primarily done by collectors and super-fans. Broadcast radio is shrinking and consolidating, and satellite radio is still hanging on. The expansion of the internet, broadband access, and wireless technology have revolutionized the way the world consumes music. It's a buyer's market in the music industry.

In this chapter, you explore the ins and outs of Google's digital music platform, YouTube Music. Upload your digital music library to YouTube Music and sync it to your Chromebook and other wireless devices. Search the YouTube Music catalog of over 70 million tracks and stream them to your Chromebook. Find out how to create playlists that you can share with other YouTube Music users, or simply search for radio stations that play an endless stream of tunes to get you through the day. There's never a dull moment with YouTube Music.

If you are a Pandora, Spotify, Amazon, or Apple streaming music user, you can fully enjoy those services on your Chromebook. Even the high-end Tidal music service is available. This chapter explores them as well.

# Getting Started with YouTube Music

At the end of 2020, Google opted to replace Google Play with YouTube Music, which is now Google's online music marketplace. It is similar to other music services offered by Pandora, Spotify, Amazon, and Apple.

 As is the case with all the applications on the Google platform, access to apps is linked to your Google Account. If you have multiple Google Accounts, make sure you're logged in to your Chromebook with the account that you want to be associated with YouTube Music. Launch YouTube Music by opening the Launcher and clicking the YouTube Music icon.

A Welcome screen appears if you're logging into YouTube Music for the first time. You need to decide what level of service you want. YouTube Music offers a free version and a paid version.

With the free version, which has limited functionality, you can

>> Upload your music collection (up to 100,000 songs) and stream it to any Chromebook, Android, iOS, laptop, or other web-enabled, internet-connected device.

>> Play music on your Chromebook, Android, iOS, or other device.

With the paid version, you get everything the free version offers, plus you can view music videos, and download music and videos for later playback, even when offline. Also, your music experience is completely advertisement-free.

In both the free and premium versions, you cannot purchase music in YouTube Music, but you can upload music purchased elsewhere into your YouTube Music library.

 There's no such thing as a free lunch. The free YouTube Music service is great, but you will hear advertising now and then. However, if you upgrade to the paid service, the ads vanish!

TIP

# Creating a Standard Account

To begin using the standard (free) version of YouTube Music, follow these steps:

1. **Open the Launcher and click the YouTube Music icon.**

   The YouTube Music app opens and asks you to pick five music artists you like.

   Go ahead and take a few minutes here. This little exercise tells YouTube Music what kinds of music you like; this influences how YouTube Music suggests new artists to you later on.

   When you click on an artist, a check mark appears. Click again to clear the check mark.

2. **Click Done with you've picked your five.**

3. **To proceed with a standard free account, click the No Thanks link at the bottom of the window.**

   The main YouTube Music window opens.

You're taken to your YouTube Music Home page, as shown in Figure 12-1. From this page, you can browse artists, albums, and songs to see what piques your interest.

**FIGURE 12-1:**
The YouTube Music main page.

*Illustration courtesy of Peter H. Gregory*

The YouTube Music main page has these features:

» **Home:** View recommended albums, artists (including the favorites you selected when you first started), music genres, suggested mix tracks, and more.

» **Explore:** View new releases, music charts, and music in various moods and genres.

» **Library:** Here is where the playlists you create, the music you save, and your subscriptions are shown. When you're just starting out, nothing will be here other than a link to create a playlist.

» **Upgrade:** Try YouTube Music Premium, free for a limited time, or just sign up.

Have a look around, after which I suggest you return to the Home or Explore tab. If you click on an artist, you'll be taken to a page that lists albums and songs. Notice that a Play icon appears when you hover over a song or album. If you hover over the three little vertical dots, a menu appears, as shown in Figure 12-2.

**FIGURE 12-2:** Possible actions related to a music selection.

*Illustration courtesy of Peter H. Gregory*

# Upgrading to a Premium Account

Are you sick of the ads yet? If you want to upgrade from the free version of YouTube Music to the commercial-free paid service, follow these steps:

**1.** **In the YouTube Music main window, click the Upgrade button.**

The Music Premium page appears.

2. **Scroll down and find a link that shows you all available plans.**

   Your subscription choices appear. Select Annual, Family, or Student.

   If you already have one or more credit cards registered with Google, it asks you to select which one to use. If you don't, you're asked to enter a credit card number. (Google will ask for your credit card even if you have a free trial, because it hopes you will think their music service is so fine that you won't cancel once the free period is over.)

**TIP**

If you see a "Purchasing unavailable" error, follow the instructions, which may direct you to visit music.youtube.com/musicpremium to make your purchase.

# Accessing Music in YouTube Music

With YouTube Music, the world is your oyster. After you've selected your favorite genre(s) and artists, YouTube Music displays popular artists, albums, playlists, and radio stations that play the music you like, as well as other music selections such as Local Favorites, Recommended New Releases, and Top Albums.

## YouTube Music Library

The YouTube Music library is where all your favorite artists, albums, songs, and radio stations reside, as well as your music uploads. In the standard (free) account, your YouTube Music view defaults to your music library. If you aren't in your library, you can get there by locating and clicking the Library link at the top of the page. Your library loads, revealing all the music that's available to play.

Your library is initially empty if you opted for the standard account and haven't uploaded any music. But as you start listening to music — whether playlists, albums, songs, artists, or radio — your library begins to populate with the following:

>> **Recent activity:** This is a list of music you have listened to and music videos you have watched. Note that certain YouTube videos will be listed here as well. For instance, I'm a subscriber to Rick Beato's channel, so when I watch his videos, they appear here.

>> **Playlists, Albums, Songs, Artists, and Subscriptions:** This section is filled with playlists you have made and the albums and songs you have uploaded. Just beneath is a list of your playlists and the ability to create a new playlist.

**REMEMBER**

With the standard free account, YouTube Music allows you to upload up to 100,000 songs. If your collection is bigger than that, just upload the music you listen to most and leave the back catalog on a jump drive.

## Playing Music on YouTube Music

There are numerous ways you can begin playing music on YouTube Music. After all, this music player lives to play music for you. Here are some ways. Explore YouTube Music on your own, and you may find even more!

From Home, Explore, or Library, scroll down. Hover over recommended radios, quick picks, listen again, mixed for you, and more. Everything you see has a Play button. Just click, and music will be playing!

When playing music, the YouTube Music app has a lot of controls, as shown in Figure 12-3:

>> **Home:** YouTube Music's main page.

>> **Explore:** View new releases, trending music, music charts, and genres.

>> **Library:** Your music library.

>> **Upgrade:** Upgrade to one of the paid versions of YouTube Music.

>> **Cast:** Cause your music to be played through a TV or external speaker.

>> **Google Account:** Manage your Google account. Also, a submenu appears that includes:

- **Your Channel:** Create a music channel with music you create and perform.

- **Get Music Premium:** See offers to upgrade to paid versions.

- **Upload music:** Upload music you already own into your YouTube Music library so you can play it anywhere.

- **History:** Show the music you have played.

- **Settings:** Change how YouTube Music works.

- **Help & Feedback:** Get help using YouTube Music.

>> **Play Controls:** These are

- **Repeat mode:** Repeats songs or albums (appears when you hover here).

- **Back:** Plays previous track.

- **Play:** Plays music.

- **Skip:** Plays next track.

- **Shuffle songs:** Plays songs in random order (appears when you hover here).

» **Queue:** Lets you view the list of songs to be played after the current selection.

» **Mini player:** Moves currently playing info into the lower right corner of the YouTube Music window (appears when you hover over the album art or video).

» **Enter full screen:** Enters full screen mode (appears when you hover over the album art or video).

» **Search:** Lets you search for music by artist, song, album, or station.

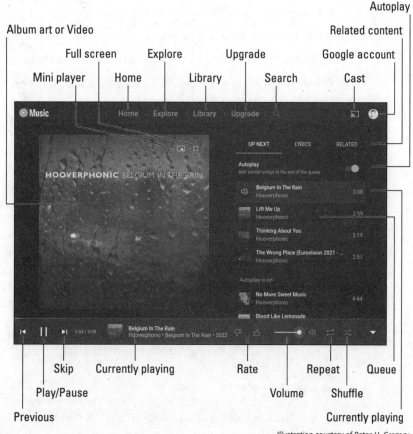

**FIGURE 12-3:**
The YouTube
Music player.

*Illustration courtesy of Peter H. Gregory*

At any time while music is playing, the name of the song playing appears at the bottom-right corner of the window. Album art may appear as well. If the selection is a music video, you'll see it if you are a YouTube Music Premium subscriber. The Play button is now a Pause button in the middle of the window at the bottom. To the right of that is the Skip button. If you have a free account, you can skip up to six times an hour; if you have a paid subscription, you can skip all you like (but if you are skipping a lot, maybe you want to choose another station). To the right of Skip, you see the length of the selection playing, the name of the selection, and thumbs down and thumbs up rating buttons. To the right of the thumbs buttons, you can see three little vertical dots; click that to see a whole list of things you can do (as shown in Figure 12-4):

>> **Start radio:** Start playing a radio station associated with this song.

>> **Play next:** Skip to the next song.

>> **Add to queue:** Add the song playing to your "play next" queue.

>> **Add to library:** Add the song playing to your library.

>> **Add to liked songs:** Just what it says!

>> **Add to playlist:** Add the song playing to a new or existing playlist.

>> **Remove from queue:** Remove the song from your "play next" queue.

>> **Go to album:** View the album.

>> **Go to artist:** View the artist.

>> **Share:** Share this song with others.

>> **Report:** Report a problem with the selection.

>> **Stats for nerds:** View a tiny pane showing technical facts about the music that is playing.

To the right of the three little dots is a tiny pointer pointing left. If you hover over it, volume control, repeat, and shuffle controls appear. And don't forget the Cast button near the upper-right corner of the window, so you can cast your music and music videos to a TV or other device with a Chromecast attached.

When you are playing music, if you hover over the album art or video (refer to Figure 12-3), you will see two tiny controls:

>> **Open mini player:** This looks like a little white square in a frame. Clicking this puts your currently playing music in a little pane in the lower-right corner of the YouTube Music window, and then displays the Home, Explore, or Library pages. In the mini player, click the similar-looking icon, and the player returns to the full window.

>> **Full screen:** This looks like four little corners in a rectangle. Click this, and YouTube Music occupies the entire screen. Press the Esc key to exit full-screen mode.

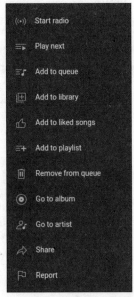

**FIGURE 12-4:**
YouTube Music song controls.

*Illustration courtesy of Peter H. Gregory*

As you explore and use YouTube Music, you'll note that your currently playing music will automatically go to the mini player if you begin exploring while listening to music.

You can also pause and restart play with the spacebar.

## YouTube Music Radio

On YouTube Music, a "radio station" is simply a music stream in a particular genre. It's not the same as AM or FM stations. It's more like the stations on Sirius Satellite Radio, but without DJs. YouTube Music "radio" stations play only music, all day and all night.

Radio stations in streaming music services are similar to "over-the-air" radio stations in that they often have a theme. Over-the-air radio stations are transmitted using AM or FM radio signals and are available in a small geographic area. Streaming radio stations are available across the entire world.

TIP

If you don't add songs or albums on YouTube Music to your library, your main option is to find and select radio stations to stream for as long as you want. If you have the free version, you hear advertisements from time to time.

YouTube Music Radio has dozens (maybe hundreds) of radio stations. From the main page, click on Home, Explore, or Library and scroll up or down to find the stations you regularly listen to as well as recommended radio stations.

TIP

If you like a radio station, you can add it to your music library. Just click the Add to Library link, and the station will be listed in your music library.

YouTube Music makes it easy to add a song you're listening to in your library. Click on the three little dots at the bottom of the window, and select Add to library. Done!

## Searching for an artist's station

Even with the free version of YouTube Music, you have an almost infinite number of stations available to play. If you search for a favorite artist in the search bar, many different stations appear, including one named for the artist. Not every song will be by that artist, but the songs will all be of the same genre — and many of the songs played *will* be by the artist so named.

## Uploading music

If you have music from another source in digital form, you can add it to your YouTube Music library. You may have your music files on an SD card, a thumb drive, an external hard drive, or online in Google Drive or even iCloud or OneDrive. Whatever your music's source, follow these steps to upload it to your YouTube Music library:

1.  **Click on the Account button (it may have your picture, an avatar, or your initials) in the upper-right corner of the YouTube Music window.**

    A menu appears.

2.  **Click the Upload button.**

    The Add Music window appears. It looks a lot like the Files app and works the same way.

3.  **Navigate to the folders on your Chromebook that contain the music you want to upload.**

4.  **Select the file(s) or folder(s) you want to upload.**

5. **Click Open.**

    When you're done, the added music appears in your library.

    YouTube Music queues the files and uploads them in the background.

You can monitor the progress of your file upload by looking at the little upload pane in the lower-left corner of YouTube Music. A progress bar shows upload progress. You can click Stop to stop the upload.

When complete, YouTube Music tells you that the song(s) have been uploaded and offers to take you to your Library where you can see it.

TIP

One thing that's really cool about YouTube Music is that you can upload music, create playlists, and change preferences — all while listening to your favorite artist, album, or radio. YouTube Music is great at doing multiple things all at once.

## Creating playlists

Playlists are the modern version of mixtapes. Back in the day, I made mixtapes on reel-to-reel and cassette tapes. Today, creating playlists in YouTube Music is easier than recording mixtapes (and you don't need Scotch Tape for splicing). A *playlist* is a collection of songs that you want to play in a specific or randomized order. You can have a playlist for working out, another for relaxing, another for working on your motorcycle, and another for romance. YouTube Music allows you to build playlists composed of songs you've uploaded to your library or with songs available from the entire YouTube Music catalog. YouTube Music enables you to have up to 5,000 songs in a playlist!

All your playlists appear in the Playlists part of your library. Even when you run YouTube Music for the first time, you may have some auto playlists that are already present in your library.

To create a playlist, follow these steps:

1. **Navigate to artists, albums, or songs in your music library. Continue until you are viewing songs you want to add to a playlist.**

2. **When viewing a song, click the More actions (three little dots) to the right of the song title.**

    **The More actions menu appears.**

3. **Click Add to Playlist.**

    If you don't have any playlists, select New Playlist. If you do have one or more playlists, they appear. Figure 12-5 shows the New Playlist window.

4. **Enter the name of your playlist in the Name text box and give it a nice description in the Description text box.**

5. **For now, keep the playlist private by keeping the Make Public selector off.**

6. **Click Create.**

   Your new playlist appears in the Playlist area of your library.

Illustration courtesy of Peter H. Gregory

**FIGURE 12-5:**
Creating a new playlist in YouTube Music.

To add more songs, simply repeat the preceding procedure by selecting songs and adding them to existing or new playlists.

## Sharing playlists

Chances are good that you'll create an epic playlist that will be remembered for all the ages. It would be nearly criminal to keep such a playlist to yourself. You need to share it! To share a playlist, follow these steps:

1. **Click Library in the YouTube Music window.**

2. **Click Playlists.**

   Your playlists appear.

3. **Click the playlist you want to share from your list of playlists.**

   Your playlist is displayed.

4. **Click More actions (three little vertical dots).**

   A menu appears.

5. **Click Share.**

   The Share pane appears, revealing all the ways you can share your playlist, as shown in Figure 12-6.

6. **Click the desired option.**

   For example, if you click Email, Gmail will open and create an email message containing a link to your playlist. Just fill in the recipients of the message and click Send.

7. **Click the X in the Share pane when you are done.**

   Your playlist is now available on YouTube Music to the persons you have shared it with.

**FIGURE 12-6:**
The Playlist share window.

If you want to share your playlist with friends through a media method not listed in the Share pane, you can generate a link to your playlist and send it out to every deserving soul in your network. Locate your playlist link by following these steps:

1. **Open the Share menu as described previously.**

   The Playlist Options menu appears.

2. **Click on Copy.**

   The URL is copied onto the Clipboard. You may then send the link to others through email or social media.

# Playing music on external devices

In addition to playing music on your Chromebook, you can connect headphones or external speakers by plugging them into the headphone jack, if it exists. But you also have more options: You can play music on Bluetooth speakers or "cast" your music to an external device such as a Chromecast connected to a TV or a monitor with speakers.

You must first "pair" the device to your Chromebook to play music to a Bluetooth device. Follow this procedure:

1. **Turn on the Bluetooth device and put it into pairing mode using the procedures for the device.**

2. **On your Chromebook, click the Status area in the lower-right corner of the Chromebook display where the time of day and battery status icons appear.**

3. **If the Bluetooth icon is gray, click it to turn on Bluetooth.**

4. **Click the menu beneath the Bluetooth icon to open the Bluetooth settings.**

5. **Wait for the device name to appear and then click it.**

    The device should successfully pair with your Chromebook. Now, if you play music with YouTube Music, the audio should play from the Bluetooth speaker.

To cast music to an external device such as a Google Chromecast or a TV with built-in cast capability, follow these instructions (assuming your Chromecast or other device is already set up):

1. **Start the YouTube Music app and select music to play.**

2. **Find and click the Cast button near the upper-right corner of the YouTube Music window.**

    The Cast pane opens. (See Figure 12-7.)

3. **In the pane, look for the name of the device you want to cast to and click that name.**

    Music should now be playing through the device.

4. **When you want to stop playing music through the device, click the device again in the Cast pane (click the Cast button to get the pane to appear if you don't see it). Then click the device to disconnect it.**

TIP

Another cool way to find artists you may like is found on the Music-Map website. Go to www.music-map.com and type in your favorite artist. The website will display artists that are similar to the one you selected. Click on any that you see on the screen, and Music-Map will show artists similar to that one.

# Enjoying Streaming Music with Pandora

If you are a fan of the Pandora music streaming service, you're in luck: It works just great on Chromebooks and offers 60 million songs. With Pandora, you merely select and listen to streaming music channels. You don't have a music library, and you don't purchase songs or albums. In truth, Pandora closely resembles the radio stations of YouTube Music.

Like YouTube Music, Pandora has free and paid subscription options. And, you guessed it: The free service includes occasional advertising, whereas the paid service is ad-free.

To listen to Pandora, follow these steps:

1. **Open a new tab in your Chrome browser.**

2. **Navigate to www.pandora.com.**

   You're now on Pandora. You see the initial screen, which looks like Figure 12-8.

You'll see the Sign Up and Log In buttons in the window's upper-right corner. However, you don't need to log in or sign up to listen to music. Just search and play!

If you're new to Pandora, you'll see an assortment of music genres. Browse to choose genres and stations you like. You can find a new station by searching a genre or artist in the search window. Pandora shows you stations as well as albums. When you see one you like, click the Option button (three little vertical dots) and then click Collect to add it to your collection. You can't add playlists to your collection, but you can listen to them.

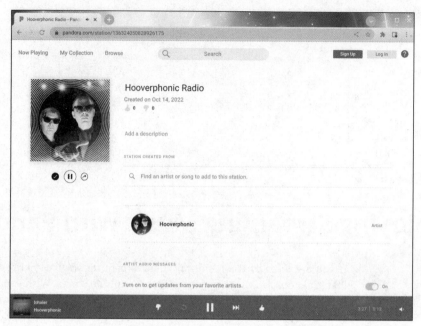

FIGURE 12-8:
The Pandora
music streaming
service.

You can share any station or playlist by clicking Share from the Option menu. Like YouTube Music, Pandora provides Facebook and Twitter Share buttons, as well as the ability to copy a link you can post on social media, email to a friend, or even save as a browser bookmark.

When you tire of the advertising on your stations, create an account and upgrade to a paid version.

If you want more capabilities, such as casting Pandora to a Google Chromecast, you need to download the Pandora — Music & Podcasts app. Just go to the Google Play Store, search for Pandora, and click Install. Then click Open to start. If you plan to use the Pandora app often, you can pin it to the Launcher.

The Pandora app, shown in Figure 12-9, is similar to the Pandora website but with a different arrangement. All the concepts are the same, however. You browse stations and playlists, add those you like, and listen to them. Unlike the Pandora website, however, you have to log in to play music.

**FIGURE 12-9:**
The Pandora app for Chromebooks.

*Illustration courtesy of Peter H. Gregory*

# Streaming with Spotify

If Spotify is the music service that floats your boat, you're in luck; it is fully supported on the Chromebook. Spotify is a bit like the streaming radio part of YouTube Music: You browse and search for genres and artists you like and build a collection of music to stream for every mood. Figure 12-10 shows the Spotify player window. With 80 million songs in their catalog, you're bound to find music you love. Start by searching the Google Play Store app for Spotify: Music and Podcasts. Click Install and then Open.

**FIGURE 12-10:**
The Spotify streaming music service web player.

*Illustration courtesy of Peter H. Gregory*

You have to create an account if you don't have one already, but it's free. And you guessed it: You'll hear commercials now and then, but you can upgrade to a commercial–free paid version.

# Amping Up Amazon Music

 If you're an avid fan of the Amazon Music service, you're in luck because it works great on a Chromebook. It's so simple that I could practically skip this section altogether.

Amazon Music offers three levels of membership:

>> **Amazon Music Free:** Choose genres and artists, and listen to pre-established playlists.

>> **Amazon Prime Music:** 90 million curated songs are included with the popular Amazon Prime membership.

>> **Amazon Music Unlimited:** 90 million songs are available in student, individual, family, and single-device (Amazon Echo or Fire TV) plans. Play any artist, song, album, or playlist you wish, and listen in HD (high-definition audio). If you're an Alexa fan, with Amazon Music Unlimited you can make more obscure requests, such as, "Alexa, play the song that goes 'There's a lady who's sure all that glitters is gold'" if you can't remember the artist or title.

To use Amazon Music in either plan, follow these steps:

1. **Start your Chrome browser and go to** `music.amazon.com`.

2. **Sign in using your existing Amazon credentials or create a new Amazon account.**

3. **Select Amazon Music Free, Amazon Prime Music, or Amazon Music Unlimited if you aren't already a subscriber.**

   If you see a pane that directs you to download the desktop app, just skip it by clicking on Continue to Amazon Music.

4. **Select Albums, Artists, Songs, Genres, or music you have purchased from Amazon in the past. (See Figure 12-11.)**

5. **Enjoy your music!**

**TIP**

The Amazon Music service plays through your Chrome browser.

There is also an Amazon Music app available from the Google Play Store. You know what to do. You'll need the app if you want to cast to a Chromecast or TV.

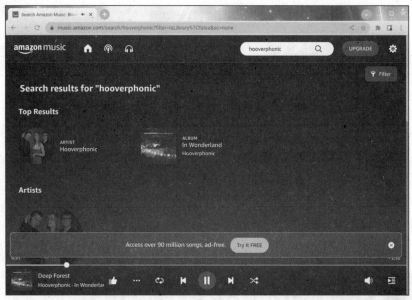

FIGURE 12-11:
The Amazon
Music service
player.

*Illustration courtesy of Peter H. Gregory*

# Rocking with Apple Music

You might think that Apple Music wouldn't be available on a Chromebook. Think again. Apple Music, the paid subscription service from Apple that launched in 2017, is available on virtually all devices: Windows PCs, Macs, Android phones and tablets, iPhones and iPads, and Chromebooks. It's fully functional as well. With 100 million songs in its catalog, you're never going to run out of music to listen to.

Like other services, Apple Music works through an installed app. To get started with Apple Music on your Chromebook, follow these easy steps:

1. **Launch the Google Play Store app.**

2. **Search for Apple Music and then click Install.**

   Apple Music is now installed on your Chromebook.

3. **Click Open.**

4. **Follow the prompts to sign in with your Apple account.**

5. **Start playing music.**

   Your player fills the screen, as shown in Figure 12-12. Like other music apps, you can play through your Chromebook speakers, a connected Bluetooth speaker, or cast to a Chromecast or TV.

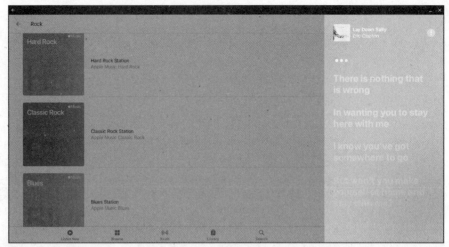

*Illustration courtesy of Peter H. Gregory*

# High-End Listening with Tidal

 If you are a high-end audiophile, I have good news for you: the Tidal music service is available on Chromebooks! Tidal was one of the first streaming music services offering high-fidelity (HiFi) sound quality.

Like the other streaming music services I describe in this chapter, Tidal's music library is enormous with over 90 million songs. If each song was a mile long, this library would reach from the Earth to the Sun!

To get started with Tidal on your Chromebook, go to the Google Play Store, search for Tidal, click Install, and launch! You'll have to log in, of course. If you haven't used Tidal, you can sign up for a free trial. Tidal offers three tiers of service:

>> **Tidal Free:** Free access to the entire music catalog, with advertising. Music plays in normal quality format.

>> **Tidal HiFi:** HiFi sound quality, unlimited skips, ad-free. Includes over 450,000 music videos.

>> **Tidal HiFi Plus:** The same as Tidal HiFi with more high-quality audio format choices.

IN THIS CHAPTER

» Using your Chromebook camera

» Transferring photos into your photo library from other devices

» Viewing your photos on a bigger screen

» Deleting and editing photos

» Sharing photos with others

# Chapter **13**

# Having Fun with Photos

The Chromebook is an excellent multimedia device. With it, you can take photos, listen to music, watch videos, share media files, surf the web, and more. Every Chromebook currently on the market has a built-in camera that allows you to video chat and capture photos for sharing on the web. Further, you can load photos from your smartphone and external media, edit the pictures, view them on a big screen, and share them across the web. The Chromebook is no slouch when it comes to multimedia.

In this chapter, you learn how to access the built-in camera to take pictures. You also discover how to edit your pictures by resizing, rotating, adding color filters, and more. I show you how to access photos on removable storage devices like SD cards. I also explore scanning documents and QR codes. You see how to get photos from your smartphone or digital camera to your Chromebook and share them with others.

# Navigating the Chromebook Camera

The Camera application that runs on your Chromebook is a native application, meaning you don't need internet access to connect to it because it resides on your Chromebook itself. You can take pictures while offline, which is handy if you ever want to take pictures while you're in an internet desert.

To launch your Chromebook Camera app, open the Launcher and click the Camera icon.

 When the Camera app is open, your Chromebook camera is activated. Two things indicate your Chromebook camera is on:

>> In the Camera app, a video appears of you sitting in front of your Chromebook. Smile!

>> The tiny light next to your Chromebook camera turns on, indicating the camera is on. This light is typically above the screen in the middle. The camera lens itself is right next to the little light.

Let's get the obvious out of the way: Chromebooks are great laptops, but unless you like taking pictures of yourself, they aren't intended to be used as a camera in the same way that a smartphone or digital camera is used.

The Camera app window has a few distinct areas you should be aware of. In the top-right corner, you have the window controls. You can make the Camera application fill the screen by clicking the square in the top-right corner. Click it again to restore the application to its default size. If you want to close the application, click the X in the top-right corner.

The large white button on the right side of the application window is used to take a photo. On the left side of the window, several smaller icons appear. (See Figure 13-1.) These icons are used to control how the Camera app works.

You can access Camera app settings by clicking on the little gear. In the settings menu, you can change picture resolution and aspect ratio (4:3 or 16:9).

Camera settings

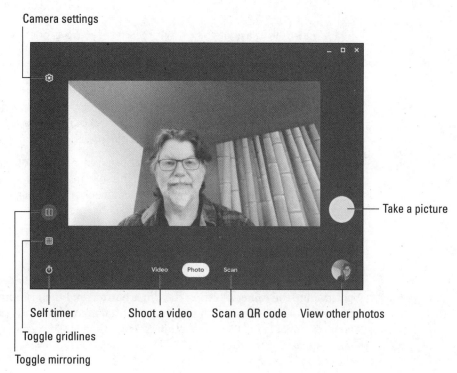

Take a picture

Self timer     Shoot a video     Scan a QR code     View other photos

**FIGURE 13-1:**
The Chromebook
Camera app.

Toggle gridlines

Toggle mirroring

*Illustration courtesy of Peter H. Gregory*

# Taking a Picture

To take a picture, launch the Camera app and follow these steps:

1. **Hover your mouse pointer over the white Picture button in the camera control bar. (Don't click it yet.)**

2. **Look at the tiny light next to your Chromebook camera.**

   This ensures you're looking straight into the camera in your photo.

3. **Click the white Picture button.**

   Your Chromebook makes an old-fashioned SLR camera noise and takes your picture.

**TIP**

Picture quality depends largely on the camera's quality and the operator's skill. Chromebook cameras are pretty good, given the size and application, but they struggle to deliver the goods in certain settings. Here are some suggestions for taking a good photo with your Chromebook camera:

>> If you're taking a photo of yourself, make sure you're as bright as or brighter than what's behind you. Avoid backlighting: Try not to take photos in front of windows or with the sun or any bright lights behind you (unless you want a silhouette shot to look like you're in the witness protection program!).

>> Make sure you're well lit (no, not intoxicated). Your background may be dim, but the camera will struggle to capture a nice photo if you don't have light shining on you. (Can you tell that light is a big deal?)

>> Most of the time, your Chromebook will be positioned lower than you; therefore, most photos appear as though someone shorter than you took them. Try to take a photo with your Chromebook angled straight on with you.

## Using the camera timer

The camera timer is the family vacation's best friend. Remember your mom or dad positioning the camera, hitting the timer button, and then running back into the frame for the awkward family photo in front of *every* sight and feature at Yellowstone National Park? Well, some things never change. The camera timer is here to stay, at least for the time being, and it's as functional as ever.

To take pictures using a timer, follow these steps:

1. **In the Camera app, locate and click on the Timer. It looks like a little stopwatch.**

    It now has a 3 in it.

    After you click the Picture button, the countdown appears on the screen and indicates the status of the countdown Timer.

2. **If you're ready to take a picture, click the white Picture button.**

    Your Chromebook beeps three (or ten) times before taking the picture and shows the countdown on the screen. You'll know the picture was taken when you hear a camera sound.

    You can configure the timer to wait three seconds or ten seconds. To view and change this setting, click the Timer button and select the desired option, as shown in Figure 13-2.

**REMEMBER**

Whenever you take a photo with the camera, with or without the timer, always look at the tiny light to ensure that you're looking directly into the camera. Looking into the camera delivers the best results unless you're going for an arty pose. Say "Cheese!"

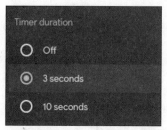

FIGURE 13-2:
Changing the
Timer setting.

*Illustration courtesy of Peter H. Gregory*

## Scanning documents and QR codes

Chromebooks can now scan documents, which can be super handy if you need to sign a document or contract and send it to some person or company. To scan a document, click Scan, and then click Document. Hold your document until it fills the picture. When you are happy with the alignment, click the Take Photo button. Next, the Camera app asks if you want to share the photo, save the photo, or save it as a PDF. Click whichever option you want.

There are many places where QR codes are used, from restaurants (to show menus) to product packaging (to show specs or a user's guide). If there's a QR code you want to scan, just click the Scan button at the bottom of the Camera app. Hold the QR code in the frame. You'll see a URL appear in the frame; when you do, you can put the object down and open the URL by clicking on it. The website will open in your Chrome browser. Cool, huh!

TIP

Okay, so I like the concept of scanning QR codes and documents with the front-facing Chromebook camera. But it's a bit awkward, too: When you put something in front of the camera, it blocks your view of the screen, making it difficult to know when you have the object positioned correctly. Ever hopeful, I'm convinced you'll get the hang of it with practice.

# Transferring Photos Taken with a Smartphone to Your Chromebook

Face it: When you're out and about, whether hiking, biking, at a sporting event, or spending time with friends, you're not lugging your Chromebook with you, taking photos. You're using your smartphone. With cameras that take incredible pictures, our smartphones are always with us, and with a moment's notice, we can snap pictures and take high-quality videos, too.

Google has made it incredibly easy to transfer photos from your smartphone to other devices. The Google Photos app makes all this both possible and automatic. Follow these steps to ensure that photos you take on your smartphone are copied to Google Photos:

1. **Install Google Photos on your smartphone.**

   It's probably already installed on your Android phone. On an iPhone, go to the App Store, search for Google Photos, install, launch, and log in to your Google account.

2. **Give Google Photos permission to access photos on your smartphone.**

   You should only have to do this once.

3. **Open Google Photos, go to Settings, and ensure that the Back up & sync setting is turned on (see Figure 13-3).**

   With this setting, you find that every photo you take on your smartphone soon appears in the Google Photos app on your Chromebook and any other devices running the Google Photos app.

**FIGURE 13-3:**
Configuring an Android phone to upload photos to Google Photos automatically.

*Illustration courtesy of Peter H. Gregory*

Similarly, you can upload photos taken with your Chromebook to Google Photos. Follow these steps:

1. **Open the Files app on your Chromebook.**

2. **Navigate to Camera.**

3. **Click a photo to upload.**

4. **Click the Share button, as shown in Figure 13-4.**

5. **Click Upload to Photos.**

   A new window opens, showing the photos you selected.

6. **Click the Upload button at the lower-right corner of the window.**

   Your photo soon appears in Google Photos.

*Illustration courtesy of Peter H. Gregory*

**FIGURE 13-4:**
Uploading photos taken with a Chromebook to Google Photos.

If you want photos taken on your Chromebook to be automatically uploaded to Google Photos, follow these easy steps:

1. **Open the Google Photos app.**

2. **Click on your photo, avatar, or initials in the upper-right corner of the window.**

3. **Click on Photos settings.**

4. **Click on Backup.**

5. **Click on Back up. Be sure it is selected, as shown in Figure 13-5.**

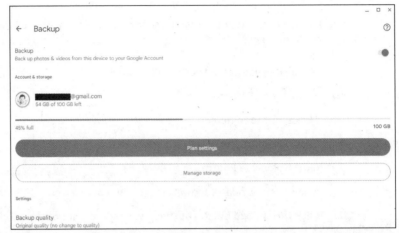

**FIGURE 13-5:**
Configuring your
Chromebook to
copy pictures to
Google Photos
automatically.

# Transferring Photos from Other Devices to Your Chromebook

You don't have to capture photos with the Chromebook Camera to be able to work with and otherwise edit, manipulate, or distribute your photos. Most major digital cameras, dashcams, and security cameras today store your photos on removable storage devices called *SD cards.* (See Figure 13-6.) Most Chromebooks on the market today have an SD-card slot for quickly accessing your data, such as photos and videos, among other things.

Some devices use a Micro SD card, a tiny version of an SD card. Most Chromebooks with an SD card slot have a full-size slot, necessitating an adaptor. Figure 13-7 shows a Micro SD card being inserted into an adaptor.

To access photos on an SD card, follow these steps:

1. **Place your SD card into the SD card slot on your Chromebook.**

   Chromebook may automatically offer to import all the photos on the SD card to Google Drive. It's entirely up to you whether you opt to do this. If you proceed, the photos on your SD card are copied to Google Photos.

2. **Click the SD card in Files to begin browsing its contents.**

   See Chapter 7 for more information about using the Files app.

**3.** **Drag and drop individual photos from the SD card to a location on your Chromebook.**

Alternatively, select multiple photos with Ctrl+click. Then, drag all selected photos at once to the desired folder on your Chromebook.

**FIGURE 13-6:**
A standard
SD card.

*Illustration courtesy of Peter H. Gregory*

**FIGURE 13-7:**
A Micro SD card
being inserted
into an SD card
adaptor.

*Illustration courtesy of Peter H. Gregory*

TIP

You can also use this technique to transfer photos to Google Drive, or even an external hard drive if you have one connected to your Chromebook.

# Viewing Photos on Your Chromebook

After you take photos on your Chromebook, the photos are stored in the Camera folder in the Files app. If you want to view your photos, follow these steps:

1. **Launch the Files app.**

2. **Click the Camera button on the left side of the Files app to navigate to your Chromebook photos.**

3. **Click the Switch to Thumbnail View button, if needed. (See Figure 13-8.)**

   Switching to thumbnail view allows you to view more photos at one time, although they're smaller.

4. **To view a particular photo, double-click the image thumbnail.**

   The photo loads.

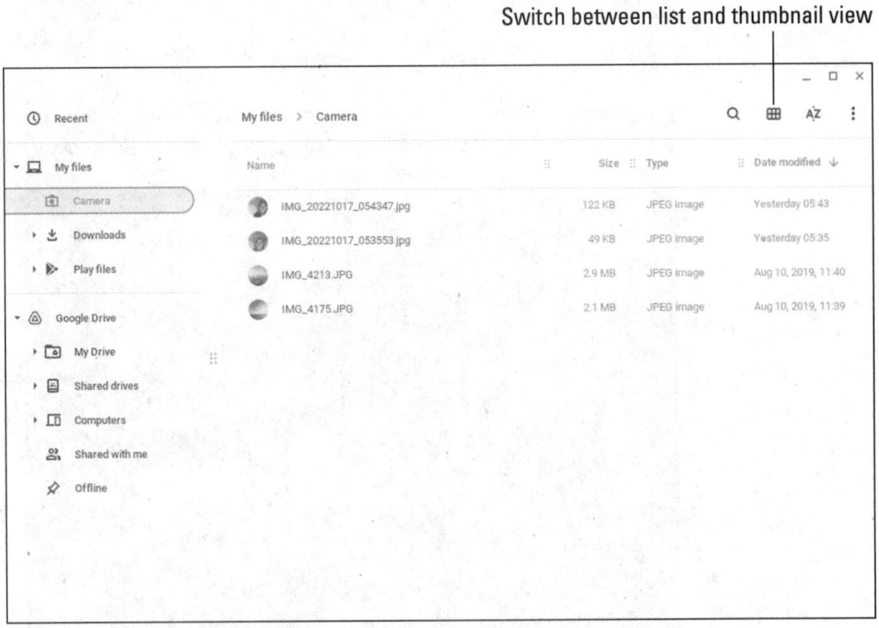

Switch between list and thumbnail view

| | | Size | Type | Date modified ↓ |
|---|---|---|---|---|
| Recent | My files > Camera | | | |
| My files | Name | | | |
| Camera | IMG_20221017_054347.jpg | 122 KB | JPEG image | Yesterday 05:43 |
| Downloads | IMG_20221017_053553.jpg | 49 KB | JPEG image | Yesterday 05:35 |
| Play files | IMG_4213.JPG | 2.9 MB | JPEG image | Aug 10, 2019, 11:40 |
| Google Drive | IMG_4175.JPG | 2.1 MB | JPEG image | Aug 10, 2019, 11:39 |
| My Drive | | | | |
| Shared drives | | | | |
| Computers | | | | |
| Shared with me | | | | |
| Offline | | | | |

**FIGURE 13-8:**
Viewing images on your Chromebook.

*Illustration courtesy of Peter H. Gregory*

# Viewing Photos on a Television

I'm old enough to remember going to friends' homes with my parents, where our hosts would break out the slide projector and show us pictures of their vacation or family reunion. Well, now there's the digital version of showing pictures on the big screen: Google Photos can be used to view photos on a television. Follow these steps:

1. **Launch the Google photos app.**

2. **Navigate to the photos/albums you want to share. Click on a photo or video.**

   The photo or video will be shown.

3. **Click the Cast button near the upper-right corner of the window.**

   If any televisions are available, they will be listed.

4. **Click the desired television.**

   The photo will be shown on the television.

5. **Click the left or right arrows to see the previous or next photos in the album.**

# Deleting Photos

Not every photo you take is beautiful and worth keeping forever. This section discusses how to delete photos from your Chromebook and from Google Photos.

## Deleting photos stored locally on a Chromebook

Photos taken with the Chromebook camera are stored locally. To delete a photo, follow these steps:

1. **Launch the Files app.**

2. **In the Files app, navigate to Camera to view the photos on your Chromebook.**

3. **Click the photo you want to delete.**

4. **Click the Trashcan icon up above on the Files toolbar.**

   The photo is deleted from your Chromebook.

## Deleting photos from Google Photos

Although you may feel that the storage in Google Photos is practically unlimited, you may still want to delete photos you no longer want to keep. To delete photos from your Google Photos library, follow these steps:

1. **Open the Google Photos app.**

2. **Find and click a photo you want to delete.**

3. **Click the trashcan icon near the upper-right corner of the window.**

   A small window appears that reads, "Remove from Google account, synced devices, and shares within Google Photos?"

4. **Click Move to Trash.**

   The photo is deleted from Google Photos and from any devices connected to Google Photos that contain it.

# Editing Photos

Chromebooks provide two different tools you can use to edit your photos:

>> **Google Photos:** This is the online service for storing your photos in the cloud and sharing them with others.

>> **Gallery app:** This is a built-in app on your Chromebook to edit photos stored on your Chromebook's hard drive, external hard drive, or SD card.

How to choose? It's up to you. You can edit a locally stored photo with Gallery, or upload the photo to Google Photos and edit it there. And, you can edit a photo already in Google Photos with the Google Photos editing tool, or download the photo to your Chromebook and edit it with Gallery. But since both Gallery and the Google Photos editing tool are similar, it probably doesn't make much difference.

And if you're a pro, you'll probably use tools like Photoshop, which you can learn more about in *Photoshop Elements 2022 For Dummies*, by Barbara Obermeier.

To edit photos with Google Photos, follow these steps:

1. **Open Google Photos, and navigate to the photo you want to edit.**

2. **Click on the photo to open it.**

3. **Click the Edit button at the bottom center of the photo.**

   The Chromebook Picture Editor allows you to modify your photos, as shown in Figure 13-9. These editing features include the following:

   - **Filters:** Select from any of four themes to make your picture really pop: Enhance, Dynamic, Vivid, and Luminous. Click each to see its effect on your photo. Click again to undo it.

     Note the tiny Google One logos (a circled number 1) in Figure 13-9. These are advanced editing features available to Google One subscribers.

   - **Crop and rotate:** Select from several standard aspect ratios, rotate, and transform. If the horizon is crooked, you can correct it by pulling left and right on the scale beneath the photo.

   - **Blur and sky:** With Blur, change how the photo is focused with Blur and Depth controls. With Sky, choose from several color-altering themes, each with a slider.

   - **Color:** Alter brightness, contrast, HDR, White point, and several other features. Each has a slider, so you can determine how much of the effect you want.

   - **Theme:** Select from several pre-configured themes with names like Vivid, Playa, Honey, Isla, and Desert. Each has its own slider.

   - **Annotate:** Draw lines and add text to your photo.

   While exploring all of these controls, you can quickly revert back to your original by clicking the X near the upper-left corner of the photo.

4. **Click Save copy to save your changes.**

   Your changes will be made to a copy of the photo. The original is still there, untouched.

   Saving a copy is helpful when experimenting with various effects so that you can compare them later.

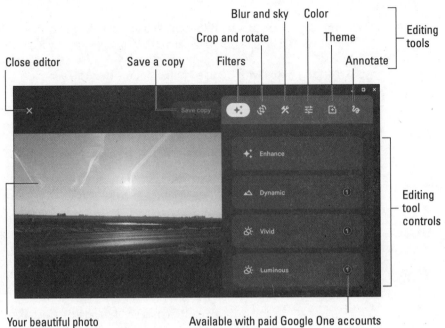

Close editor     Save a copy     Filters     Crop and rotate     Blur and sky     Color     Theme     Annotate     Editing tools

Editing tool controls

Your beautiful photo     Available with paid Google One accounts

**FIGURE 13-9:** The Google Photos photo editor.

*Illustration courtesy of Peter H. Gregory*

TIP

To change a photo from color to black and white, go to the Color control, find the Saturation item, and move the slider all the way to the left.

You can also edit photos with the Chromebook Image Editor. This is one of those "offline" tools that can be used to edit photos stored in your Chromebook (generally, this will be limited by the photos you've just taken with your Chromebook, or those you have downloaded from Google Photos). To do so, use the Files app to find the photo and double-click on it. You'll see the editing controls, as shown in Figure 13-10.

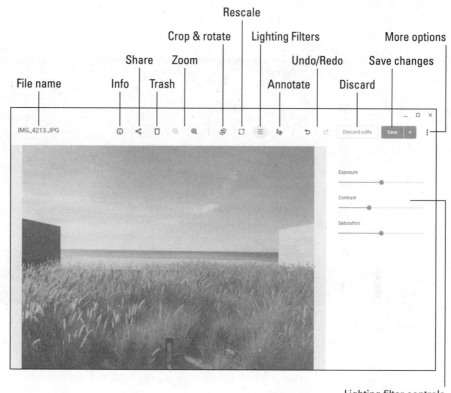

File name    Info    Share    Zoom    Crop & rotate    Rescale    Lighting Filters    Undo/Redo    More options    Trash    Annotate    Discard    Save changes

**FIGURE 13-10:**
The Chromebook's built-in image editor.

Lighting filter controls

*Illustration courtesy of Peter H. Gregory*

# Sharing Photos

Why keep all your brilliant photos to yourself? To have them be truly appreciated, you should share them with others.

Follow these steps to share photos:

1. **Open the Google Photos app on your Chromebook.**

2. **Select the photo(s) you want to share.**

3. **Click the Share button near the top right of the Google Photos window. (See Figure 13-11.)**

   A variety of sharing options appears, including email recipients. You can also create a shared album, print, or save photos online to other services such as OneDrive.

Back to album     Your beautiful photo     Cast   Favorite

Details

Share    Edit    Info    Delete

Share    Edit    Info    Delete

**FIGURE 13-11:**
Sharing photos
with others.

*Illustration courtesy of Peter H. Gregory*

# Chapter **14**

# Playing Video on the Chromebook

Watching videos used to be relegated to televisions and video playback devices like VHS, DVD, and Blu-ray players. However, thanks to the prevalence of high-speed internet access, powerful computers, and wireless broadband, the internet has become a primary delivery mechanism for streaming video content of all kinds.

Streaming video has become one of the major uses of internet bandwidth in the 21st century. Recent statistics show 91.9 percent of internet users watch video content every week, and 93.5 percent of internet users stream TV content each month. More than 2.6 billion unique users visit YouTube each month. People watch more than 1 billion hours of video each day and upload more than 700,000 videos to YouTube every day. You'll never catch up, and you'll never reach the end of the internet!

In this chapter, you find out how to play videos on your Chromebook with the internal video player. You also discover how to navigate Google's YouTube network and how to create, edit, and share videos using YouTube.

# Creating a Video with Your Chromebook

The built-in Camera app on your Chromebook can take still pictures and create videos. To record a video on your Chromebook, follow these steps:

1. **Start the Camera app using the Launcher.**

2. **In the Camera app, click the Video button at the bottom center of the window.**

   Your Chromebook is now ready to start recording a video. See how the Take Photo button has changed; it is now the Start Recording button, and it has a red dot on it.

3. **Click the Start Recording button. Smile!**

   You hear a musical clicking sound when you click the button, and the button changes to all red with a white square in the middle, indicating video is now being recorded.

   As the video is being recorded, you also see a counter on the upper center of the screen showing how many minutes and seconds you've been recording.

4. **When you are ready to stop recording, click the Stop Recording button.**

   See how easy that was? You'll be a YouTuber in no time.

# Watching Videos on a Chromebook

Video files are much larger than pictures and audio files, primarily because of the length of the videos, the quality of the video, and even the quality of the embedded audio. Although the Chromebook allows you to download video from the internet, doing so can fill up the available storage rather quickly (because a Chromebook comes with dramatically less internal storage than traditional PCs and Macs). So rather than download video files on your Chromebook, you can store them (along with other media files) on external storage devices like USB memory sticks or SD cards. You can also keep them online in Google Drive and Google Photos for instant playback on any of your internet-connected devices.

The Chromebook video player plays most video files. To access video files already on your Chromebook, follow these steps:

1. **Open the Files app and navigate to the Camera folder.**

   Or, if your video is on a USB memory stick or SD card, insert the USB stick or SD card into the appropriate plug and find it with the Files app. Figure 14-1 shows an example.

2. **Double-click the video file you want to play.**

   The Video Player app automatically starts and plays your selected video from the beginning, as shown in Figure 14-2.

**FIGURE 14-1:**
The Files app showing an external storage device.

*Illustration courtesy of Peter H. Gregory*

**TIP**

Before you remove an SD card from your Chromebook, click the Eject button and remove the card when its name disappears from the Files window. This ensures the integrity of your data on the SD card. Figure 14-3 shows the Eject button for an SD card.

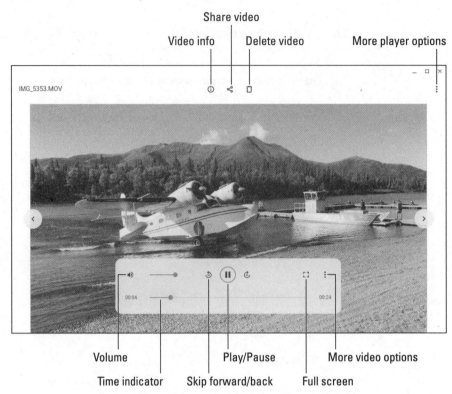

Video info · Share video · Delete video · More player options

IMG_5353.MOV

**FIGURE 14-2:**
Playing a video in the Chromebook built-in video player.

Volume · Time indicator · Play/Pause · Skip forward/back · Full screen · More video options

*Illustration courtesy of Peter H. Gregory*

**FIGURE 14-3:**
Click the Eject button before removing an SD card.

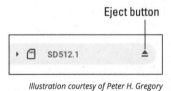

Eject button

SD512.1

*Illustration courtesy of Peter H. Gregory*

# Navigating the Chromebook Video Player

The Chromebook video player is very bare-bones, like an old-school VCR. It offers the usual Chromebook window control bar across the top of the window, which lets you minimize, maximize, and close the video player window — the same as with every app on your Chromebook.

Your video occupies the majority of the window space. Near the bottom of the video window are the controls for the video player, which include

>> Pause and Play buttons

>> Status bar with time indicator

>> Volume control

>> Full screen mode control

By default, the Chromebook video player starts your video as soon as the video loads. If you want to pause your video, click the Pause button near the lower-left corner of the window. While the video is stopped, the Pause button turns into a Play button. To resume playing, click the Play button.

TIP

You can also use the spacebar to pause and resume videos. (This also works in many other video and music players.)

## Skipping around a video

If you want to skip ahead to your favorite part of a video — or maybe resume where you left off — you can do so with the Chromebook video player. To skip around in a video, follow these steps:

**1.** **While your video is open and playing, locate the position indicator in the status bar.**

The position indicator is a little white ball that moves from left to right on a white line across the bottom of the player window as the video plays.

The video control overlay also appears at the bottom of the window, revealing several video control options, including Pause, Full screen, and Volume Control.

If you don't see these controls, give the pointer a nudge with your touchpad, and they should appear. Also make sure the window playing video is on top!

**2.** **Click and drag the position indicator forward or backward to the place in your video where you want to start watching.**

The video skips to the selected location in the timeline.

TIP

You don't have to pause your video to skip around in the video. However, you can pause the video to ensure it doesn't keep playing when you skip to different locations in the video.

## Activating full screen mode

By default, the Chromebook video player plays the video at the optimal viewing size. You can, however, make the video occupy the entire screen by using full screen mode. To engage full screen mode, follow these steps:

1. **While your video is open and playing, move your pointer over the bottom of the video player.**

   The video control overlay appears at the bottom of the window, revealing several video control options, including Pause, Full screen, and Volume Control.

2. **Click the Full screen button on the right side of the overlay.**

   The video player enlarges to fill the screen.

3. **To exit full screen mode, press the Esc key.**

## Adjusting the volume

To control the volume in the Chromebook video player, follow these steps:

1. **Locate the volume control slider on the right side of the overlay.**

   The video control overlay appears at the bottom of the window, revealing several video control options, including Pause, Full screen, and Volume Control.

2. **To mute the volume, click the Speaker icon. To unmute it, click it again.**

   When muted, the icon appears with a slash through it, indicating the volume has been reduced to zero.

3. **Increase or decrease the volume by moving the slider — to the right to increase and to the left to decrease.**

   The volume changes per the direction you move the volume slider.

TIP

You can also adjust the volume using the Chromebook volume down and volume up buttons on the top row of the keyboard.

# Using Other Video Players on a Chromebook

Although the Chromebook's built-in video player is nice, it doesn't always play every video format. You can choose among several other video player apps to try. Or, perhaps you yearn for a video player with more controls. My personal favorite is the VLC video player. I've used it for over a decade on PCs, Macs, and now my Chromebooks. To get the VLC app, go to the Google Play Store, search for VLC for Android, and install it.

To watch videos with VLC, open the app, click the Browse button on the left side, and then navigate to the movie you want to view (see Figure 14-4).

**TIP**

After installing VLC, you need to give it permission to access your photos and media. ChromeOS will ask you.

Video file name

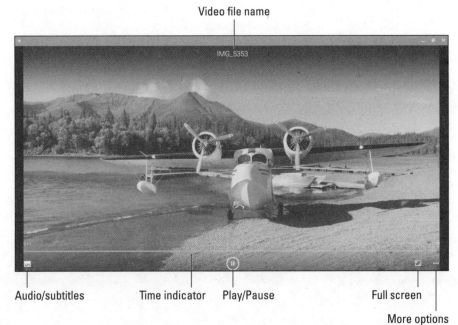

**FIGURE 14-4:**
Playing a video with the VLC video player.

Audio/subtitles          Time indicator     Play/Pause                    Full screen

More options

# Playing Videos from an Android Phone or iPhone on a Chromebook

While it is convenient to shoot pics or video with your smartphone, playing it back on a tiny screen is not so great. If you think you'll regularly — or even occasionally — view photos and videos taken with your Android phone on your Chromebook, you'll want to configure your Android phone to automatically upload photos and videos to your Google account. Follow these steps on your Android phone:

1. **Go to Settings.**

2. **Click Google services and preferences.**

3. **Click Backup.**

4. **Click Photos & videos.**

5. **Make sure Back up & sync is turned on, as shown in Figure 14-5.**

   This will automatically upload photos and videos you take with your Android phone to Google Photos.

**FIGURE 14-5:** Settings to transfer photos and video from an Android phone to Google Photos.

To transfer videos from an iPhone to a Chromebook, follow these steps:

1. **Find and install the Google Photos app from the app store.**

   Be sure the app you select is from Google LLC.

2. **In the Google Photos app, go to Settings.**

3. **Click Back up & sync.**

4. **Make sure Back up & sync is turned on. This will resemble Figure 14-5.**

   All the photos and videos you take on your iPhone will upload to Google Photos and be available to view and play back on any other device with Google Photos, including your Chromebook. Notice you may need to have the Google Photos app open for uploading photos and videos.

To view your photos and videos on your big Chromebook screen, follow these steps:

1. **Open the Google Photos app on your Chromebook.**

   The videos you recorded appear there, as do photos you've taken on your Android phone and any other device with the Google Photos app. It does take a few moments for new photos and videos to appear in Google Photos.

2. **Click the video you want to play.**

   The video begins to play.

   To play in full screen mode, click the Maximize window control at the upper-right corner of the video.

3. **To save the video to your Chromebook, click the Info button at the bottom of the video and click Download.**

   The default filename is the date and time the video was created.

   Other options are available in the Info pane, including turning the Loop video on and off.

TIP

After you upload the video from your smartphone to Google Photos, you can safely remove it from your smartphone if you are low on available space. You can always play it again directly from the Google Photos app.

# Transferring a Video from a Dashcam or Another Device to a Chromebook

If you have a dashcam, digital camera, or security camera with an SD or Micro SD card to store videos, you can play these videos on your Chromebook. Follow this procedure:

1. **Remove the SD card from your device according to the manufacturer's instructions.**

2. **Insert the SD card into your Chromebook.**

   Your Chromebook opens a new Files app window.

3. **Using the Files app, navigate to the directory where videos are stored.**

   The name of the directory will vary based on the make and model of the device recording the video.

4. **When you have found the video you want to view, double-click it.**

   The built-in video player plays the video. If you hear sound but see a black screen, you need to download the VLC app, as discussed in the section "Using Other Video Players on a Chromebook" earlier in this chapter.

TIP

You can upload photos and videos from an SD card to Google Photos to view on any of your Google-connected devices. In the Files app, click on the video or photo file(s), click Share, and click Upload to Photos.

# Getting Started with Google TV

Google TV is Google's video-on-demand service. You can buy or rent movies to play on Android, Chromebook, the Chrome browser, and more. Google TV is the part of Google Play you use to play games, download apps, or view movies and TV shows.

As is the case with all the applications on the Google platform, access to video content in Google TV is linked to your Google account. If you have multiple Google accounts, log in to your Chromebook with the account you want to be associated with Google TV.

You can launch Google TV by opening the Launcher and clicking the Google TV icon. When you do, the Google TV app launches.

## Navigating Google TV

Google TV gives you the ability to purchase movies and television shows for download as well as for streaming. Any purchases you make are tracked in the Movies & TV section of Google Play.

The first time you launch Google TV, you may be given an option to join other subscription movie apps, such as Amazon Prime, Hulu, and HBO Now.

Before purchasing movies or TV shows, you must first know how to navigate through Google TV's vast database. You can search for movies and TV shows using the Search bar at the top of the window or by browsing the Google TV charts. For example, to browse for a movie, click Movies near the top middle of the Google TV window to open the Movies page, as shown in Figure 14-6, and click Shop.

**FIGURE 14-6:** Browsing movies on Google TV.

On the Movies page, you can browse movies by category. Categories may include

>> Genres including Action, Comedy, Family, Sci-Fi, Romance, Drama, and Documentaries

>> Time periods including Recent, the 2000s, the 1990s, the 1980s, and Classic

>> Award Winning

>> Highly Rated

Browsing videos by category is a great way to discover outstanding, thought-provoking cinema and mindless entertainment.

## Purchasing movies and TV shows

Google TV gives you several options to view movies and television shows. You can either purchase and access content for an indefinite amount of time, or rent content that's available for viewing for a specified time. Renting is a cheaper option, but if you like to watch certain movies over and over again, or if you want to build a database of flicks you can dial up whenever you want, purchasing may be the way to go.

To purchase or rent a movie on Google TV, follow these steps:

1. **With Google TV open, find the movie you want to view by scrolling through the selections or searching (upper left of the Google TV window).**

2. **Click the movie you want to watch (see Figure 14-7).**

   The Movie Profile page loads.

   You may be able to view a trailer for free. The movie in Figure 14-7 has this option.

3. **Click the Rent or Buy button at the bottom of the screen.**

   A payment window appears, giving you the option to pay for your movie.

**REMEMBER**

   Newer movies and television shows are typically available for purchase or rent in 4K (highest definition) or high definition (HD). Because 4K has a much better picture quality than HD, Google asks you to pay more for 4K.

**TIP**

   If you don't have a 4K TV or monitor, you're better off buying or renting your movie in HD, if you are offered a choice. If you have a 4K TV or monitor, you can view the movie in much higher quality by selecting 4K.

**TIP**

   If you haven't set up your Google Wallet, you need to do so at this point. Follow the prompts to add the desired payment method to your Google account. After you've set up your account, you can quickly conduct purchases on the Google network.

   The payment pane appears, as shown in Figure 14-8, asking you to select your payment method and review your purchase before confirming.

4. **Click the Rent or Buy button.**

   Google may ask you to enter your Google password to prove it's you and not another person using your Chromebook who wants to watch a free movie!

   There is also a Remember me on this device box. You should only check this box if you are doing this on your Chromebook.

   The movie or show you purchased appears on Google TV and is available to play. If you rented the content, it's available on Google TV for a limited time before it's removed.

**FIGURE 14-7:**
Viewing a movie
selection on
Google TV

**FIGURE 14-8:**
The payment
window.

# Playing movies and TV shows

Purchased or rented movies and TV shows on Google TV appear in your library and are available for playing. To play your movies and TV shows, follow these steps:

1. **With Google TV open, click Your stuff on the left side of the window.**

2. **Click Movies or Shows near the top of the window to find your desired selection.**

   Your movies and TV shows are loaded.

3. **Move your pointer over the desired selection and click the Play icon.**

   Your video content begins playing.

You can pause the video by following these steps:

1. **While the video content is playing, move your cursor anywhere on the window.**

   The video control overlay, containing several video controls, appears.

2. **Click the Pause button in the middle of the screen.**

   The Pause button looks like two vertical bars.

   The video playback pauses.

3. **To resume playing your video, move your pointer back over the video control overlay and click the Play button.**

   The Play button is a sideways triangle pointing to the right.

**TIP**

If you want to view subtitles, click the Show closed captions & audio menu button near the upper-right corner of the screen. Then make your selection in the menu that appears.

To view the movie in full screen, click the Maximize window control at the upper-right corner of the window. After a few moments, the movie goes into full-screen mode.

**REMEMBER**

If you anticipate wanting to watch the movie while you are offline (for example, on a camping trip), you need to download the movie contents onto your Chromebook. To do so, click the Download icon in the lower-right corner of the movie image.

## Casting to a smart TV

*Casting* means playing back audio or video content from one device on another device, such as a smart TV. If you have a TV set up for casting, you can cast a movie you're playing on a Chromebook onto a TV. To cast a movie to a TV, follow these steps:

1. **Start playing the movie on your Chromebook.**

2. **Pause playback by clicking Pause or tapping the spacebar.**

3. **Find and click the Cast icon, which is near the upper-right corner of the window.**

If devices are available to cast, you see a menu from which you can select a device. (See Figure 14-9.)

4. **Select the device you want to cast to.**

   Movie playback now continues on your smart TV. You use the Play and Pause controls on your Chromebook to pause and resume the movie.

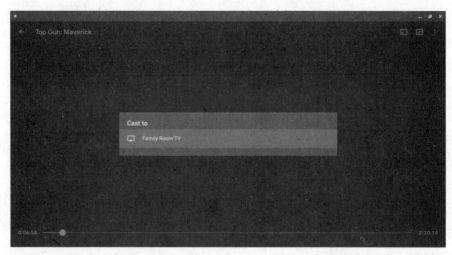

*Illustration courtesy of Peter H. Gregory*

You need to read the instructions for your smart TV to understand how to cast to it. You'll find it takes a bit of experimenting to get it working.

TIP

# Exploring YouTube

YouTube has become a free go-to source for all kinds of video: unfiltered field reporting, documentation of conflict, music videos, self-help and how-to, thought-provoking documentaries, family archives, humorous interpretations, chance happenings, TV commercials from long ago, and more. Users can create channels to store and categorize endless minutes of video. With YouTube, you can upload and edit videos, share video content around the web, keep track of video views, and so much more.

YouTube is a great tool for Chromebook users because it can serve as a bottomless repository for captured video footage. To access YouTube, open the Launcher and click the YouTube icon. When you do so, YouTube loads in the Chrome browser.

CHAPTER 14 **Playing Video on the Chromebook** 291

YouTube asks you to log in to your Google account so you can view your subscriptions and allow YouTube to suggest videos that are consistent with your interests. Also, YouTube keeps track of all videos you have viewed.

## Navigating YouTube

When YouTube has loaded, all of its available options can cause sensory overload. Covering all the intricacies of YouTube would take an entire book, but this section gives you a few tips to get you started. Chances are, you're already familiar with YouTube anyway.

The main page of YouTube contains several video options, and much of what YouTube suggests is driven by your viewing habits and subscriptions. YouTube also sells advertising placements to businesses, so you may see an advertisement or two at the beginning of a video and occasionally during a longer video. Along the left side of the screen are options for finding videos you've seen and videos you haven't seen yet.

The most helpful way to find new videos is by using the Search bar at the top of the screen. YouTube has more than 2 billion unique visitors every month, and those visitors typically search for video content just as they would search for a web page using Google's search engine. This search functionality has made YouTube one of the largest search engines in the world (the second largest, after Google Search).

Enter a term in the Search bar, click the Search button (which looks like a magnifying glass), and then scroll through the search results to find the video you're searching for. To aid in your search, YouTube ranks the results according to your query. If you haven't found the video you're looking for by the third or fourth page of search results, you may want to refine your search.

## Playing and pausing video

Playing a video on YouTube is as straightforward as searching for it. Find the video you want to play in YouTube's search results and click the image or title. YouTube loads the Video Profile page and begins playing your selection automatically.

The bottom bar of the video, pictured in Figure 14-10, contains all your play controls, status bar audio controls, and viewing settings.

To pause the video, click the Pause button on the left side of the control bar. When a video is paused, pressing Pause (or the Play button) resumes playback. You can also pause and play by tapping the spacebar.

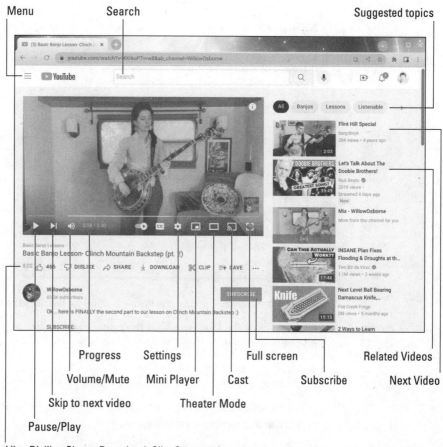

Menu    Search    Suggested topics

Progress    Settings    Full screen    Related Videos

Volume/Mute    Mini Player    Cast    Subscribe    Next Video

Skip to next video    Theater Mode

**FIGURE 14-10:**    Pause/Play
YouTube's many
controls.    Like, Dislike, Share, Download, Clip, Save, and more

*Illustration courtesy of Peter H. Gregory*

## Activating full screen mode

By default, YouTube plays the video at the optimal viewing size. You can, however, make the video occupy the entire screen by using full screen mode. To engage full screen mode, click the Full screen button on the right side of the video's control bar. To exit full screen mode, press the Esc key.

## Adjusting the volume

To control the volume in the YouTube player, follow these steps:

1. **Locate the Volume icon on the left side of the control bar.**

2. **To mute the volume, click the Speaker icon.**

When muted, the icon appears with a slash through it, indicating the volume has been reduced to zero.

3. **Increase or decrease the volume by moving your pointer over the volume icon and clicking and dragging the volume slider.**

   Move the slider left to decrease volume, and right to increase it.

TIP

You can also adjust the volume using the Chromebook volume down and volume up buttons on the top row of the keyboard.

## Casting YouTube to a smart TV

As with Google TV and Google Photos, you can cast the playing of a YouTube video to a smart TV. Follow these instructions:

1. **Start playing the video.**

2. **Pause playback by clicking the Pause button or tapping the spacebar.**

3. **Find and click the Cast icon near the upper-right corner of the video playback window.**

   You need to read the instructions for your smart TV to understand how to cast to it. You may have to experiment with it a bit to get it working.

TIP

4. **If you have devices you can cast to, you see a menu from which you can select the device you want to cast to.**

   Video playback continues on your smart TV. You use the Play and Pause buttons on your Chromebook to pause and resume the video. Volume control may be available through the TV remote and your Chromebook's volume up/down keys.

# Gaming on Chromebooks

Arguably, Chromebooks are not designed to be gaming laptops in the usual sense. Gaming laptops are high-powered machines running Windows, packed with high-performance processors, video cards, and lots of memory. This high-end package runs realistic real-time video games with vivid action and sound. Gaming computers are rather pricey, with some over ten thousand dollars!

The philosophy of Chromebooks, inexpensive laptops with less processor power, memory, and storage than even low-end PCs, is diametrically opposite of gaming machines. Simply put, if you are a hard-core gamer, you're not gaming on a Chromebook, but on a separate machine.

Stick with me here for another minute. What I've said here does not mean there is no gaming on Chromebooks. Far from it! There are numerous games and types of games that run just fine on a Chromebook, which I discuss in this section.

**TIP**

I'm now seeing "gaming Chromebooks" for sale on the market. These are a new class of more costly, high-end Chromebook designed for gaming. Many games are not yet optimized for Chromebook, so if you're a serious gamer, you'll want to go online for the latest news.

## Browser games

The term "browser games" refers to a class of games running inside a browser. Because a Chromebook is basically the Chrome browser in a laptop, browser games are a great choice. Some popular browser games include the following:

>> **Classic Minecraft:** Minecraft, the most successful PC game ever with over 100 million players, is available in browser form at `classic.minecraft.net`.

>> **Agar.io:** You are a bacterium, starting out small, eating agar that is floating around. As you grow, you can eat bigger things. But look out — larger bacteria are also out to eat you! I tried it out recently, as shown in Figure 14-11. Slither.io is another "eat to grow larger before you are eaten" game that is a lot of fun.

>> **Google Feud:** This is a guessing game where you try to figure out how Google will autocomplete searches in various categories. How good of a Google searcher are you?

>> **Antgame.io:** This is a daily puzzle game built around an ant colony simulator. For me, it's just fascinating to watch.

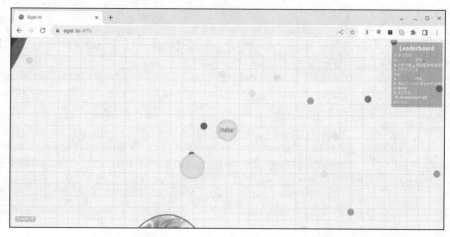

**FIGURE 14-11:** Agar.io is one of many browser-based games you can play on a Chromebook.

*Illustration courtesy of Peter H. Gregory*

# Android games

Lots of software written for Android phones runs on Chromebooks. You can access these games through the Google Play Store. Just open the Play Store and click on Games, where you'll find a vast world of games in numerous categories, including adventure games, puzzle games, role-playing games, word games, and educational games for younger children.

When you find a game you want to try, click on it, click Install, and then click Play. The game will be in your Launcher; if you think you'll play it often, you can pin the game to your Launcher so you can quickly click on it without having to find it again. Figure 14-12 shows the WGT Golf game running on my Chromebook. Other fun Android games on a Chromebook include Free Rider, Wordscapes, and Angry Birds 2. PBS Kids is great for younger children.

TIP

While Chromebooks are considered online devices where your data is stored online, Android games consume storage on your Chromebook. I discuss storage in Chapter 20.

FIGURE 14-12:
Android games such as WGT Golf run great on Chromebooks.

*Illustration courtesy of Peter H. Gregory*

TIP

Many Android games are "full screen," meaning you see only the game and nothing else. Click Alt+Tab to exit the game or do something else on your Chromebook. This should cause your Launcher to reappear so you can do other things.

**IN THIS CHAPTER**

» **Chatting and messaging with Google Chat**

» **Discovering Google Meet for video conferencing**

» **Figuring out Google Voice basics**

» **Using Zoom to stay in touch with friends and family**

» **Keeping track of everyone with Google Contacts**

Chapter **15**

# Chatting with Friends and Family

A stand-up comic mused about the paradigm shift from landline phones to mobile phones, remarking on how calling a phone number used to mean calling a *place* without knowing who was there, but today it means calling a *person*, no matter where that person is. Fast forward to today. People can communicate with text, audio, and even video, no matter where they are, with a pocket-size device. What a time to be alive.

Google is in transition with its video and text chat apps. Google Hangouts, Google's former video chat service, has been replaced by two new products, Chat and Meet. Chat is Google's instant messaging service, while Meet is Google's fully featured audio and video conferencing service. Google also offers Google Voice, with text, phone calling, and voicemail capabilities. This chapter spends time with each of these services.

Google Meet, Chat, and Voice are not the only games in town. Zoom videoconferencing, virtually unknown to consumers until the COVID-19 pandemic, is quite popular for group video calls.

All these services run on Chromebooks as well as on Windows computers, Macs, Android tablets and phones, iPhones, and iPads. You can stay in touch with people no matter where they are.

One more thing: If you want to chat with your friends and family through Chat, Meet, and Voice (as well as emails with Gmail), you need to add them to your contacts. You find out how at the end of this chapter.

# Instant Messaging with Google Chat

 Google Chat is one of Google's solutions for instant messaging. With Google Chat, you can send messages with text and pictures to anyone in your contact list, whether they have a Google Gmail account or not.

To get started with Google Chat, click on the Launcher and find the Chat app. Google Chat opens, resembling what is shown in Figure 15-1.

TIP

If you've had your Chromebook for a while, Google Chat may not be installed. Go to the Play Store, search for Google Chat, and install it. You may also have the old Google Hangouts app; if so, uninstall it by pressing Alt and clicking on the Hangouts icon, and then clicking Uninstall.

To start chatting with someone, click on their name on the left side of the Chat window. Or, start typing the name of someone you know in the Find box at the top middle of the window.

Once you find who you're looking for, you'll see the blinking cursor at the bottom, where you start typing a message to someone. Say something like, "hello are you there?" and press Enter. If the person is on their computer or smartphone and sees your message, they might reply. You'll see the messages scrolling up in the main window as you chat back and forth. You can also scroll back to view earlier messages that have rolled off the page.

There is much more you can do with Chat. Read on.

## Using spaces in Chat

In Google Chat, a Space is like a group or an imaginary meeting room. It has a name and at least two participants. You can liken it to a group conversation among a few (or a lot of) people.

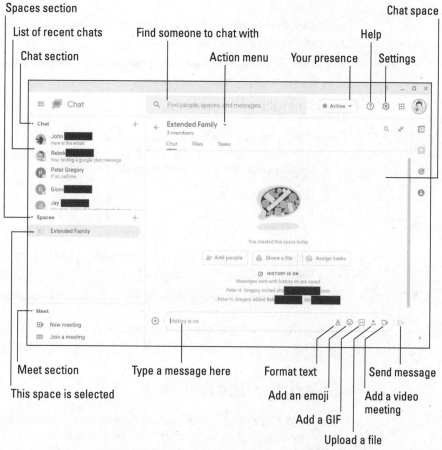

Spaces section

List of recent chats

Chat section

Find someone to chat with

Action menu

Your presence

Chat space

Help

Settings

Meet section

This space is selected

Type a message here

Format text

Add an emoji

Add a GIF

Upload a file

Send message

Add a video meeting

**FIGURE 15-1:**
The Google Chat main page.

You can look for spaces by clicking on Find a space to browse spaces you are a member of, or create one of your own. When you Browse spaces, you'll find you can only see a space if you have already been added.

You can create two main things in Spaces: a group chat or a new Space. To start a group chat, follow these steps:

1. **Click the + in Spaces.**

2. **Click on Start group conversation.**

   You're prompted to click on names that appear, who are your contacts.

3. **Click on the names of the people you want to chat with.**

4. **Click the blue checkmark to signify you are done adding people (you can add people later if you like).**

   The new group chat now occupies the main Chat window. You'll see the Add people button in the window where you can add more people.

5. **Start texting participants.**

To create a new space in Spaces, follow these steps:

1. **Click the + in the Spaces portion of the Chat window.**

2. **Click Create Space.**

   A new pane opens, where you type in the name of the Space and a short description. Chat then shows you a list of your frequent and recent contacts.

3. **Click on the names of the people you want to invite and add them to the Space.**

4. **Start sending messages in the Space to the people you added to it.**

The convenient thing about Spaces is you can jump in and out of different conversations to see what people are saying and add your messages to each of them.

## Sharing files in Chat

One cool feature of Chat is the ability to send files to others, whether individuals, group chats, or spaces. On the right side of the Space where you type in messages, you'll see an Upload file icon (indicated in Figure 15-1). When you click it, you can browse the files on your Chromebook and in Google Drive. These files can be photos, video clips, documents, spreadsheets, or anything else. If it's a file, you can send it to others.

## Incoming message requests

In Google Chat, you can receive message requests from friends or strangers. When this occurs, you see Message Requests with a number near the upper-left portion of the Chat window. Click on it, and Chat will open a pane showing incoming requests. See Figure 15-2.

If you don't recognize a person's name or email address, the message request may be spam. Click on the name, and then click Ignore in the blue Chat request window. You can also opt to block the person so they cannot chat with you again.

**WARNING**

The amount of spam in Chat can be considerable and is often associated with pornography and other scams. Please do your part by reporting the sender to Google if you receive offensive content.

**FIGURE 15-2:**
Viewing incoming message requests.

# Video conferencing in Chat

In the Chat window, the Meet button is in the lower-left corner. Click it, and you'll see two options: New meeting and Join a meeting.

>> If you click Join a meeting, you're prompted to type in a meeting code.

>> If you click New meeting, you're prompted to invite others or immediately start a meeting.

Both options launch Google Meet, the free video conferencing service by Google, which I discuss in the next section.

# Gathering with Google Meet

Google Meet is the future of video calls in the Google world, but it's so much more. With Meet, you can set up group video or audio-only calls. You can organize free video calls for up to 100 people and meet for as long as one hour.

Google Meet is already installed on your Chromebook. Open the Launcher and click on the Google Meet icon. Google Meet will start, and you'll see the app, as shown in Figure 15-3.

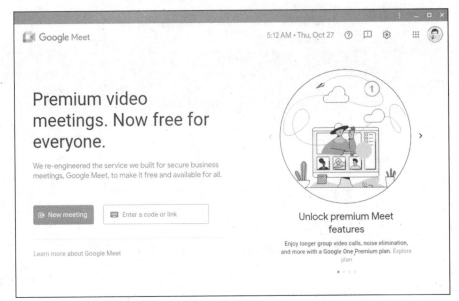

**FIGURE 15-3:**
The Google Meet landing page.

*Illustration courtesy of Peter H. Gregory*

With Google Meet, you're going to want to do one of three things:

>> Meet right now with one or more people

>> Join a meeting someone else has organized

>> Schedule a meeting to take place in the future

I explain each below.

TIP

The first time you join a meeting with Google Meet, you'll be asked to give Google Meet permission to use your Chromebook's camera and microphone. Click Allow to permit this.

## Setting up a meeting right now

To set up a meeting right now in Google Meet, follow these easy steps:

1. **Open Google Meet.**

2. **Click New meeting.**

   A small menu appears.

3. **Click Start an instant meeting.**

   Your meeting will be set up. Your camera will start, and you'll see your smiling face looking back at you. See Figure 15-4 to orient yourself with the controls.

4. **Add others to the meeting.**

   You have two options. You can click Add others, on the middle left side, and type their email address(es) in the open pane. Or, you can copy the meeting link and send it to them via email, chat, or some other way. Once they join, you'll see them in your Google Meet window, and you can start talking.

**TIP**

Skip down to the section "Meeting in Google Meet," where I discuss how some of the meeting controls work.

## Joining a meeting by invitation

If you have been invited to a Google Meet meeting, follow these steps:

1. **From Google Calendar, find and click on the meeting. Click Join Meeting. The meeting will open in Google Meet.**

2. **Directly from Google Meet, open the Google Meet app and type the meeting code in the Enter a code or link field.**

   Google Meet will open, and you'll be connected to the meeting.

## Scheduling a meeting for later

To set up a meeting to take place at a later time, follow these steps:

1. **Open Google Meet.**

2. **Click New meeting.**

   A small menu appears.

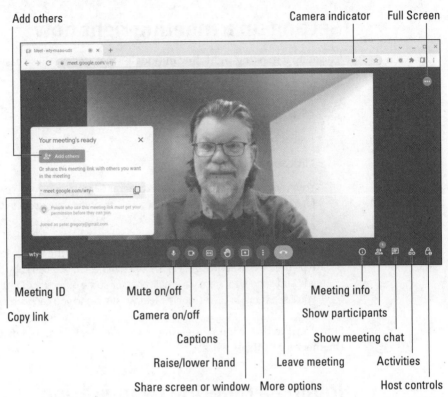

Add others        Camera indicator    Full Screen

Meeting ID       Mute on/off        Meeting info

Copy link       Camera on/off        Show participants

Captions       Show meeting chat

Raise/lower hand       Activities

Share screen or window    More options      Host controls

**FIGURE 15-4:**
A meeting in
Google Meet. It's
time to invite
others!

*Illustration courtesy of Peter H. Gregory*

3. **Click Schedule in Google Calendar.**

   Google Calendar opens in a new tab in the Chrome browser and shows the
   New meeting window, as shown in Figure 15-4.

4. **Type the name for your meeting where it says Add title.**

5. **Click on the date and time fields to specify the start and end dates and
   times for your meeting.**

6. **Invite your guests. Type the email addresses of your guests.**

7. **Set the reminders if you want them different from what is shown.**

8. **Scroll down and type any meeting description in the Add description
   text box.**

9. **Click Save.**

At the time of the meeting, you and any guests you've invited will need to click on Join with Google Meet to join the meeting. Google Meet will open, and you'll see each guest as they join.

TIP

When you join the meeting, your Chromebook may ask you if you want to join by using the Google Meet app or your Chrome browser. You can join in the browser, but you'll find the experience somewhat richer if you join with the Google Meet app.

## Meeting in Google Meet

When you're in a Google Meet meeting, you'll find a rich assortment of controls to enhance your experience. Figure 15-5 shows a Google Meet window with a group meeting in progress. Here are some of the useful controls you can use:

>> **Mute/Unmute:** Temporarily turn off your microphone, so others on the call don't hear whatever you don't want them to hear: coughing, dogs barking, whatever.

>> **Camera on/off:** Same concept as mute/unmute but for your camera. What's that between your teeth?!

>> **Chat:** You can send text messages through the meeting chat feature. For instance, you can send a web page URL to participants so they can later open the web page you are showing or describing.

>> **Participants:** You can see the list of participants in the meeting. You can invite participants to the meeting by clicking on Add. As a meeting organizer, you can mute and even remove participants from a meeting.

>> **Hang up:** Click the big red button to leave the meeting. The meeting organizer can leave the meeting and leave everyone else in the meeting, or the organizer can end the meeting for all.

>> **Share:** You can share an app window or your Chromebook's entire screen, so others in the meeting can see your window or screen. You can share pictures with family and friends, a website, or anything else on your Chromebook.

TIP

If you have a Google One premium account, you are also permitted to record a meeting with up to 25 participants for up to one hour in length.

Screen sharing is handy for helping another person with Chromebook settings. You can have them share their screen and walk them through any steps, so their Chromebook works the way they want it to.

## Sharing your screen

Follow these steps to share your screen on a Google Meet call:

1. **During a Google Meet meeting, click the Share button at the bottom middle of the window.**

   The Share menu opens in a small pane.

2. **Click Your entire screen, A window, or A tab, corresponding to what you want to share.**

   If you click A window or A tab, another pane will open that shows windows or tabs, directing you to select which one you want to share. Click on your choice and then click Share.

   Your video will be moved to the lower-right corner of the Meet window, and most of your window will show the Chromebook window you are sharing. This is what participants will also see.

3. **To stop sharing, click the Share button again, then click Stop presenting.**

   The Meet window will revert to the video view of you and other participants. It's simple!

## Meeting host controls

As a meeting host, there are other things you can do to control the call, including:

>> Whether others can share their screen, or only you

>> Whether others can send chat messages in the meeting

>> Whether others can turn on their video or microphone (this can be handy for a webinar where only you, the speaker, use a mic and camera, with everyone else just watching and listening)

To enable these features, click Host controls; then, in the Host controls pane, click Host management; and then select the desired features.

**TIP**

A couple of years ago, this was called Hangouts, then Duo, and now it's called Meet. I don't know when or why Google might rename this or any service (and it's not just Google, but Microsoft and others as well). The basic concepts about Meet will endure, even if they rename it and rearrange things. These types of changes are all a part of the information revolution!

This participant is muted

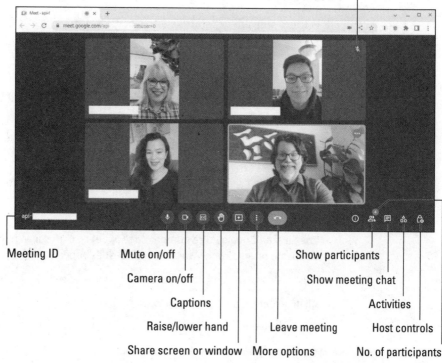

Meeting ID

Mute on/off

Camera on/off

Captions

Raise/lower hand

Share screen or window

More options

Leave meeting

Show participants

Show meeting chat

Activities

Host controls

No. of participants

Illustration courtesy of Peter H. Gregory

FIGURE 15-5:
A Google Meet
meeting in
progress.

# Calling and Texting with Google Voice

Google provides a lot of choices when it comes to communicating with others. One of those options is a nifty service called Google Voice, which lets you make phone calls and send and receive text messages using a new "virtual" phone number.

With Google Voice, you are assigned a new free phone number from Google. You configure your Google Voice service to ring on your mobile phone, landline, or Chromebook. You can set up voicemail, call forwarding, and text with this new number. Plus, you can make local and long-distance phone calls within the United States and internationally.

TIP

You must have a mobile or landline number to use Google Voice. Using Google Voice doesn't change your existing mobile and landline phone services — those numbers continue to work as before. With Google Voice, you get an *additional* number that can ring on any or all of your existing phones and other devices, such as your Chromebook. You're able to make and answer actual phone calls with your Chromebook!

# Setting up Google Voice

Follow these steps to get started with Google Voice:

1. **Go to** `voice.google.com` **with your browser.**

   The main Google Voice website launches. You can scroll down to read all about Google Voice to see if this is something you're interested in trying out.

2. **Click the For Personal Use button to proceed.**

   A small menu appears.

3. **Select Web.**

   The Welcome page appears.

4. **Click Continue.**

   The Select a Google Voice number page appears. In the search field, type in a city name or area code. Available nearby cities appear.

   A list of available numbers appears. Click More to see more numbers.

5. **Click Select on a number you want to use.**

   The verification process begins.

6. **Click Verify and follow the instructions.**

   You need to provide an actual phone number (landline or mobile). Google then sends a code (via text or a phone call), which you type in the Verify field to complete the process.

After you set up your Google Voice account, it's available on all your devices, including Windows laptops, Macs, Android phones and tablets, iPhones, iPads, and, oh yeah, Chromebooks! You can send and receive phone calls, voice mail, and text, all via the web or Google Voice apps.

On your Chromebook, after your Google Voice account is set up (and after you've been using it for a while), your main window will resemble Figure 15-6.

TIP

You can use Google Voice with your browser or download the Google Voice app from the Google Play store. You'll need to give the Google Voice app permission to access your contacts the first time you use it.

# Sending text messages with Google Voice

Texting with Google Voice is the same as texting on a mobile phone. With your Google Voice number, anyone with a mobile phone can send a text to your Google

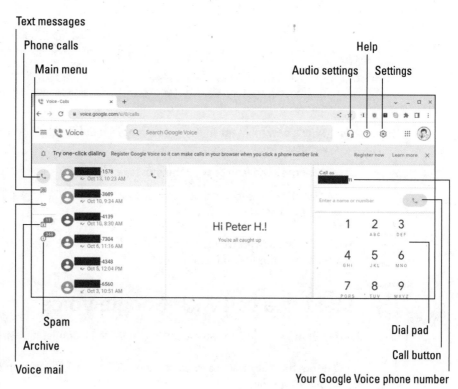

Text messages

Phone calls

Main menu

Help

Audio settings   Settings

**FIGURE 15-6:**
The Google Voice
main screen. The
author's contacts
are redacted for
their privacy.

Spam

Archive

Voice mail

Dial pad

Call button

Your Google Voice phone number

*Illustration courtesy of Peter H. Gregory*

Voice number, and it shows up in Google Voice. Furthermore, unless you tell your contacts you are texting with your Google Voice number, they'll have no way of knowing that you are using Google Voice. To them, your Google Voice number is your mobile number. How cool is that!

Sending text messages with Google Voice is easy; just follow these steps:

1.  **From the Google Voice main window, click the Messages button on the left side of the window.**

    Your history of recent messaging appears on the left side of the window.

2.  **Click Send New Message.**

    The cursor moves to the To field, where you can begin typing in a person's name. A list of suggestions from your contact list will appear, so you can scroll through and select one if you prefer.

3.  **Select a recipient from the list or enter a new phone number.**

The contact list continues to appear, in case you want to send a group text to two or more people. When you are done selecting recipients, click in the Type a message field below.

The message history appears if you've exchanged messages with this person(s) before.

4. **Type a new message in the Type a message field at the bottom of the window.**

5. **Click the Send icon to send the message.**

The Send icon is to the right. Messages you send, and messages sent to you, appear in the main window.

REMEMBER

You can send and receive messages in Google Voice with other Google Voice users, as well as any mobile phone numbers.

## Making a call with Google Voice

Although making phone calls with Google Voice is simple, here are the steps:

1. **From the Google Voice main window, click the Call button on the left side of the window.**

A list of recent calls appears on the left side of the window. A dial pad appears on the far right.

2. **Select a recipient from your contacts by typing a name or number in the Enter a Name or Number field. Or tap the numbers on the keypad to call a number.**

The recipient's phone rings. If the recipient accepts the call, you can begin talking.

Be sure your audio settings are correct so you and the recipient can hear each other.

3. **Tap the hangup icon to end the call.**

WARNING

Google Voice cannot be used for "911" or "999" (police, fire, ambulance) calls in many locations.

## Other Google Voice features

All the features of Google Voice could easily fill an entire chapter, but in this section, I give you a few pointers to other features:

- » **Voice mail:** People can call you and leave a voice mail if you don't pick up. Google Voice can send you an email (or text) transcript of the voice mail message.

- » **Call screening and pick-up:** When someone calls your Google Voice number, you can have the incoming call ring on one or more of your phones simultaneously. You can pick up the call, and Google Voice will tell you who is calling. You can accept the call or send it to voice mail. If you send it to voice mail, you can listen to the caller's message while the caller is still talking, or you can pick up the call and talk live if you want.

- » **Calls on any device:** You can send and receive calls with your Google Voice number on any device on which you have the Google Voice app installed. This includes mobile phones, tablets, laptop computers, and desktop computers.

- » **Call schedules:** People can call your Google Voice number 24 hours a day, but you can set a schedule, so your mobile and landline phones don't ring during certain hours.

- » **Send a photo:** On the texting portion of Google Voice, you can send a photo, just like you would if you were texting on your Android phone or iPhone. In the Send a message field, click the Add image and select one or more photos from your Chromebook, Google Drive, or Google Photos.

- » **One-click dialing:** On your Chromebook, when you visit a website or other app with a phone number link, you can click the link to call the number with Google Voice.

You can explore many other features and settings by clicking the Settings button near the upper-right corner of the Google Voice window.

While you can install and use the Google Voice app on your Chromebook, the web version is better on a Chromebook. You will, however, want to install it on your mobile devices, so you can keep in touch with people on all of your devices.

# Videoconferencing with Zoom

Zoom videoconferencing has been around for nearly a decade, but quickly became a household term when many businesses and schools used it as a virtual meeting platform during the COVID-19 pandemic. Zoom is a free service and is great for family and friends to get together on video.

## Zooming over to Zoom

To use Zoom, head over to the Google Play Store, where you can search for and install the Zoom for Chrome app. The first time you run the Zoom app, you can join a meeting or log in. If you want to host your own meetings, click Sign In and scroll down to click on Sign in with Google. After you type in your email address, you should be able to log in with your Google user ID and password. Once you do, you'll see the main Zoom page, as shown in Figure 15-7.

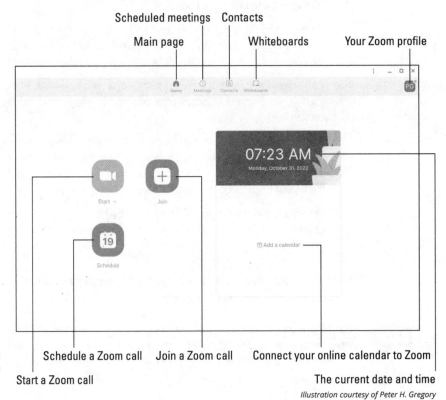

Illustration courtesy of Peter H. Gregory

**FIGURE 15-7:** The Zoom main page.

- Scheduled meetings
- Contacts
- Main page
- Whiteboards
- Your Zoom profile
- Schedule a Zoom call
- Join a Zoom call
- Connect your online calendar to Zoom
- Start a Zoom call
- The current date and time

**TIP**

If you can't log in to Zoom with your Google user ID and password, you may need to create a separate account.

## Joining a Zoom call

If you've been invited to join a Zoom call, follow these easy steps:

1. **Open the Zoom app.**
2. **Click the Join button.**

3. **Type in the meeting ID and the password if the meeting is password protected.**

    You're now on the Zoom call!

4. **Unmute your mic and turn on your camera.**

5. **Enjoy your meeting!**

6. **To leave the meeting, click the End button at the lower-right corner of the Zoom window. Then click Leave Meeting.**

    Zoom will return to the main page.

## Starting your own Zoom call

To start a Zoom video call, you have two choices: start a call now, or schedule a call to take place later. To start a call right now, follow these simple steps:

1. **Open the Zoom app and log in.**

2. **Click Start.**

3. **Click Join audio by computer.**

    The first time you use Zoom, you'll need to give Zoom permission to use the microphone.

4. **Click the audio button to unmute and the video button to start your camera.**

    You'll also need to give Zoom permission to use your camera. You only need to do this once.

    Your video call is up and running, and you should see yourself on the screen.

5. **To invite others to your call, click on Participants, then click the Invite link.**

6. **In the Invite window, you have several choices. You can type in the names of contacts, or you can click the Email button in the Invite window and then click Gmail.**

    Zoom will write an email from you; all you have to do is add the participants and click Send. Everything they need to know will be included in the email.

    People you invite to Zoom calls don't need to have a Zoom account or the Zoom app. They can join right from their browser.

**TIP**

There are many more things you can do in Zoom — Figure 15-8 has some hints. Explore the Zoom adventure!

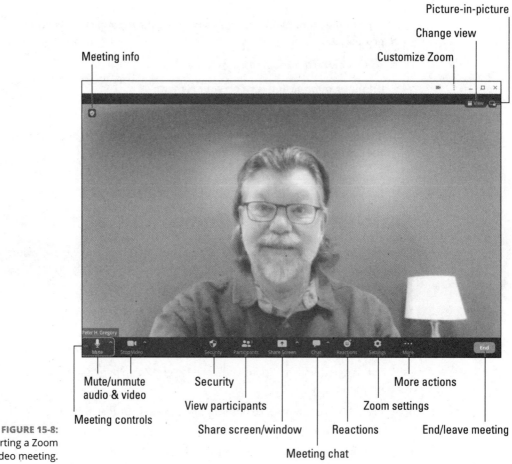

Picture-in-picture

Change view

Customize Zoom

Meeting info

Mute/unmute
audio & video

Security

View participants

Share screen/window

Meeting chat

Reactions

Zoom settings

More actions

End/leave meeting

Meeting controls

**FIGURE 15-8:**
Starting a Zoom
video meeting.

*Illustration courtesy of Peter H. Gregory*

# Other Text and Video Applications

Many other texting and video applications are used in the world besides those described in this chapter. Here, I briefly describe a few of interest.

>> **Microsoft Teams:** Popular in the corporate world, Teams is similar to Google Voice and Google Meet combined, with videoconferencing, texting, file sharing, and screen sharing. Yes, Virginia, there is a Teams app you can install on your Chromebook if you want to participate in your corporate meetings (check with your company's policy about using personally owned devices first).

>> **Slack:** A nifty collaboration tool, Slack is free to use (with some limitations) and is the home of popular Slack "channels," or private chat rooms. You can also do

audio calls with Slack. Go to www.slack.com to sign up. At the time of this writing, there is no Slack app for Chromebooks, but you can use your browser.

» **Webex:** The original videoconferencing app, Webex is still used in the corporate world. If you attend a webinar, it may be on Webex. With Webex, you can install the Webex app or join a meeting with your browser.

» **GoToMeeting:** Another one of the original corporate videoconferencing services. Like Webex, you can join meetings and webinars with the app or through your browser.

» **Signal:** This highly secure texting app utilizes "end-to-end encryption" that makes eavesdropping virtually impossible. As of the writing of this book, Signal is not yet available on Chromebooks, but you can use it on your Android or iPhone, as well as PCs and Macs.

I'm merely scratching the surface here. People use numerous other apps and services to communicate through text, voice, and video. You can find them in the Google Play store when you search for "video conferencing."

# Working with Google Contacts

Google Contacts is just that: a list of the people you communicate with via phone, email, video, text, and even good old-fashioned snail mail. When you use Google services, Google Contacts is your online address book, accessible from all your devices and any other device (such as a hotel kiosk computer).

Point your browser to contacts.google.com. You see the Contacts main window, as shown in Figure 15-9.

TIP

There *is* a Google Contacts app that may or may not be on your Chromebook. It displays in a skinny vertical format as though it is running on a smartphone. Use it if you like — it works with your contacts, just like the instructions in this section. Personally, I prefer the web version.

## Adding contacts

You can easily add a contact to Google Contacts by clicking the Create contact button near the upper-left corner of the Google Contacts window. Next, select Create a contact. The Create contact window appears, as shown in Figure 15-10, where you can fill in the contact's name, phone number, email address, and other details. If you have a photo of the contact (or an image that reminds you of the contact), you can upload that, too. When you are done, click Save.

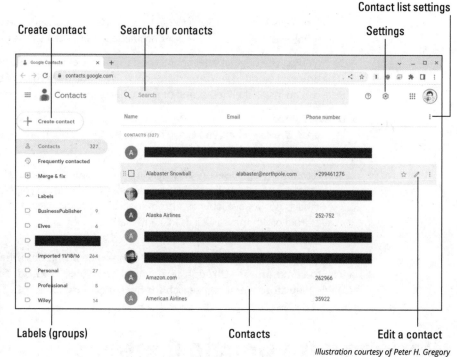

Create contact      Search for contacts      Contact list settings

Settings

Labels (groups)      Contacts      Edit a contact

**FIGURE 15-9:**
The Google
Contacts main
window. The
author's contacts
are redacted for
privacy.

*Illustration courtesy of Peter H. Gregory*

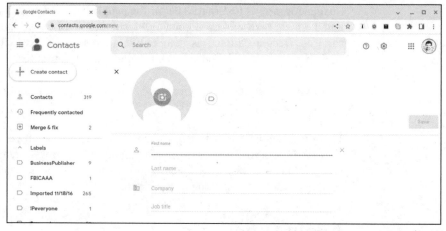

**FIGURE 15-10:**
Adding a new
contact with
Google Contacts.

*Illustration courtesy of Peter H. Gregory*

# Viewing and editing contacts

You can browse Google Contacts to see whether you already have a particular contact there by typing the contact's name, phone number, or email address in the Search field. As you type, Google Contacts displays contacts just below the search bar. If any of the visible contacts is the one you are looking for, you can click it to view it.

To edit a contact, click the pencil icon to the right of the contact's phone number, as shown in Figure 15-9. If you click on the contact to view their information, find and click the Edit button over to the right. You'll then see the contact's details. You can update any existing fields or add new information, as shown in Figure 15-11. When you're done making changes, click Save. If you messed up, click the X near the upper left.

If you have contacts you frequently correspond with or need to refer to from time to time, you can add them as favorites, which causes them to go to the top of your contacts list. Just click the star next to the contact.

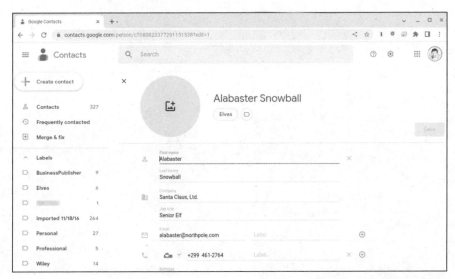

**FIGURE 15-11:** Updating contact details with Google Contacts.

*Illustration courtesy of Peter H. Gregory*

Chapter **16**

# Reading Ebooks on the Chromebook

An ebook, short for electronic book, is a digital format of a book that is stored and read on electronic devices. The benefits of ebooks are numerous, but perhaps the biggest is convenience. With ebooks, you no longer have to lug around heavy paper books; now, you can store hundreds of books on a single slim device.

Although ebooks will never entirely replace the experience of turning pages or writing notes in the margins, reading books on your Chromebook is an excellent way to enjoy a good novel, particularly when you are on the go. The Google Play Books library is home to nearly 7 million titles, and that number continues to grow.

In this chapter, you find out how to load Play Books on your Chromebook and how to navigate the Play Books library. I show you how to add new books to your library — and many books in the Play Books library are available for free! Using your Chromebook, you can read your books online and offline, regardless of where you are. And in case you're one of the millions of Kindle users, you're in luck because this chapter explains how Kindle works on Chromebooks.

# Navigating Google Play Books

One way to read books on the Chromebook is with Play Books. Play Books is where you search for and purchase titles and where you can find all your book purchases and uploaded books.

 To launch Play Books, open the Launcher and click the Google Play Books icon. For a similar experience, you can use your browser and go to play.google.com/books.

**TIP** If Play Books doesn't appear among the choices in your Launcher, add it by following these steps:

1. **Open the Launcher and click the Play Store icon.**

   The Play Store opens.

2. **Type the words Play Books into the Search bar and press Enter.**

   Google Play Books & Audiobooks appears as the first or second search result.

3. **Click Install or Open.**

   Google uses the name "Google Play Books & Audiobooks" in the Play Store, but everywhere else, Google calls it Google Play Books.

## Searching and purchasing books

If this is the first time you've worked with Play Books, you may not have much to see when you open the app. However, you can change that situation quickly. Open Play Books by clicking Play Books in the Launcher and then click the Shop link near the lower-right corner of the window. Play Books gets you started on your search for books, whether by genre, top-selling, new, or free.

To purchase a book, follow these steps:

1. **In the search bar at the top of Play Books, enter the name of the book you're searching for. Press Enter.**

   The search results populate the screen, as shown in Figure 16-1.

2. **Browse through the search results to locate the desired book and click the thumbnail of the cover.**

   If the book you're looking for doesn't appear in the search results, revise your search to use fewer words and thus expand your search results.

**TIP**

You can search for books by author, title, and subject.

After you click the book cover image, the book profile page loads. On this page, you can read a description of the book, read reviews, search for similar texts, view a free sample of the book's contents, and purchase the book for reading on your Chromebook.

3. **If you're ready to purchase the book, click the Buy button near the bottom of the window.**

   A Google Wallet window appears, as shown in Figure 16-2, asking you to confirm your purchase. If you don't have a payment method on file, you must first add one before you can purchase the book. See Chapter 12 to find out how to set up payments with Google.

4. **Click Buy ebook.**

   The purchase is completed, and the book is added to your Play Books library.

**FIGURE 16-1:**
Google Play
Bookstore search
results.

*Illustration courtesy of Peter H. Gregory*

Even if you don't want to spend money, you can still add new books to your library by choosing one of the free books available in the Play Books library. The free books are mixed into the Play Books bookstore, but you can get access to a list of the top free books by following these steps:

1. **Scroll down in Play Books and click on Free just beneath where you see the words Ebooks charts.**

FIGURE 16-2:
Paying for a book
in Google Play.

*Illustration courtesy of Peter H. Gregory*

2. **Click the right arrow to the right of Ebooks charts.**

   A long list of free books appears.

3. **Browse through the list and click the thumbnail of a book you're interested in.**

   The book's profile page loads.

4. **If you want to read the book, click the Get for free button below the title.**

   The window refreshes, and the Get for free button is replaced by the Read button, as shown in Figure 16-3.

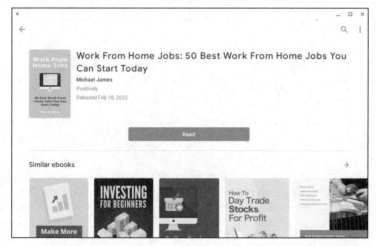

FIGURE 16-3:
Adding a free
ebook to your
library.

*Illustration courtesy of Peter H. Gregory*

# Previewing a book

You may be interested in a book but want to take a peek before you buy it — the way you can flip through a book in a bookstore. Play Books lets you do this. To preview a book, follow these steps:

1. **Select a title that interests you.**

   The Free Sample button appears next to the price if a preview is available.

2. **Click Free Sample.**

   Play Books opens the book using the reader (more about that later in this chapter). You can scroll through some of the book's pages, as shown in Figure 16-4. The reader tells you how many pages are available in the sample, and you can use the progress bar at the bottom to quickly scroll through the content available in the preview.

**FIGURE 16-4:** Scrolling through a book preview.

*Illustration courtesy of Peter H. Gregory*

# Reading and Listening to Ebooks

Every book you purchase or preview through Play Books is stored in your Play Books library in the cloud and is accessible from any device with an internet connection. This accessibility is a great feature, allowing you to access your library on all your devices.

Just click the thumbnail image in your Play Books library to start reading a book. As you read, you can advance through pages by *scrolling* — using the touchpad of your Chromebook — or by clicking near the left or right edges of the screen. Scrolling is a great way to advance quickly to a spot in the book.

You can access books in your library from all your devices, and Play Books keeps track of your reading progress. If, for instance, you begin reading a book on one device and later resume on another, Google keeps track of where you left off. It's practically magic.

## Reading in Full screen mode

When you start reading an ebook with the Play Books app, you start on the book's first page. To advance pages, scroll sideways with your mouse or trackpad to turn the page forward or backward. Or, click anywhere on a page, and the progress bar appears so you can see how far along you are in the book, as shown in Figure 16-5. Click again, and the controls disappear, and the pages are made a little larger.

The reading controls work like this: You can slide the little blue ball left and right to quickly move forward or backward in the book. Click the Chapters button to view the list of chapters, and click a chapter to immediately go to it. Near the upper-right corner, you can search for content in the book and change the size and color of the text, as described in the next section. Clicking the Menu button displays a list of other items you can see and the actions you can take.

## Personalizing your view

While reading your book, you can personalize the density of the lines of text, increase or decrease the size of the letters, and even change the typeface of the ebook text. To customize your view, follow these steps:

1. **In your Play Books library, click the book you want to read.**

   The book loads into the window.

2. **Click the Aa icon near the top-right corner of the window. (If you don't see it, tap the image of the book in the reader to expose the controls at the top and bottom of the window.)**

   The Display options pane appears, revealing several options for customizing your ebook view, as shown in Figure 16-6.

   You can change the text by clicking on the Text link at the top of the Display options window, and you can change the lighting (how the book appears on the screen) by clicking the Lighting link.

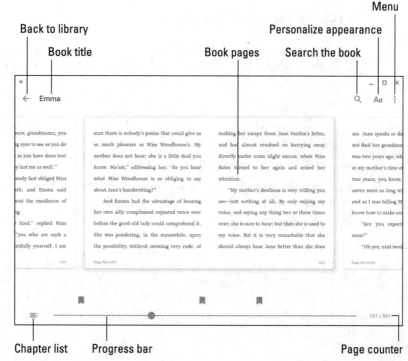

**Menu**

**Personalize appearance**

**Back to library**

**Book title**   **Book pages**   **Search the book**

Emma

**FIGURE 16-5:**
Controls in the
Play Books
reader.

**Chapter list**   **Progress bar**   **Page counter**

*Illustration courtesy of Peter H. Gregory*

3. **Make the desired changes.**

   Google applies those changes to the text in real-time.

4. **When you're finished making changes, click outside the Display options window.**

   The pane disappears.

**FIGURE 16-6:**
Changing display
options when
reading an ebook.

*Illustration courtesy of Peter H. Gregory*

# Using bookmarks

You may want to place a bookmark as you read through your ebooks to remember your place. With Play Books, you can place multiple bookmarks to quickly return to those pages. Place a bookmark by following these steps:

1. **In your Google Play Books library, click the book you want to read.**

   The book is loaded into the window.

2. **Turn to a page you want to bookmark.**

3. **Click the menu icon in the top-right corner of the window. (Refer to Figure 16-5.)**

4. **Click Add bookmark.**

   A bookmark appears on the page, as shown in Figure 16-7, indicating that the page has been bookmarked. When you can see the reading controls, a bookmark appears above the scrollbar at the bottom of the reading window.

**FIGURE 16-7:** Bookmarked pages in the Google Play Books reader.

*Illustration courtesy of Peter H. Gregory*

To quickly navigate to your bookmarked pages:

1. **Tap anywhere on the page to view reading controls if needed.**

2. **Click any bookmarks just above the timeline, as shown in Figure 16-7.**

   You're taken immediately to the desired bookmarked page.

# Viewing the definition of a word

While reading, you may encounter a word you aren't familiar with. If you're reading while connected to the internet, you can quickly see the word's definition by Alt-clicking it or tapping it with two fingers. A window appears, as shown in Figure 16-8, containing the popular definitions of the word. Click anywhere outside of the definition window to make it disappear.

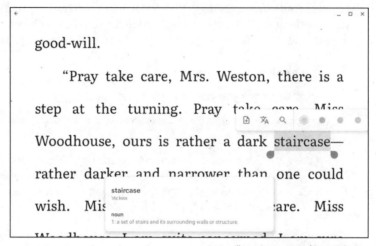

*Illustration courtesy of Peter H. Gregory*

**TIP**

Using Alt-click or a two-finger tap, you can highlight the word in one of several colors, as shown in Figure 16-8.

# Reading ebooks offline

As is the case with most of what you do on a Chromebook, all your books are stored in the cloud in your Play Books library. Further, if your Chromebook has enough space, Play Books also downloads your book to your Chromebook. If you want to read a newly purchased book offline, chances are that you'll be able to without having to do anything!

If you are a voracious reader and have an extensive library, eventually, you'll need to make room for new ebooks. Follow these steps to remove a downloaded book from your Chromebook (note, though, that you're *not* removing it from your library; you're just no longer storing it locally on your Chromebook):

1. **Open your Play Library.**

2. **Scroll to a book you want to remove from local storage on your Chromebook.**

3. **Click the menu icon (three little vertical dots) to the right of the book's cover image.**

4. **Click Remove download.**

   The locally stored copy of the book is removed.

You can remove a book regardless of whether you're online.

If you are anticipating being offline for a while (such as for a trans-Atlantic airline flight without Wi-Fi), you may want to make sure the books you want to read are stored locally — that is, on your Chromebook. Follow these steps:

1. **While online, launch Play Books.**

2. **Scroll to a book you want to make available locally.**

3. **Check to see whether the book is already stored locally and download if needed.**

   If there is a blue checkmark to the right of the book, it is already stored locally on your Chromebook. If, instead, there's a "download" icon to the right of the book, it is not stored locally. Click the download link to create a locally stored copy on your Chromebook. (See Figure 16-9.)

Click to download a copy

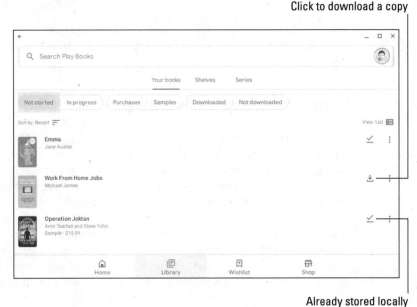

**FIGURE 16-9:** Making a book available for offline reading.

Already stored locally

*Illustration courtesy of Peter H. Gregory*

# Reading ebooks on the Google Play Books website

You don't have to use the Play Books app to read ebooks. Instead, you can enjoy a similar experience right within the Chrome browser. To get to your library on the website, go to `play.google.com/books`. Your library appears, as shown in Figure 16-10. To read an ebook, just click its image.

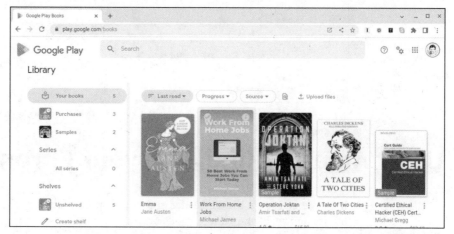

*Illustration courtesy of Peter H. Gregory*

**FIGURE 16-10:** Google Play Books in the Chrome browser.

# Listening to Audiobooks

When you launch Google Play Books, the app assumes you want to read ebooks. However, you can easily search for, purchase, and buy audiobooks. Click Audiobooks from the main Play Books screen, and Google's world of audiobooks will open to you.

Like with ebooks, you can browse genres, view best sellers, and listen to previews. Figure 16-11 shows a preview of Hitchhiker's Guide to the Galaxy, narrated by Stephen Fry.

TIP

When viewing individual audiobook titles, you'll often see the "Switch to the ebook" link if you want to consider an ebook instead.

**FIGURE 16-11:**
Previewing an
audiobook in
Google Play
Books.

*Illustration courtesy of Peter H. Gregory*

# Using Amazon Kindle on your Chromebook

If you're already a Kindle reader and have a Kindle library, you can access your library and read your Kindle books on your Chromebook.

To read Kindle books in your library, you first need to download the Amazon Kindle app by following these steps:

1. **Go to the Google Play Store.**

2. **Search for the Amazon Kindle app.**

3. **Click Install.**

When you have the Kindle app, you start it with the Launcher. The Kindle app opens, displaying featured books available to read, as shown in Figure 16-12.

**TIP**

You can also read Kindle books in your web browser if you prefer.

Click on the Library icon at the bottom of the Kindle window to get started. If you are not logged in, a Sign In button will appear. Click that to continue.

Log in to your Amazon account. If you don't have one, click Create a new Amazon account to make one. If you are already an Amazon customer, you have a Kindle account; use your Amazon login credentials to log in to Kindle. After you log in, your Kindle library appears, as shown in Figure 16-13. If you are already a Kindle user, you'll recognize the books in your Kindle library.

*Illustration courtesy of Peter H. Gregory*

Note the book thumbnail at the bottom center in Figure 16-13. The thumbnail indicates this book is currently being read — click on the thumbnail to resume reading. Also, the tiny headphones icon indicates this is an Audible book you can listen to with your Kindle reader.

*Illustration courtesy of Peter H. Gregory*

## Purchasing Kindle books

To shop for Kindle books from your Chromebook, go to Amazon.com on your browser to search for and purchase Kindle books. The titles you purchase will automatically appear in your Kindle library. Be sure to be signed in to your same Amazon account when you purchase Kindle books.

## Reading Kindle books

To read a book in your Kindle library, click its cover image. The book opens to the first page (or the page you last read if you were reading the book on this or another device).

No reading controls appear when reading your Kindle book — but they are there. To view the reading controls, click near the middle of the reading window to make the controls appear, as shown in Figure 16-14. If you click too far to the right or left, Kindle will think you are turning pages. Don't worry — you'll soon get the hang of it.

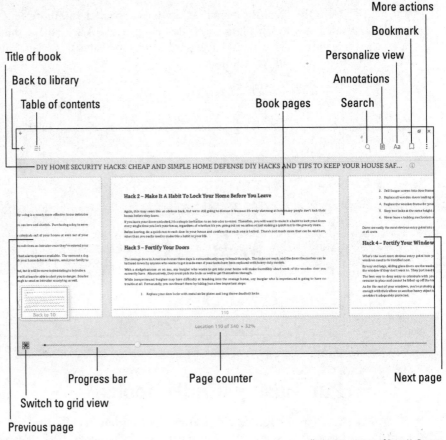

Illustration courtesy of Peter H. Gregory

**FIGURE 16-14:** The Kindle reader controls.

# Reading Kindle books offline

You can download Kindle books to your Chromebook to read offline. To see which books are in the cloud and which are downloaded, go to your Kindle library and click the Library link at the bottom of the Kindle window. Your entire library of books appears. Next, click the Downloaded link at the top of the Kindle window to see which ones are already on your Chromebook.

To download a book so you can read it offline, follow these steps:

1. **Click and hold on the book cover.**

   A check mark will appear.

2. **In the upper-right corner of the Kindle window, click the Download icon.**

   The book will be downloaded and stored locally.

Later, if you run short on local storage space on your Chromebook, you can remove downloaded books from your Kindle library. To do so:

1. **Go to your Kindle Library. Click Downloaded to see a list of locally stored books.**

2. **Find the book to remove from local storage.**

3. **Click and hold on the book's image.**

   A check mark will appear over the book's cover.

4. **Click the More options button at the upper-right corner of the Kindle window.**

   It appears as three little vertical dots.

5. **Click Remove Download.**

   The book is not removed from your Kindle Library — just from being stored locally on your Chromebook. You can still read the book when you are online.

# 4

# Advanced Chromebook Settings

IN THIS CHAPTER

» **Personalizing your screen and using an external display**

» **Moving and hiding the shelf**

» **Linking Bluetooth devices**

» **Dealing with notifications**

» **Enlisting assistance with "Hey Google!"**

# Chapter **17**

# Customizing Your Chromebook

hromebooks are made to be easy to use. Out of the box, a Chromebook user can be up and running in less than five minutes. By default, the features and functionality of a Chromebook make the user experience top-notch without any customization. However, Google recognizes that all people are different. Although Google's user-experience designers are some of the best in the world, how people use technology isn't a one-size-fits-all proposition. For that reason, you can customize several look-and-feel aspects of your Chromebook.

In this chapter, you discover how to customize your display with your own wallpaper images, change the resolution of your display, and add a monitor to your Chromebook. You also find out how to customize the appearance and position of your shelf. I explain how to manage notifications so you can stay informed about what's happening in your Chromebook. And finally, I help you turn your Chromebook into a Google Assistant!

# Customizing Your Display Settings

Out of the box, your Chromebook's default settings are what the manufacturer found to be the ideal settings for viewing, computing, and so on. Your display defaults to the best screen resolution to show as much detail as possible. Your Chromebook likely also comes with some standard background images, called *wallpapers,* that you can use to change the look of your desktop area. However, if you would like to customize your display to better match your personality, you can do so in several ways.

To view your settings, go to the Settings menu. Click the Settings area in the bottom-right corner of the shelf, which reveals a list of options — the Settings panel — and choose Settings, the little gear-like icon.

## Changing your wallpaper

When you start your Chromebook, the image that fills your desktop background is called wallpaper. Your device manufacturer provides several options for wallpaper that you can try. You also have the option to change the wallpaper to almost any photo that you desire. To change your Chromebook wallpaper, follow these steps:

1. **Open the Settings panel on the shelf and choose Settings.**

   Your Chromebook Settings window appears, as shown in Figure 17-1.

2. **Click Personalization on the left side.**

3. **Click on Set your wallpaper & style in the Personalization section.**

   The Wallpaper and Screen saver window appears, as shown in Figure 17-2. Click on the little right-arrow to the right of the word Wallpaper to view the categories of wallpaper images available. Click on any of the categories to view available images.

4. **If you have an image of your own that you would like to use, click My Images in the upper-left corner of the Wallpaper selection window to view your own images. You can also select from any of your images in Google Photos.**

5. **Select the desired wallpaper image by clicking the image.**

   Your Chromebook's wallpaper changes to match your selection.

TIP

   In each of the image libraries already on your Chromebook, note that in the first image, you can click the Change daily selector to display a different image from that collection every day. Variety is the spice of life!

6. **Click the X in the top-right corner of the Wallpaper window.**

   The window closes, and the Chromebook Settings window reappears.

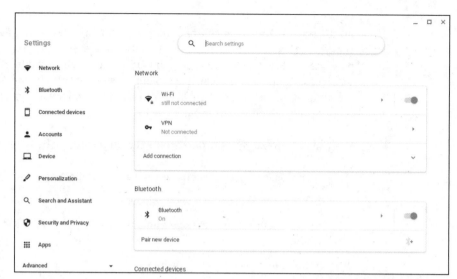

**FIGURE 17-1:**
The Chromebook
Settings window.

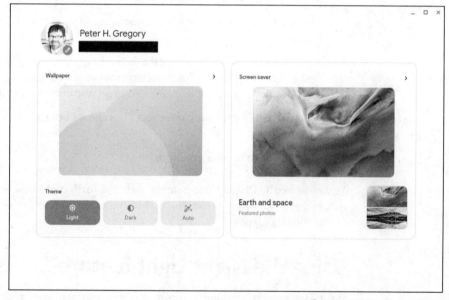

**FIGURE 17-2:**
Chromebook's
wallpaper and
screen saver
browser.

# Changing your screen resolution

*Screen resolution* is the measure of the sharpness and clarity of your screen. Resolution is expressed in terms of horizontal rows and vertical columns of pixels. A *pixel* is a tiny area of illumination on a display. Think of each pixel as a dot that can vary in color and brightness; together, all these dots make up the images you see on the screen. For instance, the typical flat-screen television may have a resolution of 1920 x 1080, which means that the image is 1920 pixels wide and 1080 pixels tall, and a 4K display is 3840 by 2160 pixels. When you increase or decrease your resolution, the physical size of your screen doesn't change. What changes is the number of pixels you're packing into that physical area. High resolution equals more pixels, which equals greater clarity.

You can customize your Chromebook's screen resolution by following these steps:

1. **Open the Settings panel on the shelf and click Settings.**

   Your Chromebook Settings window opens.

2. **In your Chromebook Settings window, click Device on the left side of the window.**

3. **In the Device section, click Displays.**

   The Displays Settings window appears, as shown in Figure 17-3.

4. **Scroll the Display Size slider back and forth to choose a new resolution.**

   As you scroll, the resolution (the horizontal and vertical pixel count) is indicated.

   Your Chromebook display automatically adjusts to match your selection. Figure 17-4 shows what the screen may look like at an extremely low resolution. Such a setting makes text on the screen larger and potentially easier to read.

5. **When satisfied with your selection, click the X in the window's top-right corner.**

   The Chromebook Settings window closes.

TIP

As you move the Display size pointer back and forth, note that one of the settings will include the word "(Native)." This indicates the actual resolution of your Chromebook's display.

## Using the Night Light feature

Many laptops, tablets, and smartphones are now equipped with a "night mode" display setting. This setting lowers the "color temperature" of the display from a bright blue-white to a yellowish display. The science behind this feature is related to how the human brain interprets bright white light. The brain thinks it's sunlight. If you use your device late at night, your brain might think it's daytime, and consequently, you could have trouble falling asleep. (In other words, bright smartphone and laptop displays are the new caffeine.) The night mode, called Night Light on a Chromebook, automatically adjusts your display color to appear more yellowish (akin to candlelight or firelight) at night.

**FIGURE 17-3:**
The Chromebook
Displays Settings
window.

*Illustration courtesy of Peter H. Gregory*

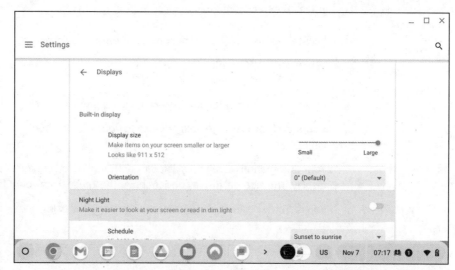

**FIGURE 17-4:**
Chromebook's
display with a low
resolution.

*Illustration courtesy of Peter H. Gregory*

Night Light does not adjust the actual brightness of the display but rather its color temperature. Follow these steps, and you'll see what I'm talking about:

1. **Click Settings on the shelf and then click Device on the left side of the Settings window that appears.**

2. **Click Displays and then scroll down until the Night Light section appears, as shown in Figure 17-3.**

3. **Click the Night Light selector.**

4. **Use the Color Temperature slider to adjust the degree of color shift.**

   Setting the slider to the Cooler setting is like having no Night Light set at all. Sliding it to the right shows you what the display looks like at night. Adjust it where you like.

5. **Set the schedule for Night Light.**

   The default setting is Sunset to Sunrise (adjusted to your time zone and latitude), but you can set a Custom Schedule in which you specify the time of day that the Night Light turns on and off. By default, the Custom Schedule is set to On at 6 p.m. and Off at 6 a.m. When creating a Custom Schedule, move the slider to the desired times.

## Using an external display

Working with a laptop all day long can result in eyestrain for some people. Thankfully, you can use an external display device with your Chromebook. To add and customize an external display device, follow these steps:

1. **Locate the display (HDMI) port on your Chromebook.**

   The majority of Chromebooks on the market come with at least one HDMI port, such as the one shown in Figure 17-5.

2. **Ensure that your external display device is powered on.**

3. **Connect the external display device to your Chromebook using an HDMI cable.**

   Your Chromebook screen may flicker briefly as it auto-configures the new display. The external display device shows the image from your Chromebook.

   You can now begin working from your Chromebook using both screens.

**FIGURE 17-5:**
A Chromebook HDMI display port.

HDMI port

*Illustration courtesy of Peter H. Gregory*

**TIP**

If you have a flat-screen television, you can connect your Chromebook to your TV for an extra-large display. This capability can be great for viewing your pictures, movies, YouTube, and so on.

An external monitor can work with a Chromebook in two ways:

>> **Mirrored:** This means that everything you see on your Chromebook display is shown on the external display. The external display is a "mirror" of your Chromebook display.

>> **Extended:** The external monitor represents *additional* ("extended") space to show apps and windows.

To switch between mirrored and extended display as well as to change other settings, follow these steps:

**1.** **Open the Settings panel on the shelf and click Settings.**

Your Chromebook settings appear.

**2.** **Click Device in the left margin of the Settings window and then click Displays.**

The Displays Settings window appears, as shown in Figure 17-6, and you see the Arrangement configuration, where your two (or more) displays are shown side-by-side in the Displays Settings window.

The Arrangement configuration allows you to choose whether your external display is mirrored or extended.

**3.** **Select or deselect the Mirror Internal Display checkbox to change this.**

When you change the display, a notification appears.

**4.** **(Optional) If you choose not to mirror the displays, configure the arrangement of the two monitors by dragging the depictions of the displays to match the orientation of the actual displays.**

Configuring the arrangement of the representative monitors allows you to logically arrange how your physical monitors work with one another. For example, if your external monitor is to the left of your Chromebook, you can drag the little boxes representing the displays so that their orientation on the screen resembles their physical orientation, which comes in handy when you move the mouse pointer between the two displays. When the displays on the Arrangement configuration screen are arranged like the actual displays, the mouse pointer can move smoothly from one display to the other.

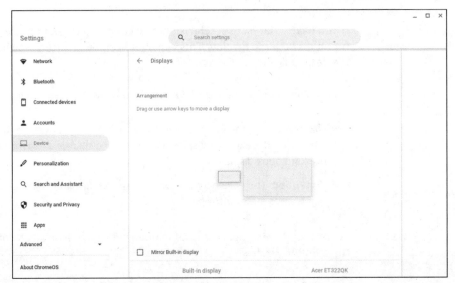

Settings

Q  Search settings

Network
Bluetooth
Connected devices
Accounts
Device
Personalization
Search and Assistant
Security and Privacy
Apps
Advanced
About ChromeOS

←  Displays

Arrangement
Drag or use arrow keys to move a display

☐  Mirror Built-in display

Built-in display                    Acer ET322QK

**FIGURE 17-6:**
Manage the
arrangement of
multiple displays.

*Illustration courtesy of Peter H. Gregory*

You can also adjust the resolution of an external display. To do so, follow these steps:

**1.** **Open display settings, as in the previous procedures in this section.**

**2.** **Click the external display symbol in the Arrangement section and then scroll down past the Arrangement section.**

The configuration settings for the external display appear, as shown in Figure 17-7. In this section, you can adjust the resolution (the number of rows and columns of pixels), the size of text that appears in windows and apps, and whether your external display is oriented in the usual way or rotated 90, 180, or 270 degrees.

**3.** **If the image on the external display is too big or too small, click Overscan to open the Overscan section of the display configuration settings.**

Symbolic arrows appear on the external display to assist in this effort, as shown in Figure 17-8. Instructions appear on your Chromebook display.

**4.** **Press the arrow keys on your keyboard to adjust the image size. Hold the Shift key down and press the arrow keys to adjust the position.**

You want to adjust the settings until the four gray arrow points touch the edge of the display, as shown in Figure 17-8.

**5.** **To accept your changes, click OK; to ignore your changes, click Reset.**

FIGURE 17-7:
Configuring an
external display.

*Illustration courtesy of Peter H. Gregory*

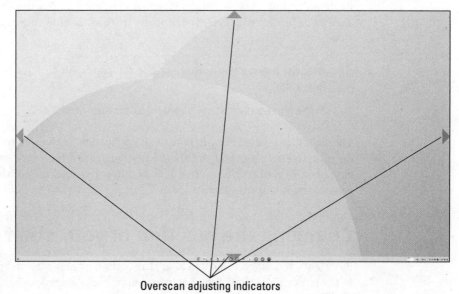
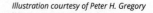

FIGURE 17-8:
Configuring the
Overscan setting
to correct
external display
positioning.

Overscan adjusting indicators

*Illustration courtesy of Peter H. Gregory*

**TECHNICAL
STUFF**

Your external monitor may also have settings to adjust the size and position of the image on the screen. Consult your monitor's owner's manual for more information.

**TIP**

Mirroring your Chromebook display onto an external display device is helpful when presenting or demonstrating a task to a larger audience. Display devices can be televisions, monitors, or even projectors.

# Customizing Your Shelf

The shelf is the home base for controlling what happens on your Chromebook. By default, the shelf is located along the bottom of your screen. Your app menu (similar to the Start button on a Windows PC) appears on the left side of your shelf. Next to the Launcher icon are shortcuts to your favorite apps. You can find your notification panel and status area on the right side of your shelf. (Flip to Figure 2-1 in Chapter 2 to take a quick look at these elements.)

## Hiding your shelf

By default, your shelf is always visible on the screen. You can, however, set the shelf to be hidden when you're not using it. To auto-hide your shelf, follow these steps:

1. **With the pointer somewhere on the wallpaper, Alt-click (or two-finger tap).**

2. **In the pop-up menu that appears, select Autohide Shelf.**

The shelf hides whenever you launch an application to give you more usable space on your screen. To reveal the shelf when you're working in a browser window, simply move your pointer so that it hovers over the shelf area at the bottom of the screen, and it will reappear.

## Changing the position of your shelf

By default, your shelf is located along the bottom of your screen. To move the shelf to the left or right side of your screen, follow these steps:

1. **Alt-click (or two-finger tap) the background of your Chromebook.**

2. **In the menu that appears, hover your cursor over Shelf Position.**

   A submenu appears, as shown in Figure 17-9.

3. **Select the option that corresponds with the side of the screen to which you'd like to move your shelf.**

   The shelf relocates to the designated side, as shown in Figure 17-10.

**FIGURE 17-9:**
Relocating the
shelf.

*Illustration courtesy of Peter H. Gregory*

**FIGURE 17-10:**
The shelf on the
left side of the
display.

Additional launcher icons here

*Illustration courtesy of Peter H. Gregory*

**TIP**

If the shelf is located at the bottom of the screen and contains a lot of app icons (as mine does), they won't all show if you move the shelf to the left or right side of the screen. This spillover is indicated by an icon displaying a tiny down arrow icon. Click this icon to make the remainder of your app icons appear.

# Connecting Bluetooth Devices to Your Chromebook

Bluetooth, which has saved the world from the tangle of headphone and speaker wires, is a wireless protocol that you can use to connect devices up to a distance of 30 feet apart.

You connect Bluetooth devices through a process known as "pairing." To connect devices, both need to be put into "pairing mode," which allows them to make a new connection. It's like introducing a couple of your friends on a blind date: You introduce them to each other, and from then on, what happens is up to them.

The devices you can connect to your Chromebook include speakers, headphones, earbuds, and external pointing devices such as a mouse or trackpad. Other more specialized devices qualify, such as those little tags you put on your keychain so you can find it when you misplace it — again (they're also handy to affix to checked baggage on airline flights). (In my household, we also have one of those little automotive diagnostic plugs that you plug into the diagnostic port of your car so that an app on a smartphone or Chromebook can read the codes and give us an idea of how our car is feeling today.)

 To connect a Bluetooth-enabled device to your Chromebook, follow these steps:

1. **Click the Settings area on the shelf and click the Settings gear.**

   The Chromebook settings window opens.

2. **Click Bluetooth in the Bluetooth section.**

   The Bluetooth settings window opens. See whether the word *Off* or *On* appears just below the Bluetooth logo.

3. **If Bluetooth is off, turn it on by clicking the button to the right.**

4. **Click the Pair new device icon, a Bluetooth symbol with a little + next to it.**

5. **Read the instructions, if necessary, for the device you're using to find out how to put it into pairing mode.**

   Pairing a device often involves holding down its Power button, or another button, for some seconds.

6. **Click the device's name when it appears under the Available devices heading, as shown in Figure 17-11.**

   The word "Pairing. . ." appears, and your Chromebook attempts to pair with the device. This takes a few moments.

7. **If your Chromebook and the device agree to pair, the device name appears in the Currently connected list of devices, as shown in Figure 17-12.**

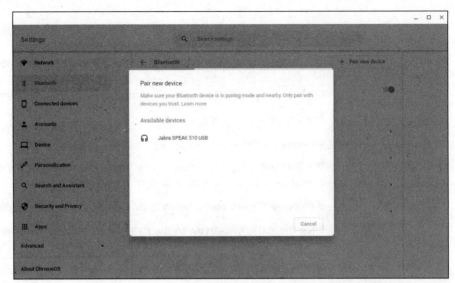

FIGURE 17-11:
Getting ready to
pair a Chrome-
book to a
Bluetooth device
for the first time.

Illustration courtesy of Peter H. Gregory

FIGURE 17-12:
Chromebook has
successfully
paired with a
Bluetooth device.

Illustration courtesy of Peter H. Gregory

In the future, your Chromebook should automatically pair with the same device if both are turned on and near each other, and if Bluetooth is active on your Chromebook. Some devices need a little nudge. If so, follow these instructions:

1. **Click the Settings area on the shelf and click the Settings gear.**

   The Chromebook settings window opens.

2. **Click Bluetooth in the Bluetooth section.**

   The Bluetooth settings window opens. See whether the word *Off* or *On* appears just below the Bluetooth logo.

3. **If Bluetooth is off, turn it on by clicking the button to the right.**

4. **Click the little right-arrow to the right, next to the on-off switch.**

   A list of devices you have connected to in the past appears. If the device you want to connect does not appear here, go to the preceding steps on pairing a device for the first time.

5. **Click the device you want to connect.**

   If the device is turned on, it should pair in a few moments.

Later on, to disconnect a device, you can just turn it off. Or you can turn off Bluetooth on your Chromebook. Yet another way is to go into the Bluetooth Settings window, click the device name, and click Disconnect. If you want your Chromebook to forget about your device forever, click the device in the Bluetooth Settings window and click Forget.

TIP

In my experience, some Bluetooth devices are rather friendly and pair and re-pair easily, whereas others are cranky or even cantankerous, at which time I have to tell my Chromebook to forget about a device entirely and re-pair it as though I'd never used it before. Can't we all just get along?

You can also control Bluetooth on your Chromebook in the Settings window on the shelf. Click *on* the Bluetooth logo to turn Bluetooth on and off. Click *below* the logo to pair or unpair known devices, as shown in Figure 17-13. You can do it all from here!

*Illustration courtesy of Peter H. Gregory*

# Managing Notifications

A lot can go on "under the hood" of your Chromebook, and your Chromebook can get rather chatty in telling you about it through notifications. Some of these notifications may just be noise to you, but others are potentially useful. Sometimes the noise is so loud that you may feel like foregoing notifications altogether; however, a few are vital, such as those for software updates.

*Notifications* are the messages that appear on the lower-right side of the Chromebook display — and sometimes, they can run all the way to the top-right side of the display!

To close individual notifications, click the tiny *X* in the upper-right corner of the notification, as shown in Figure 17-14. To manage notifications settings, follow these steps:

1. **Open the Settings window on the shelf.**

2. **Click the word Notifications that appears beneath the Notifications logo.**

   A window showing a list of apps appears, as shown in Figure 17-15. Note that the list may be longer than the display window; scroll through the list to view apps that can send notifications.

3. **To prevent an app from sending notifications, uncheck the checkbox next to its name.**

For example, uncheck the box next to Camera if you don't want the Chromebook's camera app to notify you every time you take a picture.

4. **To temporarily suspend all notifications, click the Do Not Disturb selector.**

You can also click the Notifications logo in the Shelf Settings window. Great shortcut, right?

To turn notifications back on, click the Do Not Disturb selector again.

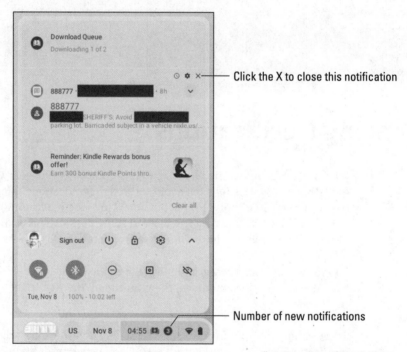

Click the X to close this notification

Number of new notifications

**FIGURE 17-14:**
A notification on the Chromebook display.

TIP

Here's a nice shortcut for Notifications: On the shelf near the clock, battery, and Wi-Fi symbols, a small circle with a number appears if you have notifications waiting. If you click that circle, the Shelf Settings window appears, and the notifications appear above it. (See Figure 17-14.)

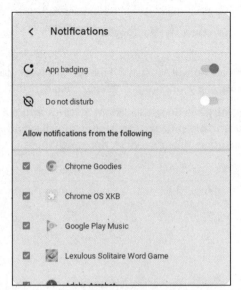

# Using Hey Google!

 You can turn your Chromebook into your very own Google voice-activated assistant. Any time you say, "Hey Google!", your Chromebook will respond to your beck and call, just like those dedicated voice assistant devices. There's a wide array of things that Google Assistant can do for you, from playing your favorite music to dimming the lights for that romantic dinner or getting the latest weather report.

To turn on and configure Google Assistant, follow these easy steps:

**1.** **Open the Settings panel on the shelf. Click the clock area at the lower-right corner of the screen; then click the little gear.**

Chromebook's settings menu appears.

**2.** **Click on Search and Assistant.**

**3.** **Click on Google Assistant.**

The Google Assistant settings page appears, as shown in Figure 17-16.

**4.** **If Google Assistant is off, click the little switch to the right to turn it on.**

5. **You may want to also turn on Hey Google.**

   If you haven't done this before, you'll be asked to click on a short agreement, and you'll need to train Google Assistant on the sound of your voice. This takes only a minute or two, and your Chromebook steps you right through it.

6. **Scroll down, and you'll see Google Assistant Settings, which opens a new window containing many settings about where you live and work, your vehicles, transportation, music services, and much more.**

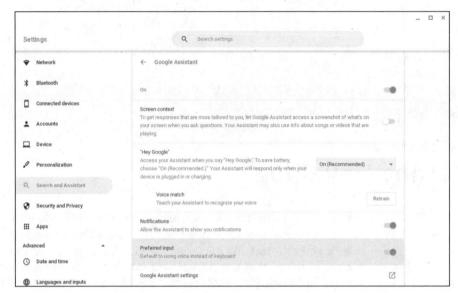

**FIGURE 17-16:**
Configuring Google Assistant on a Chromebook.

Google Assistant is your connection to Google Home, where you can set up home automation, including features like viewing security cameras, unlocking your door, turning lights on and off, adjusting the thermostat, and so much more.

# Other Chromebook Customizations

I've only scratched the surface regarding customizations you can do on your Chromebook. There are more options than I could fit in this book, but I mention a few others here.

>> **Touchpad:** You can change how your touchpad works in terms of scrolling speed and direction, clicking, tapping, and more. I discuss this in Chapter 4.

>> **Keyboard:** You can change your keyboard language, and even rearrange a few of the keys like Ctrl, Alt, Shift, and Search. This may be especially useful if you use an external keyboard whose labels are different from a normal Chromebook. I discuss this in Chapter 4.

>> **Language:** You can change the language of your Chromebook to something else. For instance, you may be living in the United States but formerly lived in England, and you've decided you like the English way of spelling things. I discuss this in Chapter 1 on setting up a Chromebook.

>> **Wi-Fi networks:** You can set up your Chromebook to connect to more than your home Wi-Fi network. For example, you may take your Chromebook to work (be sure to check the policy on the use of personal devices on company networks), or maybe you hang out at that coffee shop on Saturday mornings. Chapter 1's section on connecting to the internet discusses this.

>> **Other user accounts:** You can set up your Chromebook so multiple family members can use it, each with their own user account. On the login screen, click Add Person at the bottom of the screen. You can create an entirely new Google account or log in to one that exists already. Once a new or existing account has been logged in on your Chromebook, it will appear among the accounts available for logon.

>> **Unlock with an Android smartphone:** Instead of typing your password in to unlock your Chromebook, you can unlock it with your connected Android smartphone (which must be unlocked). How cool is that! I cover this in Chapter 18.

>> **Dark mode:** If you prefer a dark screen with white lettering, you can configure your Chromebook to operate in dark mode. Head over to Settings, Device, Personalization, Set your wallpaper and style. Then, in the Wallpaper and Screen saver screen, scroll down and click on Dark in the Theme area.

>> **Screen saver:** Google has a dazzling array of photos in Earth and Space, as well as Featured Photos. You can choose your own photos from Google Photos if you prefer.

>> **Customize the Shelf:** You can determine what apps sit on the shelf, giving you rapid access to your favorite apps. I cover this in Chapter 2.

# Chapter **18**

# Securing Your Chromebook

I n the context of computers and the internet, countless cybercriminal organizations, gangs, and lone hackers lurk with the intention of pilfering, stealing, defacing, and destroying — for profit, enjoyment, and because they can. Doubtlessly, you've heard about breaches, small and large, and ransomware, viruses, and other issues.

The good news is that you have a Chromebook! Chromebooks are not targeted like Windows, Macs, Android phones, and iPhones. Chromebooks themselves are pretty secure and are fitted with the latest safeguards. But that doesn't mean you don't have to be careful. Cybercriminals have many ways to try to trick people out of information and money.

Sometimes increased usability can mean increased security concerns. The more protection you put in place, the more hassle there is. You can add or remove as much security as you want, but there are consequences both ways — and unfortunately, security isn't always convenient.

In this chapter, you discover how to protect against malicious invaders and manage your access to your Chromebook through user accounts and Guest mode. You see how to increase your peace of mind by locking your screen, managing your passwords, and ensuring that you aren't leaving valuable information around by managing your privacy settings. You can even get the ultimate protection through Google Advanced Protection. Also, this chapter tells you about webcam filters, privacy screen filters, and cable locks for keeping prying eyes and hands away.

# Conducting User Management

Google takes security seriously, and thus the Chromebook is no slouch when it comes to security. To access a Chromebook, you must have a Google Account. This requirement is just as much about enhancing your interaction with the Chromebook and the Google platform as it is about securing your interaction. By default, when you first use your Chromebook, you can log in with a Google Account or use the Chromebook as a guest. Guest users don't get any of the privileges that registered users get. In fact, Guest mode is a lot like surfing the web incognito because none of your traffic is tracked, stored, or otherwise logged in the Chromebook.

When you log in to your Chromebook with a Google Account, that user account becomes the master account, or *Owner account*. With this account, you can administer and manage all other users who access the Chromebook, or you can restrict users whom you don't want to access the Chromebook.

## Adding and deleting users

Account management is an essential part of securing your Chromebook. By default, anyone with a Google Account can log in and utilize your Chromebook. The good news is that Chromebook doesn't allow each user to access other users' data; however, you may not want your computer to be accessible to everyone on the planet. If you would like to limit access to your Chromebook to specific users, follow these steps:

1. **Log in to your Chromebook with the Owner account's username and password (that's probably you).**

2. **Open the settings panel on the Shelf and click Settings.**

   The Settings window opens.

3. **Click Security and Privacy.**

4. **Click Manage other people in the Security and Privacy section.**

   The Manage other people window appears.

**5.** **Enable the Restrict sign-in to the following users selector.**

A form below this selector activates, revealing all the users who have logged into your device already, as shown in Figure 18-1.

**REMEMBER**

If you're the only person who has accessed the Chromebook up to this point, the only account you see in this box is yours. Notice that next to your account name is the word *Owner,* which means that your account is the owner of the Chromebook. With the Restrict sign-in to the following users option enabled, the only users who can access your Chromebook are listed with your account.

**6.** **To add users, click the Add user link beneath the list of users. In the Add user text box, as shown in Figure 18-2, enter the email addresses for the Google Accounts to which you want to grant access. Click Add.**

The names are added to the list of approved Google Accounts.

**TIP**

The Add user form calls for an email address. To save on headaches or errors, use only the email addresses assigned to the Google Accounts that will access your Chromebook.

To delete a user from being able to use your Chromebook, click the *X* to the right of the user's name in the list. No X appears to the right of the owner's name because the owner's access can't be revoked. Users who aren't listed as the owner can't modify the user settings for your Chromebook.

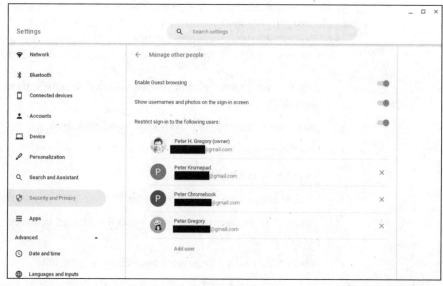

**FIGURE 18-1:** Viewing active user accounts on a Chromebook.

*Illustration courtesy of Peter H. Gregory*

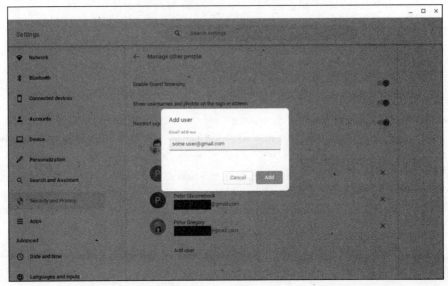

**FIGURE 18-2:**
Adding names to the list of users allowed to use your Chromebook.

# Hiding users on the login screen

When you add new users to your Chromebook, their names and profile pictures are shown on the login screen. Showing these can make access for frequent users easy and convenient. However, it also reduces security: The approved user accounts are in plain sight, so potential intruders don't have to work so hard. Instead of guess-ing a username and a password, intruders need to guess only a password. To hide users so that they don't appear on the login screen, follow these steps:

1. **Log in to your Chromebook with the Owner account's username and password.**

2. **Open the settings panel on the Shelf and click Settings.**

   The Settings window opens.

3. **Click Security and Privacy.**

4. **Click Manage other people in the Security and Privacy section.**

5. **Deselect Show usernames and photos on the sign-in screen selector, as shown in Figure 18-3.**

6. **Verify that your settings were applied by logging out.**

   To log out, reopen the Settings window in the Shelf and click Sign out.

   You're signed out of your Chromebook, and the usernames and photos disappear from the login screen. Instead, a generic login box requires you to enter your full account username (your Gmail address) and password.

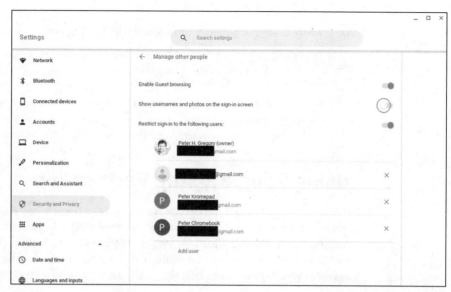

**FIGURE 18-3:** Hiding user accounts on the login window.

# Guest mode

*Guest mode* is an easy way to allow anyone to use your Chromebook without putting your personal account — or your Chromebook's settings — at risk. Key features, such as saving data to the device, changing settings, or otherwise modifying the Chromebook, are disabled. Any changes, downloads, or tweaks done to the Chromebook while in Guest mode are deleted when the Chromebook is powered off or when the guest logs out. If you ever want to give someone quick access without creating a user account, Guest mode is the way to go!

Even so, you may find that Guest mode leaves you more vulnerable than you like. In that case, you can revoke guest browsing by following these steps:

1. Log in to your Chromebook with the Owner account's username and password.

2. Open the settings panel on the Shelf and click Settings.

3. Click Security and Privacy.

4. Click Manage other people in the Security and Privacy section.

5. Deselect the Enable Guest browsing selector (see Figure 18-3).

6. **Verify that your settings were applied by logging out.**

   To log out, reopen the Settings window in the Shelf and click Sign Out.

   You're signed out of your Chromebook.

   If you successfully disabled Guest mode, the option to use the Chromebook as a guest disappears from the login screen. If you want to turn Guest mode back on, log back in and follow the steps above, enabling the selector in Step 5.

## Using Google 2-Step Verification

Using only user IDs and passwords isn't as safe as it once was. Criminals use malware and other tricks to steal your *login credentials.* Google comes to the rescue with Google 2-Step Verification, a mechanism that goes further than your user ID and password and serves as an additional safeguard to ensure that, even if attackers steal your login credentials, they still can't log in to your Google Account.

With Google 2-Step Verification, you log in to Google with your user ID and password. Then, Google pops up a window on your smartphone and asks whether you are currently trying to log in on your Chromebook. Answer No if you aren't the person attempting to log in. If you are logging on to your Chromebook, of course, you answer Yes. Voilà — you're logged in.

**REMEMBER**

The security behind 2-Step Verification is that if a hacker steals your login and password and tries to log in to Google as you, you unexpectedly receive an "Is this you?" alert on your smartphone. Answer No! Then you should change your Google password as soon as possible.

To set up Google 2-Step Verification on your Google account, follow these steps on your Chromebook:

1. **Log in to your Google Account with your smartphone.**

2. **Log in to your Google Account on your Chromebook.**

   Logging on to Gmail or any other Google service is sufficient.

3. **On your Chromebook, click the Google Account settings near the upper-right corner of your browser, on the tab where you signed on to Google.**

   You click your photo or avatar if you set one up to go here. Otherwise, click the little circle in the upper-right corner of the window.

4. **Click Manage Your Google Account.**

A page opens that lets you manage virtually every aspect of your Google Account.

5. **Click Security on the left side of the window.**

6. **Scroll down until you see the Signing In To Google section and, in that section, click the arrow to the right of 2-Step Verification.**

The 2-Step Verification window opens.

7. **Click Get Started and provide your password, if prompted to do so.**

Google shows your smartphone's make and model and asks if you have it.

8. **On your smartphone, answer Yes that you are trying to change how you sign in to Google.**

Google may ask other questions to verify that you have your phone with you and are proceeding with 2-Step Verification.

9. **Click Try It Now.**

On your smartphone, a window pops up asking whether you are trying to log in from your Chromebook. Your location is shown as well.

10. **Click Yes if you are indeed the user trying to log in. (See Figure 18-4.)**

Google asks whether you want to set up a backup method for logging in. Google will ask you for your mobile number.

11. **Enter your mobile number, select whether you want Google to call you or send you a text message, and click Send.**

Google calls your phone or sends a text to your phone with a code.

12. **Type in the code received in the text message and click Turn On.**

This setup gives you a backup method to log in to Google in case you don't have your smartphone (back in Step 11, you can have Google call a landline phone).

When you set up 2-Step Verification, every time you log in to Google, this one little extra step gives you the peace of mind of knowing that others can't access your Google Accounts easily. But if you want to get even more serious about your Google Account security, read on.

# Using Google Authenticator

Google Authenticator is a tool used by Google and hundreds of other services to improve your account security, by using a method known as "multi-factor authentication." It works like this:

» On your smartphone, you download and install the Google Authenticator app. You can find it in the Google Play Store for Android phones and in the App Store for iPhones.

» For each online account for which you want to improve security, you do a one-time setup by associating your online account with Google Authenticator.

» When you log in to an online account where you've set up Google Authenticator, you provide your user ID and password. Then you're prompted to enter the code for this online account from your Google Authenticator app.

» Any cybercriminal who has been able to steal your login credentials (that is, your user ID and password) will not be able to log in to your account if you have Google Authenticator tied to it. When prompted to enter your Google Authenticator code, they won't be able to because they don't have your smartphone with the Google Authenticator codes listed on it. Foiled!

Multi-factor authentication, sometimes called two-factor authentication, makes it difficult for cybercriminals to log in to your accounts because they don't have your smartphone in their possession. Only your smartphone contains the secret codes (which change every minute to new, unpredictable values).

To set up Google Authenticator for Google, follow these steps:

1. **Install Google Authenticator on your smartphone. Look in the Google Play Store for Android phones or in the App Store for iPhones.**

   You'll need to do this only once.

2. **Log in to any Google service (such as Gmail) on your Chromebook.**

3. **Click on the Google Account at the upper-right corner of the window.**

   This will be your photo, avatar, or initials.

4. **Click Manage Your Google Account.**

5. **Click on Security.**

6. **Scroll down to Signing in to Google.**

7. **Click on 2-Step Verification. Enter your Google password if you are prompted for it.**

8. **Scroll down and click on Authenticator app.**

9. **On the next page, click on + Set up authenticator.**

   A QR code will appear on the screen, as shown in Figure 18-5.

10. **On your smartphone, open the Google Authenticator app. Click the colorful + symbol near the lower-right corner.**

11. **Click Scan a QR code.**

    Your smartphone camera activates.

12. **Point your smartphone at the QR code on the screen from Step 9.**

    The code will be added to your Google Authenticator app. Find the code for Google that you just added. (If you are using Google Authenticator for the first time, it will be the only one shown.)

13. **Back on your Chromebook, in the window displaying the R code, click Next.**

14. **On the Chromebook, type in the six-digit code associated with the account in Step 12. Click Verify.**

    Google Authenticator is now set up on your Google Account.

The procedure for setting up Google Authenticator on your other online accounts is similar. Each service will have a Settings feature that you can use to manage your account. You'll be able to find a place where you can set up Google Authenticator.

This may seem like a complicated procedure, but I promise you that it will soon be routine. The peace of mind is worth it!

TIP

Once you have set up Google Authenticator for one or more of your online services, you'll have to have your smartphone with you when you log on to those services so that you can read the six-digit code from Google Authenticator to complete your login.

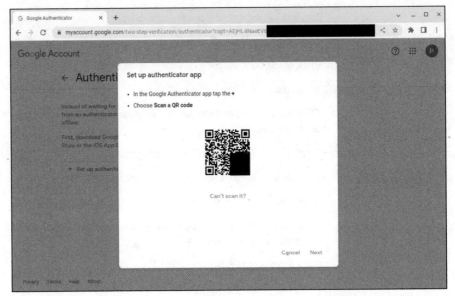

FIGURE 18-5:
Setting up Google
Authenticator for
signing in to
Google.

Illustration courtesy of Peter H. Gregory

When you upgrade your smartphone to a newer model, you can easily transfer all of you Google Authenticator codes to your new phone. However, if you lose your smartphone, your codes cannot be recovered.

WARNING

Under *no* circumstances should you *ever* provide the numbers from Google Authenticator to any person. If you are ever asked to provide those numbers, know that a cybercriminal is trying to trick you so they can log in to your account. Don't do it!

# Obtaining ultimate security with Google Advanced Protection

If Google 2-Step Verification is not enough security for you, you will be glad to know that Google has developed Google Advanced Protection. This service offers the ultimate protection for your Google Account, making it virtually impossible for anyone but you to ever access your Google Account.

Here are a few things to know about Google Advanced Protection:

» You purchase two tiny, inexpensive security devices you need to carry. (I carry mine on my key ring.) You have to purchase them only once.

» You need to use those little security devices only the first time you log in to any Google application on each device, and on any device from which you have logged out.

» Google Advanced Protection works not only on your Chromebook, but also on Android and Apple phones, iPads, Windows computers, and Macs.

» On Windows, Macs, and Chromebooks, to log in to Gmail and other Google services, you must use the Chrome browser. Firefox, Edge, Safari, and other browsers won't work.

» On Android phones and iPhones, you must use the Gmail app to access email in your Google Account. Using other email apps won't work.

» If, after using Google Advanced Protection, you decide it isn't for you, you can always turn it off and go back to using Google Authenticator or just your user ID and password. Please consider using Google Authenticator at least.

TIP

I've been using Google Advanced Protection for more than five years, and speaking as a 20-year cybersecurity professional, I have found it to be rock solid and reliable and have never had a bit of a problem with it.

Figure 18-6 shows me using my Google Titan key to log in to Google on my Chromebook. To find out more about Google Advanced Protection, go to landing. google.com/advancedprotection.

**FIGURE 18-6:**
Using a Google Titan USB key to complete logging on to a Chromebook with Google Advanced Protection.

# Managing and Protecting Your Passwords

Using the internet involves having multiple user accounts that require user IDs and passwords. Trying to remember so many passwords can be downright frustrating. In this section, I discuss three methods for storing them that can make your use of passwords easier and more secure. You can store them in an online password vault, in your browser, or a hard-copy book.

**TIP**

There are some fundamental rules about passwords that I want you to understand clearly. If you learn anything from this book, it should be these password safeguards. You can find these rules in Chapter 23.

## Using an online password vault

My preferred method for storing user IDs and passwords is a password vault, which securely stores all your user IDs and passwords and provides them to you when you need them. My favorite password vaults are LastPass (at www.lastpass.com), Keeper (at www.keepersecurity.com and shown in Figure 18-7), and Dashlane (at www.dashlane.com).

FIGURE 18-7:
Using the Keeper
password vault to
store a user ID
and password.

*Illustration courtesy of Peter H. Gregory*

With an online password vault, your passwords are available on all your devices. Here are some of the essential principles regarding the use of an online password vault:

>> The password for your password vault is the only password you need to remember (other than your Google password for logging in to your Chromebook). Thus, ensure that your vault password is strong and not easily guessed by others. If anyone guesses your password vault's password, they will have *all* your passwords!

>> Use multi-factor authentication for your password vault. Your passwords are the most vital pieces of information you have, as they enable access to all of your other information.

>> Use the password-generating feature of your password vault to ensure that every password is strong and different from every other password you use. This way, if a website is hacked and the intruder obtains your password, it will work *only* for that one website and no other.

TIP

Selecting a password vault solution is crucial because you're entrusting another party to keep your passwords safe. This is why using known, trusted brands like those mentioned in this section is essential. These companies are, after all, storing all your important login credentials. If this prospect makes you squeamish, consider using a hard-copy book, as discussed later in this chapter.

## Storing passwords in the Chrome browser

In case using a password vault (see the preceding section) isn't for you, an alternative for your internet password storage is to use your Chromebook's default feature for storing and managing your passwords. This feature of the Chrome browser made it into the Chromebook, and it's great if you have several passwords for several online products.

REMEMBER

Don't worry: Chrome doesn't store your passwords without your permission. You must approve storing a password the first time you enter it on a particular web page, as shown in Figure 18-8.

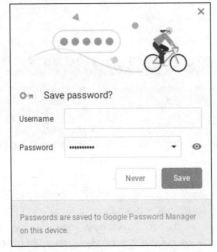

**FIGURE 18-8:**
The Chrome browser offers to store your password.

If you choose to store your password, Chrome encrypts it and stores it in your account for later use. Later, when you log in to the website, the Chrome browser automatically types it in.

TIP

If you ever forget a password, you can go to the Password Manager and click the password you've forgotten. A Show button appears that reveals your password when clicked.

You don't *have* to save passwords in your browser; however, you may find that saving them makes your web-browsing experience better. If you opt not to save a password but change your mind later, you need to delete the website from the Never Saved section of your Password Manager. To do so, follow these steps:

1. **Open the Chrome browser. You can be on any website.**

2. **Click on the three little vertical dots at the upper-right corner of the browser.**

   When you hover over the three little dots, it says Customize and control Google Chrome.

3. **Click Settings.**

4. **Click Autofill.**

5. **Click Password Manager.**

   The Password Manager window appears, revealing every stored password.

6. **In the Never Saved section, click the _X_ to the right of any website where you want Google Chrome to save your password the next time you log in.**

   Now, the next time you return to that website and enter your login credentials, you're prompted with the option to save your password, which you can approve.

## Storing passwords in a hard-copy book

You can keep your user IDs and passwords in a "little black book." This method can be the most secure of the three described in this chapter, provided that you guard that book diligently — and don't lose it!

You can purchase special-purpose, hard-copy password journals from online merchants. But seriously, you can get a small journal book and write your passwords down there. See Figure 18-9 for an example.

**TIP**

If using a password vault is intimidating, using a hard-copy notebook is a good alternative — as long you still use unique, complex passwords and keep the book safe.

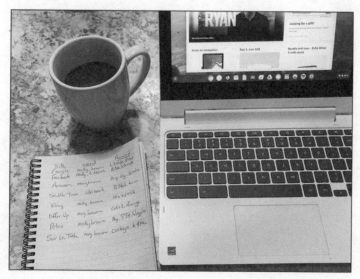

**FIGURE 18-9:** Writing your passwords down in a little black book.

*Photo courtesy of Peter H. Gregory*

# Locking Your Screen

Walking away from your Chromebook without first logging out or shutting it off can leave you vulnerable, even for only a brief moment. Locking your screen is a great way to ensure that your device, email, or Google Account isn't tampered with while you're away. You have three ways to lock your Chromebook screen:

>> Press and hold your Power button for a moment. A window appears onscreen that lets you power down, sign out, lock, or provide feedback. Click Lock.

>> Open the Settings menu on the Shelf and click the Lock button, as shown in Figure 18-10.

>> If your Chromebook has a Lock key on the keyboard (see Figure 18-11), press it for about a second, and your Chromebook will lock and display the password screen for your Google Account.

To unlock your Chromebook, enter your Google password.

The Lock button

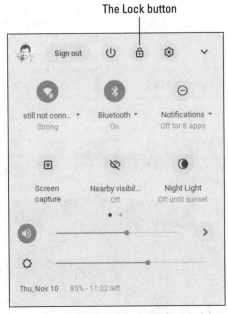

**FIGURE 18-10:** Locking your Chromebook with the Lock button in the Settings window.

*Illustration courtesy of Peter H. Gregory*

The Lock key

**FIGURE 18-11:**
Locking your
Chromebook with
the Lock key on
the keyboard.

# Setting a secure wake-from-Sleep mode

To add more security to your Chromebook, you can require a password to wake your Chromebook from Sleep mode. *Sleep mode* is a mode your Chromebook uses to conserve power when not in use. Your Chromebook automatically goes into Sleep mode after eight minutes of inactivity when plugged in and six minutes of inactivity when not plugged in. Still, you can put the Chromebook into Sleep mode immediately by closing the lid.

By default, a sleeping Chromebook is still vulnerable. Entering Sleep mode doesn't log you out or lock your screen. So, enabling a wake-from-Sleep password is probably a good idea if you rarely turn off your computer. To set this feature, log in to your Chromebook and then follow these steps:

1. Open the Settings panel on the Shelf and click Settings.

2. Click on Security and Privacy.

3. Click on Lock screen.

4. Enable the Lock in sleep mode or when the cover is closed selector, as shown in Figure 18-12.

   You may be prompted to enter your password at any point in these steps. This helps keep a bystander from changing your security settings.

From here on out, you'll need your account password to bring your computer out of Sleep mode!

**TIP**

You can also use your Android smartphone to unlock your Chromebook by toggling the Smart Lock setting shown in Figure 18-12.

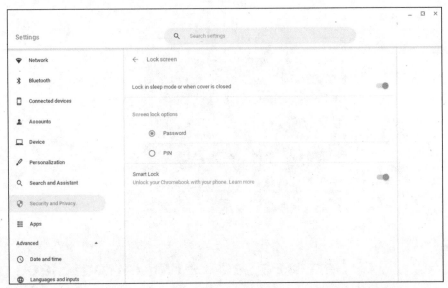

**FIGURE 18-12:**
Enabling locking
in sleep mode.

# Unlocking your Chromebook with a PIN

You can create a PIN that you can use to unlock your screen. Using a PIN instead of your password can be handy if you have a strong, complex password on your Google account, but want to quickly unlock your Chromebook without typing that long password in every time. To set up a PIN, follow these steps:

1. **Open the Settings panel on the Shelf and click Settings.**

2. **Click on Security and Privacy.**

3. **Click on Lock screen and sign-in.**

   You'll now be asked to enter your password.

4. **Type in your password.**

5. **Under Screen lock options, click on PIN or password, then click Set up PIN.**

   The Enter your PIN pane appears.

6. **Type in a PIN of six or more digits and click Continue.**

   You can use the keyboard or click the numbers on the screen.

7. **Type in the PIN a second time and click Confirm.**

   Your PIN is now set up, and you can use it to unlock your Chromebook.

# Protecting Your Network Traffic with VPN

Public hotspots such as those found in coffee shops, airports, and hotels are convenient, but most do not encrypt your data as it crosses the airwaves, which means that an attacker may be able to see the data you're sending and receiving. If you need to send sensitive data in public places, you may want to download a VPN app that encrypts your network traffic to keep it away from prying eyes.

**TECHNICAL STUFF**

VPN is short for "virtual private network," a fancy-pants way of saying that your network transmissions are encrypted from your Chromebook to the VPN service.

My favorite VPN software is Nord VPN (www.nordvpn.com), but some other good ones are available, including ExpressVPN (www.expressvpn.com) and CyberGhost VPN (www.cyberghostvpn.com). I use Nord VPN on all my devices, including Chromebooks, MacBooks, iPhone, and Android phone.

To obtain and install a VPN program, go to the Google Web Store and search for one of those mentioned here.

**WARNING**

I must caution you here: There's no such thing as a free lunch. Good VPN software comes with a modest subscription fee, typically from $35 to $75 per year. Stay away from *free* VPN services. Providing VPN service costs money, and if it's free, it's probably doing the opposite of what you want — slurping up your data and selling it.

**TIP**

Although VPN provides essential protection, occasionally, you may find some app that doesn't function while using the VPN. One of my online banking apps does not work unless I momentarily turn off the VPN software.

# Keeping Your Chromebook Up-to-Date

From time to time, Google releases software updates for the ChromeOS. Sometimes these software updates are security related, and installing them when they're available is always a good idea.

To check for updates, follow these steps:

1. **Go to Settings.**

   If a software update is available for your Chromebook, you see a message like the one shown in Figure 18-13.

2. **Click Restart to Update.**

   Your Chromebook downloads the update and restarts.

Here's another way to check for updates:

1. **Go to Settings.**
2. **Scroll down and click About ChromeOS.**
3. **Click Check for updates.**

   If a new update is available, you'll be prompted to restart your Chromebook to install the update.

   If no update is available, it will say Your Chromebook is up to date.

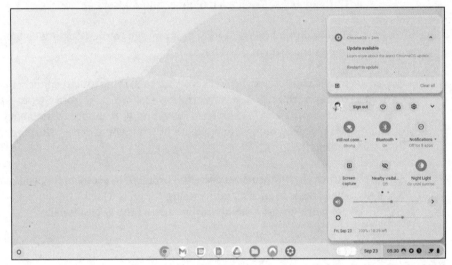

Illustration courtesy of Peter H. Gregory

**FIGURE 18-13:** Checking your Chromebook for updates.

When you click Settings, you may also see a message like the one shown in Figure 18-14 that tells you that apps you downloaded from the Google Play Store have updates available. When you see this message, click Update All.

You can check proactively for app updates if you don't see a notification like the one in Figure 18-14. Follow these steps:

1. **Open the Google Play Store.**
2. **Click on your photo, avatar, or initials in the upper-right corner.**

3. **Click Manage apps and device.**

4. **On the next screen, look for the words Updates available, as shown in Figure 18-15.**

5. **Click Update all.**

   The apps on your Chromebook with available updates will be updated.

**FIGURE 18-14:**
Updating
software from a
notification.

*Illustration courtesy of Peter H. Gregory*

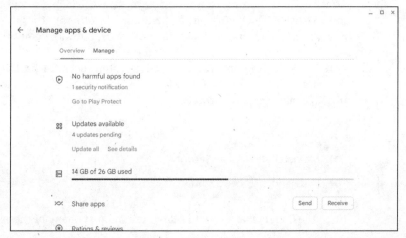

**FIGURE 18-15:**
Updating
software in the
Google Play
Store.

*Illustration courtesy of Peter H. Gregory*

**TIP**

In checking for ChromeOS updates, you're just looking at your notifications. It's a good idea to get into the habit of glancing down at the lower-right corner of the screen at the notifications area to see whether ChromeOS wants to tell you things, such as about updates and other issues.

# Protection from Viruses and Other Malware

Microsoft products MS-DOS and Windows have been plagued with computer viruses and other malware since practically the beginning of time. Android phones are now the biggest target of malware, and even the Apple Mac and iPhone are attacked. What about Chromebooks? Well, because ChromeOS is functionally similar to Android, it's safe to say that hackers are working on attacks on Chromebooks.

Even if few or no viruses target Chromebooks specifically, two potent threats exist that are highly relevant: attacks on the Chrome browser, and malicious Chrome browser extensions. Because Chrome is the world's most popular browser, attacks against Chrome occur regularly.

Attacks against Chrome can, for instance, steal the login credentials you use to log in to websites (including online banking and others). These password-stealing attacks are one of the most significant threats, but they're not the only ones.

Anti-malware programs for Chromebooks stop such attacks. I highly recommend that you select one of the following apps and install it to protect you from these invisible but very potent threats:

>> AVG AntiVirus & Security (see Figure 18-16)

>> Malwarebytes Mobile Security

>> Bitdefender Mobile Security

Go to the Google Play Store to search for and install any of these.

**TIP**

Although you may be protected from internet hazards by one of the tools mentioned earlier or something similar, you should not throw caution to the wind and assume that these programs will bail you out of every kind of trouble. The nature of cybercrime makes it better for you to remain diligent even if you are protected by one of these programs.

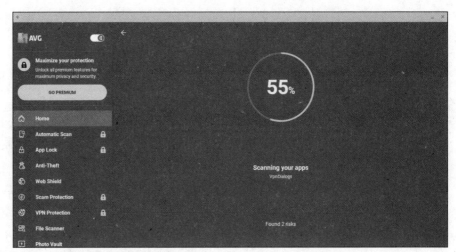

**FIGURE 18-16:**
AVG scanning a
Chromebook
for security
threats and
vulnerabilities.

# Protecting Your Chromebook from Prying Eyes and Thieves

Covering your webcam or using a screen filter is an easy and inexpensive way to protect your privacy, and using a cable lock is a great way to secure your Chromebook in a public space.

## Cover your webcam

Your Chromebook most likely has a built-in camera that faces you so you can do live video chats, as I discuss in Chapter 15. As a security precaution, I recommend that you employ some sort of a cover for your webcam when you're not using it. You may forget to end a video call, or an attacker could figure out how to access Chromebook webcams. (This advice doesn't apply only to Chromebooks but also to some smart TVs — but good luck locating a secret camera on a TV!) You're better safe than sorry, particularly if your Chromebook is in private areas of your home, such as your bedroom.

Several methods are available for covering your webcam. You can use a purpose-made webcam cover (search "webcam cover" online to see what they look like). These are available at online retailers for minimal cost, and they're often given away at computer and electronics trade shows. Or you can take the budget route and use a small piece of washi tape, masking tape, or a part of a sticky note.

# Use a privacy screen filter

If you spend much time working with sensitive content on your Chromebook and find that you're doing this in public places like coffee shops and airports, you may want to consider getting a computer screen privacy filter for your Chromebook. A privacy filter makes it easy for you to view the content on your screen but more difficult (and nearly impossible) for others to view what's on your screen. In case you're not sure what I'm talking about, Figure 18-17 shows a typical privacy filter on a Chromebook.

**FIGURE 18-17:**
A privacy filter makes it more difficult for others to view the data on your screen.

*Image courtesy of 3M*

A computer screen privacy filter is a thin, semitransparent piece of plastic that goes over the top of your laptop screen. Often it's affixed with an adhesive that lets you remove the filter when you want to. The filter permits anyone directly in front of the laptop (you, and anyone right behind you) to view the screen, but anyone to the left or right of you is unable to view what is on your screen.

# Preventing the theft of your Chromebook

If you are concerned about the actual theft of your Chromebook (and who wouldn't be!), you'll be glad to know that most Chromebooks come with a Kensington lock slot that allows you to attach a specially made security lock to your Chromebook to deter theft. In Figure 18-18, you can see how I lock my Chromebook with one of my security cable locks.

Photo courtesy of Peter H. Gregory

**FIGURE 18-18:**
Locking your
Chromebook
with a security
cable lock.

IN THIS CHAPTER

» **Troubleshooting network connections and browser issues**

» **Rectifying power issues**

» **Finding Chromebook help online**

» **Utilizing the Chromebook Recovery Utility**

» **Resetting your Chromebook to factory settings**

Chapter **19**

# Troubleshooting Your Chromebook

Technology is great until something breaks. The reality is, we live in an imperfect world, and nothing works perfectly all the time, even well-designed technology. It's always good to consider those areas in which life with your Chromebook can occasionally go sideways.

This chapter shows you how to troubleshoot network connectivity issues because you can't use your Chromebook to the fullest without internet access. You also find out how to troubleshoot and possibly remedy problems with your battery. If the sky starts falling and your Chromebook operating system becomes corrupt, you want to be sure you have a restore disk available to reinstall ChromeOS and get back to work as fast as possible. If all else fails, Google has a vast database of helpful resources online to provide solutions for any Chromebook problem. This chapter tells you where to go and how to search through these resources to get answers fast!

# Resolving Internet-Connectivity Problems

Chromebooks require a connection to the internet to serve their full purpose in the portable-computing ecosystem. Every Chromebook comes equipped with high-speed Wi-Fi. Some Chromebooks even come with cellular connectivity, allowing them to get online wherever a cell signal is present.

Generally speaking, once you configure your Chromebook to connect to a Wi-Fi access point to reach the internet, your Chromebook will remember the network and its settings. You should never have to worry about its Wi-Fi settings again (unless the network owner changes its password).

If you're having trouble connecting to a wireless network, check these possible solutions before calling tech support:

» **Ensure that the Chromebook's Wi-Fi controller is turned on.** Check the Wi-Fi indicator in the settings panel of the shelf. If the Wi-Fi indicator is gray and the words Not Connected appear beneath it, as shown in Figure 19-1, the wireless adapter has been shut off. (For your reference, Bluetooth is turned on, so you can see the difference.) Turn Wi-Fi on by following these steps:

1. **Open the settings panel on the shelf and click the Wi-Fi icon.**

2. **In the menu that appears, click the Wi-Fi icon.**

   Your wireless adapter turns on, and the Wi-Fi logo turns from gray to blue, allowing you to select from all available Wi-Fi networks.

» **Make sure your Chromebook is connected to a Wi-Fi network.** Look at the Wi-Fi indicator in your shelf's settings area. If you're still having trouble, verify that you're connected to the correct network by following these steps:

1. **Click anywhere in the settings panel on the shelf.**

   The settings menu appears, revealing several options. Just below the Wi-Fi logo is the name of the network to which your Chromebook is connected.

2. **If the connected network isn't the network you want to connect to, click the text just below the Wi-Fi icon.**

   The Wi-Fi Network menu appears.

3. **Scroll through the list to find the desired network, and then select it by clicking it.**

   Figure 19-2 shows Wi-Fi network controls, indicators, and a list of available networks to connect to.

Wi-Fi is turned off

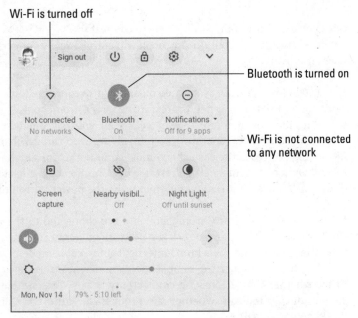

Bluetooth is turned on

Wi-Fi is not connected
to any network

Illustration courtesy of Peter H. Gregory

**FIGURE 19-1:**
The wireless
adapter is
turned off.

Previous menu     Network info     All Chromebook settings

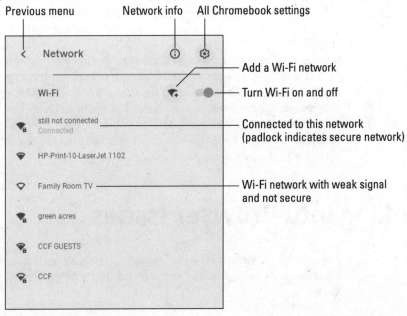

Add a Wi-Fi network

Turn Wi-Fi on and off

Connected to this network
(padlock indicates secure network)

Wi-Fi network with weak signal
and not secure

**FIGURE 19-2:**
Selecting a Wi-Fi
network for an
internet
connection.

Illustration courtesy of Peter H. Gregory

**TIP**

Once you configure your Chromebook to connect to a Wi-Fi network, including the network's password, your Chromebook will automatically connect to that network when it is available.

If your wireless controller is turned on and you're connected to a network but still can't connect to the internet, try restarting your Chromebook. This restart flushes your Chromebook memory, power cycles all your Chromebook hardware, and restarts the ChromeOS operating system, giving everything a chance to start fresh. Restarting devices is the easiest and most common fix for glitches like connecting to a network or the internet. To restart your Chromebook, click on the status area of the shelf, click Shut Down, and then press the power button to restart.

If you've restarted your Chromebook and are connected to the network but still can't connect to the internet, ask the network owner to restart the internet gateway. The gateway may be a home internet router, cable modem, or DSL modem. If you're at home, in an office, or at school, you may want to check with other users to see whether they are having connectivity issues. This simple troubleshooting should quickly indicate whether the problem is with your Chromebook or the Wi-Fi network itself.

**TIP**

To test the speed and health of your internet connection, open your browser and go to www.fast.com. You'll see how fast your internet connection is. You'll get a "site unreachable" error if you can't reach the internet.

If your smartphone can provide a mobile Wi-Fi hotspot, you may want to turn it on and see whether your Chromebook can connect to it and access the internet. A word of caution: Unless you are on an unlimited data plan, you want to do this only temporarily as a test to see whether your Chromebook can reach the internet via a different Wi-Fi access point. If you can reach the internet through your smartphone's Wi-Fi hotspot, then the other Wi-Fi network you are trying to connect to is probably having problems.

# Looking into Browser Issues

From to time, browsers seem to take a holiday and not work quite right. Sometimes, though, it's just the website that's being ornery. But how can you know?

Some of the problems you're likely to run into include:

>> Websites won't load, or they are "stuck."

>> Websites seem to load partially but are missing images, or pages look incomplete.

>> Websites can't be reached.

When I'm troubleshooting issues like this, these are the actions I try:

>> **Close the tab and then try the website on a different tab.** Believe it or not, this approach sometimes works.

>> **Close and restart the browser.** I usually configure my browser to continue where I left off, meaning all the tabs I had open when I last used my browser will still be there when I restart it (or restart the Chromebook itself). Figure 19-3 shows the Continue where you left off setting, under On start up in the Settings window.

>> **Remove any recently-installed browser extensions.** Sometimes, a browser extension will change how your browser works, often in subtle ways. You can disable or remove a browser extension if you recently installed one. In the Chrome browser, hover over the icon near the upper right corner that looks like a jigsaw puzzle piece (the word Extensions appears). You can turn extensions off and on. After doing this, you may want to restart your browser also.

>> **Try another browser.** On every device I use for internet access, I have the browser that the system came with (Safari on iPhones, iPads, and Macs; Chrome on Android phones and Chromebooks), and I have at least one other browser. I usually have *two* spare browsers, as follows:

- **Firefox:** This is a very secure and user-friendly browser that is popular and has been around for a long time.

- **Brave:** This browser is very much like Chrome itself, and it will run most — if not all — Chrome browser extensions. In every way that matters, Brave is like Chrome, except that it does not send tracking information to Google.

  Brave and Firefox are available in the Google Web Store. Click the launcher, click Google Web Store, search for Firefox or Brave, and install it.

>> **Disconnect Wi-Fi and then reconnect to it.** I cover this suggestion earlier in this chapter. It just may help!

- » **Sign out of your Chromebook.** Signing out and then signing back in may fix things. Figure 19-5 shows the Sign Out icon in the upper-left corner of the settings pane. Click in the status area (where the date and time appear) to show this pane.

- » **Try browsing as Guest.** To see whether you have an issue with your user account on the Chromebook, try signing out and then signing back in as Guest. Remember, though, as a Guest, you can't save any files or access or save a bookmark. However, this is a handy little test to see what works and what doesn't.

- » **Clear the browser cache and cookies.** Now and then, one or more websites won't load or work correctly because the browser and the website get confused and can't get along. The remedy: clearing the browser cache and cookies. To do this, follow these steps:

  1. **In the Chrome browser, click on the settings icon (three little vertical dots).**

  2. **Click Privacy and security.**

  3. **Click Clear browsing data.**

     The Clear browsing data pane appears.

  4. **Make sure you are on the Basic tab.**

  5. **Check the Cookies and other site data and Cached images and files boxes, and uncheck the other boxes. See Figure 19-4.**

  6. **Click Clear data.**

     Go back and try the websites you had trouble with again.

     Note that this procedure will log you out of any websites you were logged into. This is a byproduct of clearing cookies.

- » **Restart your Chromebook.** Sometimes, restarting (also called rebooting) your Chromebook is the only action that helps. Click Shut Down (refer to Figure 19-5), and then, after your Chromebook has powered off, press the Power button to restart it.

If none of these efforts fix your problem, skip to the "Finding Help Online" and "Using the Chromebook Recovery Utility" sections, later in this chapter.

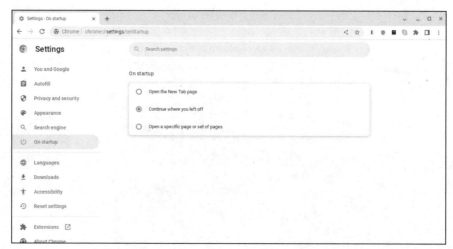

FIGURE 19-3:
Configuring
Chrome to restart
where it left off.

FIGURE 19-4:
Clearing the
Chrome browser
cache and
cookies.

TIP

You should download and run — at least once — an alternative browser today. If Chrome is giving you fits, you may also have trouble using the Google Play Store to find, download, and install another browser.

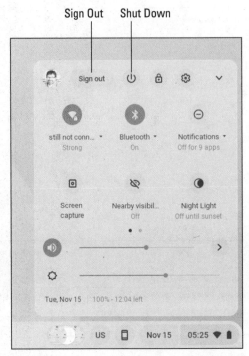

Sign Out    Shut Down

**FIGURE 19-5:**
The Sign out and Shut down icons.

## GOOGLE AND PRIVACY

Google has a marvelous ecosystem of computers (Chromebook, Chromebase, Android) and online services (Gmail, books, movies, chat, meet, search, and so many more) that work well to enrich users' internet experience. Sometimes, it seems as though Google (and others, which I won't name here, but you know who they are) knows a little too much about its users. I've heard anecdotal stories that make some people feel creepy, like, "We were talking about getting a new ski parka today, and now I'm seeing ads for ski parkas online."

If you feel like your privacy is being invaded, there are a couple of things that you can do. First, configure the Chrome browser's Do Not Track feature. Or, go further and stop using Chrome altogether. Use the Firefox or Brave browser instead. (You should configure Do Not Track on those browsers also.) Although you would still be using a Google-powered computer, the feeling of improved privacy is sure to improve your peace of mind.

# Resolving Power Problems

Sometimes batteries go bad. Sometimes they even go out in a literal blaze of glory. Don't worry: The odds of such happenings with your Chromebook battery are lower than your chances of winning the lottery. However, Chromebooks — just like other brands of laptops — can have power problems like the following:

» **Your battery's charge doesn't last nearly as long as it should, or its capability to stay charged decreases with each use.** Refer to your device manual (which could be a single sheet of paper with a URL or QR code) or look online to identify estimated battery life based on your level of device usage. Then verify your Chromebook's battery consumption by following these steps:

1. **Plug your Chromebook into the power charger until you reach a 100 percent charge.**

2. **Verify your battery's charge level by opening the settings panel on your shelf and examining the battery indicator at the bottom.**

3. **Verify that the battery indicator says Battery Full before disconnecting your power charger.**

Take note of the time and begin working with your Chromebook. Recheck the battery indicator to monitor how quickly it reduces in charge. When the battery is low enough to justify plugging it in, take note of the time again to see how long it lasted. If it's within normal usage limits as defined by the manufacturer of your Chromebook, you may want to adjust your usage. Maybe your screen is a bit on the bright side, for instance. Reducing the brightness level also reduces battery usage. If you have a backlit keyboard, you can try turning down the brightness.

On the other hand, if your battery loses charge faster than your manufacturer's specifications, follow these steps before returning your Chromebook to the manufacturer or point of purchase:

1. **Plug your Chromebook into a power source and charge the battery to 100 percent.**

2. **When the Chromebook has reached 100 percent, unplug it and use the device until power dwindles to 5 percent or less, but not until it shuts off.**

3. **Repeat this process at least ten times before testing to see whether the battery life has extended.**

If your battery still won't maintain a charge, return it to the point of purchase or contact the manufacturer for service. If your Chromebook is no longer under warranty, you may be able to have a local computer repair shop replace the battery. Or, maybe it's time for a new Chromebook.

Another influence on battery life to consider is your browser. One of the tabs on your browser may be running code on your computer nonstop. Unfortunately, no easy way exists to confirm this suspicion. Closing specific browser tabs, or exiting the browser altogether, may help you to isolate the problem of excessive CPU usage. Another app running in the background can also be the culprit: Try exiting all the other apps running on your Chromebook to see whether doing so helps.

» **The battery won't charge, so your Chromebook must stay connected to the power adapter, or your Chromebook won't turn on when plugged in**. Try using another power adapter. If the symptoms persist with the other power adapter, your battery is likely toast. If the other power adapter rectifies the situation, you likely have a faulty power adapter.

If your Chromebook is one of the newer models with USB-C power (see Figure 19-6 for an example), you may be able to easily find another power adaptor to try. USB-C is becoming the new standard for laptop power plugs. If, on the other hand, your power cord is the "metal tip" variety like the one shown in Figure 19-7, you'll probably need to obtain another battery from the manufacturer.

Always invest in a good surge protector for your Chromebook. I don't mean a cheap power strip, but a decent surge protector — the kind that comes with a "we'll replace your damaged equipment" guarantee. Dirty power, with spikes, dips, surges, and so on, affects a laptop's power supply.

**FIGURE 19-6:**
A USB-C style power adaptor.

*Illustration courtesy of Peter H. Gregory*

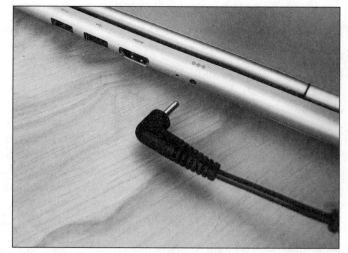

FIGURE 19-7:
A "metal tip" style
power adaptor.

*Illustration courtesy of Peter H. Gregory*

# Finding Help Online

If you ever find yourself in a situation you can't solve with this book or your Chromebook's help manuals, try the Chromebook Help Center online. You can visit the Help Center, shown in Figure 19-8, at support.google.com/chromebook. The Help Center answers some of the most common Chromebook questions relating to setup, connecting a Chromebook to the internet, printing, working with media, and more. If your question is a little more refined and technical, you can explore the Chromebook Help Forum, where you can ask questions and receive helpful answers — or find others who have had the same issues, with helpful answers waiting to be found.

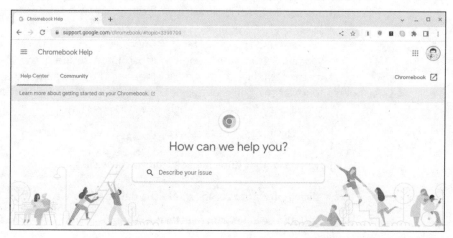

FIGURE 19-8:
The online
Chromebook
Help Center.

*Illustration courtesy of Peter H. Gregory*

After arriving at the Help Forum, you can search or browse topics. The easiest way to get started is to type your problem or issue in the Search bar and press Enter. For example, if you're having issues with the battery in your Chromebook, search with the following query: **Chromebook battery problem**. Or you can get more specific: **Chromebook battery will not hold a charge**. Several results will appear for you to browse through.

**TIP**

If you have a question you want to post, make sure to do a thorough search through the Forum before posting your question. Forums are websites where the general public can converse on a specific topic or range of topics. Although the Google forums (including the Chromebook Help Forum) are moderated to ensure that everyone is playing nicely, you may still rub people the wrong way if you post a question that has already been asked and answered.

**TIP**

If your problem seems more related to your Chromebook's hardware than its software, you can contact the manufacturer's website for help. Fortunately, the Chromebook Help Center can guide you to it. On the main page of the Chromebook Help Center, scroll down and click Find device support. Then click Get Help From Your Chromebook Manufacturer. There you see a page with all the Chromebook manufacturers, along with support telephone numbers and links to support websites.

# Powerwashing Your Chromebook

*Powerwash* is the term used to return your Chromebook to its factory settings. You may be selling your Chromebook or giving it to a friend or family member, at which point it's a good idea to erase all of your files and your account(s). You may also feel like it's gone awry and may have even been advised through Google's Chromebook Help to powerwash your Chromebook.

**WARNING**

You can't undo powerwashing any more than you can unbreak an egg. After you click Restart, your Chromebook becomes a secure, power-cleaning machine. Nothing on the device will be left. The good news is that it won't touch anything on your Google Drive or other web services. But anything stored locally on your Chromebook will be gone forever.

Your Chromebook restarts, as clean as can be — just like new.

To powerwash your Chromebook, follow these easy steps:

1.  **Click in the status area (where the date and time appear).**

2.  **Click the Settings icon (a little gear).**

3. **Scroll the menu on the left all the way down and click Reset settings.**

   The Reset settings section appears.

4. **Click the Reset button to the right of Powerwash, as shown in Figure 19-9.**

   The Restart your device pane appears, telling you that your Chromebook must be restarted to commence the powerwash.

5. **Click Restart if you are sure you want to continue.**

   Your Chromebook will restart and be reset. You'll see the welcome screen you saw when you first got your Chromebook and turned it on.

**FIGURE 19-9:** The Powerwash feature completely resets your Chromebook to factory settings.

*Illustration courtesy of Peter H. Gregory*

# Using the Chromebook Recovery Utility

ChromeOS is great, but it's not an infallible operating system. Things can go awry with your Chromebook. If your Chromebook ever gives you a message saying ChromeOS Is Missing or Damaged, you may have to reinstall the operating system. Reinstalling the operating system removes all locally stored data from your Chromebook, but if you're getting the missing-or-damaged error, chances are you've already lost your data.

Google has provided a way for you to recover your Chromebook. The process is relatively simple; it involves downloading a recovery program and storing it on an external USB drive or SD card. If your Chromebook is dead or dying, chances are you can't use your Chromebook to do this. But the good news is you can create a recovery program using another computer, even a Windows or a Mac.

Reinstalling the ChromeOS operating system requires a recovery drive (such as a USB jump drive or an SD card) to get you back up and running. To create a recovery drive, follow these steps:

1. **Do one of the following:**

   - **If you are on a Chromebook, open the Chrome Web Store and search for Chromebook Recovery Utility.**

   - **If you are on a PC or a Mac, open the Chrome browser and go to the Chrome Web Store at** chrome.google.com/webstore. **Search for Chromebook Recovery Utility.**

     You may need to log in to your Google account as well.

     If the utility isn't found, try a Google search for Chromebook Recovery Utility.

2. **Add the extension to your browser.**

   Figure 19-10 shows this app. As the figure shows, I did this on my Mac to show how you can use another computer to jumpstart your Chromebook.

3. **Launch the utility when the browser extension has been added, as shown in Figure 19-11.**

   The Chromebook Recovery Utility launches.

4. **Follow the prompts until you're asked to enter the model number of your Chromebook.**

5. **Click Continue.**

   The Utility asks you to insert a USB drive or SD card, as shown in Figure 19-12.

6. **Select the media you want to use as your recovery drive and click Continue.**

WARNING

Anything still on your USB drive or SD card will be deleted after you create the recovery image. Now is the time to ensure that you use the right media.

7. **Click Create Now.**

   Your Chromebook begins downloading and installing the software needed to make your recovery drive.

TIP

Right about now, you should be getting a cup of coffee and reviewing your stocks because this process takes 10–20 minutes.

Chromebook notifies you when your recovery media has been successfully created.

8. **Remove your SD card or USB drive from your Chromebook and click Done.**

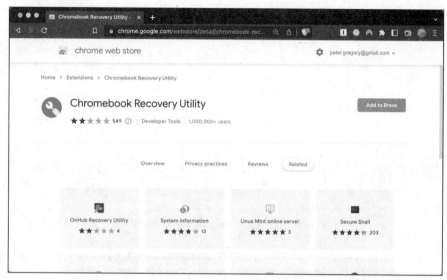

**FIGURE 19-10:**
Installing the
Chromebook
Recovery Utility.

*Illustration courtesy of Peter H. Gregory*

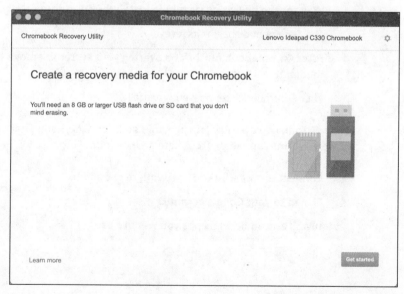

**FIGURE 19-11:**
Launching the
Chromebook
Recovery Utility.

*Illustration courtesy of Peter H. Gregory*

Insert your USB flash drive or SD card

Select the media you'd like to use.

SMI USB DISK - 29.3 GB

Learn more                                                    Go back        Continue

**FIGURE 19-12:**
Insert your USB
drive or SD card.

*Illustration courtesy of Peter H. Gregory*

To recover your Chromebook by reinstalling ChromeOS, follow these steps:

1. **At the ChromeOS Is Missing or Damaged screen, insert the recovery media into your Chromebook's USB or SD slot.**

   Your Chromebook automatically detects the recovery media.

2. **Wait for the operating system to install the OS automatically.**

   The Chromebook begins its recovery.

3. **After Chromebook finishes recovering your system, remove the recovery media.**

   Your Chromebook reboots automatically.

Your Chromebook is now in the same state as when you first purchased it and powered it on. Your steps from here are the following:

1. **Connect to a nearby Wi-Fi network to get online.**

2. **Sign in to your Google account.**

3. **Install any additional apps you want to use.**

## BACK UP YOUR DATA

Although most of the data you work with on your Chromebook is already online, important data can still be stored locally on your Chromebook. If this is the case, copying this data to Google Drive or a local storage device, whether to a hard drive or SD card, is essential. If your Chromebook suffers a ChromeOS malfunction requiring you to recover your Chromebook, or if your Chromebook is lost, stolen, or develops a serious hardware problem, chances are that any data that resides *only* on your Chromebook is gone forever, unless you first took the time to make a copy.

If you're reading this, hoping there may be a way to recover data stored only on your dead or dying Chromebook, I'm sorry, but you may be out of luck. If you're not in such dire straits, remember: The time to back up your data is today, while you still can.

All your Google experiences, such as Gmail, books, docs, sheets, photos, movies, and chats, will be right where you left them. Also, if you are a Microsoft Office 365 user, your documents and spreadsheets will be waiting for you. All you will have lost is any data stored locally on your Chromebook.

**TIP**

I've used multiple Chromebooks daily for four years, including a couple used by relatives and friends. At no time has it ever been necessary to powerwash a Chromebook, nor recover it as discussed here. ChromeOS is a solid product.

# 5

# The Part of Tens

Chapter **20**

# Ten (Plus One) Hardware Features to Consider When Buying a Chromebook

I f you haven't purchased a Chromebook yet, the tips in this chapter will help you figure out what features will best serve your needs. If you already own a Chromebook, this chapter explains how to understand the hardware in your Chromebook and how it contributes to your Chromebook experience. I point out the most important features to most users so that you can choose wisely and get the best Chromebook for your money.

If you're a serious, detail-oriented shopper, write down the features that are most important ("have to haves") and those that are less important ("nice to haves"). Knowing what activities you expect to use your Chromebook for can make the more critical features evident.

I recommend shopping for Chromebooks in person, rather than online, so you can become familiar with the *feel* of Chromebooks, particularly with the size of the screen and keyboard. Some stores have a display area with computers turned on where you can try ChromeOS in guest mode.

If, while shopping for a Chromebook, you find a nice Windows laptop with features you like, keep moving. You want a Chromebook, and it must say Chromebook (or Chrome) to be a Chromebook. Chromebooks don't run Windows, and Windows laptops and tablets don't run ChromeOS. They may look the same from a distance, but they're not the same.

In this chapter, I tell you about important features that are sure to make a difference in the usefulness and enjoyment of your Chromebook.

# Screen

When it comes to Chromebook specifications, it's all about the screen. Through the screen, you see the world on your Chromebook, whether you're working or running your business, viewing vacation pictures, chatting with friends over video, or checking your banking transactions online.

Here are the five primary aspects of the screen that are important to understand:

>> **Size:** Measured diagonally from one upper corner to the opposite lower corner, the size of the screen directly translates into your viewing experience. Generally, the larger, the better — to a point. A larger screen makes for a larger Chromebook. I prefer nothing smaller than 13 inches, but your needs may differ. You can go as big as a whopping 17 inches.

>> **Resolution:** This specification is all about the level of detail you want to see on the screen. You want at least *Full HD* quality, which requires a resolution of 1920 x 1080, meaning 1,920 pixels (dots) in width and 1,080 pixels (dots) in height. This pixel count is the resolution of a standard movie you view on Netflix, Hulu, or Amazon Prime. Bigger numbers mean that images will be even more detailed: There are 4K Chromebooks with a resolution of 3840 x 2160.

>> **Touchscreen:** Many Chromebooks are equipped with a touchscreen. The touchscreen makes your Chromebook's screen perform like a tablet or smartphone: You can touch it to launch apps, scroll in windows, draw, and even type.

- » **Stylus:** Some Chromebooks come with a *stylus*, also called a *pencil*, an electronic pencil used instead of your finger on a touchscreen. A stylus can also be purchased separately if your Chromebook has a touchscreen (a few Chromebooks come with one).

- » **Convertible:** Some touchscreen Chromebooks are *convertible*, which means that the screen pivots around to the back, turning your Chromebook laptop into a tablet computer. My Lenovo C330 Chromebook does this, and it's like having two computers in one: You have a laptop when you want it, and you have a tablet when you want it. It gives you the best of both worlds.

One crucial point about screen size: Chromebooks with screens that are smaller than 13 inches have a keyboard that may seem small and crowded. If you type a lot, you may be dissatisfied with an 11-inch Chromebook; the keyboard may seem awfully cramped. You could, however, get an external keyboard, but for the money you would spend on that, you could get a Chromebook with a larger screen — 13, 15, or even 17 inches.

# Processor

Also known as the CPU (an acronym for *central processing unit*), the *processor* is the brain of every computer. Here are the two main factors to know about the CPU:

- » **Processor speed, measured in gigahertz (GHz):** This rating indicates how fast your processor can perform calculations. The higher the number, the faster the calculations.

- » **Number of cores:** Each core can perform one operation at a time. *Multiple cores* means that multiple processes can happen simultaneously. Hence, having more cores equals a faster processor.

These two components are key drivers in overall processor performance, and more, in this case, is better.

However, the faster the processor and the more cores it has, the more expensive it is and the more electricity it consumes, shortening battery life. Believe me when I tell you that Chromebooks don't need much power: The processor doesn't need to be over-the-top fast!

# Memory

Another critical factor in the performance of a Chromebook (and any other computer) is the quantity of memory present. *Memory* is high-speed, short-term storage, often referred to as RAM. When you open a program, the program is loaded into memory so that it can be run. Naturally, the more memory you have, the more browser tabs you can open and the more apps you can run simultaneously. Chromebooks, however, don't load many programs into memory. Therefore, a large amount of memory is not necessary. A computer's memory is measured in gigabytes (GB), and your Chromebook should have anywhere from 4 GB to 16 GB. Four gigabytes (4-8 GB) is adequate for the average user. Avoid Chromebooks with 2 GB of RAM.

# Storage Capacity

Formerly called the *hard drive,* a computer's ability to store data is often just called its storage capacity.

Look for at least 64GB of storage. If you plan to store a lot of photos and videos directly on your Chromebook, look for 64GB or more. This will seem tiny compared to Windows and Macs, whose storage capacity ranges from 250GB to 1,000 GB (the same as 1 TB, or *terabyte*) and even more! But remember, a big part of the Chromebook experience is the fact that the Chrome OS itself is very small, and most of your content is stored online. (See Chapter 7 for the skinny on using online content on Google Drive.)

**TECHNICAL STUFF**

Virtually all Chromebooks' storage is on some form of electronic-based storage, called an SSD (solid state drive) or eMMC (another form of solid-state drive). Few, if any, new Chromebooks have mechanical hard drives, known as HDD. Hard drives are a thousand times slower than their SSD and eMMC counterparts.

# Webcam

Virtually all Chromebooks come with built-in webcams. If you are interested in video chats with coworkers, friends, or family, a webcam built into your Chromebook is a must; otherwise, you need to buy one and plug it into a USB port.

If high video quality is essential to you (in the case of a webcam, this means the image quality of *you* that people view on *their* computers), look for a webcam that is at least HD (1920p) quality. Most, though, are lower — 720p, for instance — and are adequate for most purposes.

# Internet Connection

To be fully useful, Chromebooks require an internet connection. The connection can come in three forms:

» Built-in Wi-Fi to connect to wireless networks. All Chromebooks have this.

» A hardwired connection to an Ethernet cable, which, for virtually all Chromebooks, requires an adaptor that typically plugs into a USB port.

» Cellular options that you use to activate a wireless internet data plan with a national provider such as Verizon, T-Mobile, or AT&T. Some Chromebook models come with these options. Cellular capability may be termed LTE or 5G, which are cellular data protocols. Of these, LTE is decent, but 5G is much faster — if you live in an area with good coverage.

If you expect to frequently visit locations with no accessible Wi-Fi, and you don't have a mobile hotspot or a phone that can produce a mobile hotspot, you should consider purchasing a Chromebook with the cellular option built in. Otherwise, you'll be "tethering" your Chromebook with your smartphone's built-in Wi-Fi hotspot (check your smartphone specs *and* your mobile carrier's data plan).

Many Chromebooks are listed as having "faster Wi-Fi," or Wi-Fi with the latest high-speed standards such as "Gigabit Wi-Fi," Wi-Fi 6, or 802.11ax. Mostly, this claim means nothing if most of your Chromebook work involves visiting websites. That's because if you have a 15 Mbps internet connection, web pages will load no faster than that, no matter how fast your Wi-Fi is — whether it's just as fast or 50 times faster. Ultra-fast Wi-Fi matters *only* if you are doing advanced work, such as connecting wirelessly to a storage server and transferring large amounts of data. With a few exceptions, the speed of your Wi-Fi is governed by the speed of your internet connection.

# Battery

Battery life, which is usually a big deal with portable devices like laptop computers, smartphones, and earbuds, is an essential feature of the Chromebook. If you compare the specifications of different devices, you find that the battery life of more powerful devices is typically shorter. Although this situation is also the case with the Chromebook, a Chromebook tends to have a *longer* battery life because its operating system is streamlined and doesn't run much software or require ultra-powerful hardware.

If battery life is important to you, the only battery-centric specification that matters is the number of hours of battery life you can expect to get. However, as with fuel economy in an automobile, *your mileage may vary.* On a laptop, you can greatly influence battery life by adjusting the brightness of the screen and by turning off Wi-Fi and/or Bluetooth when not in use.

# SD Card Slot

An *SD card* is a tiny, inexpensive storage device you typically find in digital cameras, home security cameras, and dashcams. Some Chromebooks come with an SD card slot, which enables you to view content easily from these devices. SD cards are also handy for storing and transferring photos and videos between computers, among other file types. The ability to quickly add external storage with a collection of SD cards is valuable, especially if you have an extensive library of photos, videos, movies, or other files that you want to access quickly.

# HDMI Port

*HDMI,* which stands for High-Definition Multimedia Interface in case you're curious, is a type of interface primarily used for high-definition video and audio. If you want to connect your Chromebook to a high-definition external monitor or a flat-screen TV, you should ensure that your Chromebook comes with an HDMI port.

TIP

HDMI ports enable you to use your television as an external monitor. Connecting your Chromebook to your TV via HDMI turns your Chromebook into a portable media center! In many cases, however, you can also "cast" your content wirelessly to your smart TV, but the quality won't be quite the same.

# USB Ports (Including USB-C)

USB is the standard for attaching devices to laptops and desktop computers. It has also become the standard for digitally powering and charging electronic devices. The question you need to ask yourself when selecting a Chromebook is not *whether* it has a USB port, but *how many* USB ports it has. If you use a USB mouse and need another port for a USB keyboard or external storage device, you should ensure that your Chromebook has more than one USB port. (Many people opt for a wireless Bluetooth mouse and keyboard to save their USB ports for other uses, such as external hard drives.)

You want to be sure that your Chromebook is USB 3.0 instead of the older USB 2.0. If you connect an external hard drive to your Chromebook to copy data into or from your Chromebook regularly, you immediately see the difference between the newer and older USB: Data transfers about ten times faster with USB 3.0 than with USB 2.0.

USB-C is becoming a standard on laptop computers, including Chromebooks. If you have any USB-C–connected devices that you want to use with your Chromebook, you may want to look for a Chromebook with at least two USB-C ports. If you are looking at a Chromebook that charges through a USB-C port, find out whether that same port can *also* be used to connect a device like an external hard drive.

TIP

If the Chromebook you are looking at has only USB-C ports and you have devices with the older USB-A port, take heart: inexpensive adaptors are available from better computer stores and online merchants.

# Backlit Keyboard

If you use your laptop in a dimly lit room or on nighttime airline flights, you'll want a backlit keyboard. A backlit keyboard makes a big difference in low light even if you are a good touch typer.

Chapter **21**

# Ten (Plus One) Handy Chromebook Shortcuts

A Chromebook is made to be easy to use right out of the box. It's not a self-driving car, but it's almost as easy. Get it out, plug it in, turn it on, and follow the prompts: You'll be up and running in minutes. Still, even though Chromebook is very usable, you may want to do further customization. This chapter contains eleven tips, tricks, and shortcuts to make your Chromebook experience more productive — or at least a little more fun.

## Search from the Launcher

The Google platform is baked into the Chromebook and ChromeOS through and through. The point, when the Chromebook was created, was to showcase the extensive Google ecosystem of applications. One way the Google platform is integrated into ChromeOS is the Chromebook Search feature. A search bar is revealed when you open the Launcher or press the Search button on your keyboard. Type a search query into the bar and press Enter. Chromebook serves you Google search results, as though you had opened a browser and gone to Google.com to find something.

# Do a Quick Reboot

No computer is perfect, and although some manufacturers like to make you think that you'll never need to reboot your computer, you almost always will at one point or another. The longer you use your Chromebook, the more gunked up the memory becomes with remnant websites, applications, data, and so on. You can reboot your computer a few ways, but the fastest way to reboot is to press the Power and Refresh buttons simultaneously. Like a flash of light, your Chromebook restarts with fresh memory in just a few seconds.

Note, however, that when you start the Chrome browser after a reboot, it picks up where you left off if you configured Chrome to do so (as described in Chapter 3). But when you do a quick restart, Chrome asks whether you want to restore pages, meaning just that: You can pick up where you left off by clicking Restore, or you can ignore it and start anew. Figure 21-1 shows these options.

**FIGURE 21-1:**
Chromebooks ask whether you want to continue from where you left off before a reboot.

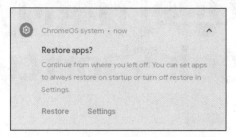

*Illustration courtesy of Peter H. Gregory*

# Control Chromebook with the Omnibox

If you're familiar with Chrome from using it on devices other than your Chromebook, you may already know that Chrome has several high-powered features you can access by entering Chrome shortcuts into the Omnibox (the search or URL field). Naturally, Chrome on Chromebook has the same set of features. Following are some of the shortcuts you may find the most helpful:

>> **chrome://power:** View how much charge your Chromebook has and how much power you use.

>> **chrome://settings:** Load and configure your Chromebook settings.

>> **chrome://extensions:** See and manage all your Chrome browser extensions.

>> **chrome://quota-internals:** Quickly view how much storage space you have on your Chromebook.

- » **chrome://sys-internals:** See current resource usage, which updates every second.

- » **chrome://chrome-urls:** Check out a complete list of all these Chrome URLs. There are dozens of them.

# Lock Your Screen

Ever been in a public place working on your computer and need to get up to go to the bathroom in a hurry? Or maybe someone is barging into your room, and you don't want them to get into your business and see what you're doing on your Chromebook. You can lock your screen by holding your Power button for 400 milliseconds (about half a second) and then clicking Lock. But sometimes you need to lock your screen in 1 millisecond. Never fear: Press the Lock key (shown in Figure 18-11 in Chapter 18) to lock your screen instantly!

# Launch Apps in the Shelf

One way to save time on your Chromebook is by pinning frequently used apps to the shelf. In doing so, you save yourself the extra click and scrolling through pages of applications to find the one you want. If you're serious about keyboard productivity, you can save yourself the need to even click: Load a pinned app by pressing Alt and the number corresponding with the placement of the application on the shelf (counting from left to right or top to bottom). No longer will you be bogged down by the long journey of a mouse pointer to a click.

# Do a Barrel Roll

Sometimes, you just need to have a little fun with your day. Google has hidden a few Easter eggs in your Chromebook. Make your screen do a barrel roll. That's it. No productivity, usefulness, or work-changing functionality here. It's just fun to make your screen go bananas for a brief moment. Press Ctrl+Alt+Shift+Refresh to make your focused browser window roll around and then snap back to normal. (If all apps are minimized and you see only your wallpaper, nothing will happen.)

# View Chromebook Tasks

Have you ever wondered why your Chromebook has slowed down but weren't sure which tab was responsible? Find out by going to the Chrome browser, clicking the menu button (just under the *X* used to close the window), clicking More Tools, and then clicking Task Manager. A new window opens, showing the tasks running on your Chromebook. Click CPU, and Chrome sorts the list, showing the biggest users first.

Further, if you think a tab is causing browser problems, fix it by clicking the corresponding row in Task Manager and then clicking End Process. Also, if you see the error message, "Aw snap. . .something went wrong," click Refresh to reload the tab.

# See All Your Open Windows

If you have been busy multitasking on your Chromebook, you may have many apps open. Press the Show All Open Windows key (shown in Figure 21-2) to show all the apps and windows on your Chromebook immediately. (See Figure 21-3.)

the Show All Windows key

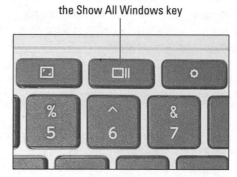

**FIGURE 21-2:**
The Show All
Open Windows
key on a
Chromebook.

*Illustration courtesy of Peter H. Gregory*

What to do from here? Press the Show All Open Windows key again to return to what you were doing before. Or, click any open windows to switch to the one you want.

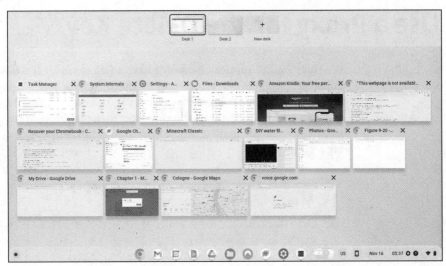

Illustration courtesy of Peter H. Gregory

**FIGURE 21-3:** Viewing all open windows.

# Perform Math, Conversions, and Definitions with Search

Google Search is a major feature that's available on a Chromebook. Have you ever used Google to perform conversions or calculations, or look up a word for you? If you haven't, you should. Your Chromebook can give you that service through the Search bar. Give it a try with these steps:

1. **While logged into your Chromebook, click the Launcher.**

   The app menu opens, and the Search bar appears.

2. **Enter your math problem or search query into the Search bar.**

   For example, type **4+4**. The second result will be the answer: 8. You can even ask for conversions: Type **15 ounces to grams**. The second result is 425.242847 grams.

3. **Enter a word to define into the Search bar.**

   For example, type **define viola**. The result is "an instrument of the violin family, larger than the violin and tuned a fifth lower."

Google Translate is also available on Chromebook through the Chrome browser. Go to translate.google.com, and Google can translate words and phrases from one language to another.

# Use a Proxy for the Delete Key

It's true: Your Chromebook doesn't have a Delete key. It has a Backspace key, but no Delete key (unless you're one of the fortunate few). Here's the difference between these two keys: Delete removes the character to the right of your cursor, whereas Backspace removes the character to the left of your cursor. The following shortcuts come in handy if you're typing an email message or composing or editing a document:

>> **Alt + Backspace:** Deletes characters to the right of your cursor. Characters to the right are deleted one by one.

>> **Ctrl + Backspace:** Deletes entire words to the left of your cursor. The words start to vanish one by one.

# Give Google Assistant a Nudge

As I discuss in Chapter 17, saying "Hey Google" to quickly interact with your Chromebook is handy. But if, after training the Google Assistant, it stops responding to "Okay Google" or "Hey Google," just press the Search + A keys to force it to wake up.

IN THIS CHAPTER

» **Playing some great games**

» **Accessing your Chromebook remotely**

» **Editing video and photos**

» **Securing your passwords**

» **Checking your internet speed**

» **Listening to podcasts**

Chapter **22**

# Ten Great ChromeOS Apps

pps are all people hear about today. Apple, Android, and Google all have application stores. With literally millions of apps available, we are in application overload. Still, many beneficial apps are available for Chromebook users. This section gives you a brief overview of ten apps that make your life on Chromebook more enjoyable, productive, and entertaining.

## Wordscapes

Wordscapes from PeopleFun is one of those word games that displays a crossword puzzle–like grid and a set of letters below. You swipe through the letters to form words that fit in the grid. As you continue playing, it gets more difficult. If you love word games, Wordscapes is just the ticket. I'm a fan of word games; I like to think they keep me young, but maybe I'm just fooling myself. . . .

Swipe-through-letters games are great on a Chromebook with a touchpad, and better yet on a convertible Chromebook where you can play games with your finger right on the screen.

# Angry Birds

You've been living under a rock for the past decade if you haven't heard of Angry Birds. Angry Birds is a fun way to kill time with your Chromebook. The game's premise is to fling birds at the evil pigs and make their makeshift towers fall with a spectacular crash. Quite a bit of strategy is involved, especially in the more advanced levels, because you have to toss birds that can smash through different materials to get to the evil green pigs. The one thing that makes the game genuinely remarkable, aside from the hilarious audio, is the fantastic physics engine that calculates trajectory, velocity, and the force and sound of impacts. But don't kid yourself: This game doesn't develop mental strength. Still, Angry Birds is one of the most popular computer games ever, with way over 100 million downloads.

Today, you have many different Angry Birds games to choose from: Angry Birds 2, Angry Birds Friends, Angry Birds Journey, Angry Birds Transformers, and many more!

# Chrome Remote Desktop

Sometimes you may need to get work done on a machine other than your Chromebook. Or maybe you have some files that reside on another device that's miles and miles away. Chrome Remote Desktop, shown in Figure 22-1, is a great way to remotely access your other computers without having to be in the same room, or even in the same city. The Chrome Remote Desktop client must be installed in each Chromebook you want to control. You also have to ensure that the other computers are connected to the internet and that the Chrome browser is open.

You can also remotely access, and even control (with the owner's permission), someone else's Chromebook. You can do this with your friend's Chromebook or your own, from a Mac, PC, or another Chromebook. My mother has a Chromebook, and sometimes when she has a question, I can access her Chromebook and remotely control it to show her how to do something. This type of access is great for someone who is the IT department for relatives and friends.

Chapter 5 takes you through the steps of remotely accessing your Chromebook.

**WARNING**

Only give control of your computer to someone you know and trust.

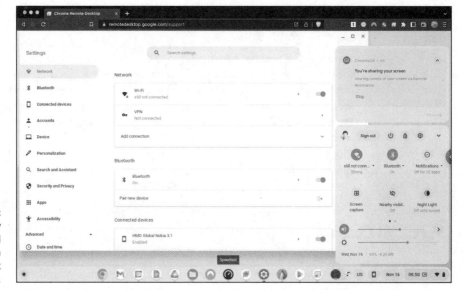

**FIGURE 22-1:**
Remotely
accessing and
controlling a
Chromebook
from a MacBook.

# Canva

Canva is an online graphic design tool used to create visual content, and it works great on a Chromebook. For videos, you can resize, split, and trim your clips, and then add music, voiceovers, or narration. For photos, you can access an array of editing tools that allow you to add text, adjust brightness, or alter colors. Better yet, Canva offers filters and photo effects to make your photos look more fun and edgy. Many of the tools on Canva are free, but they also offer a pro version that includes many more features, such as removing the background of a picture in a single click!

# Sketchbook

This app is the Adobe Photoshop Sketch app for Chromebook. The ultimate in sketch tools, Sketchbook lets you create digital art, whether you're just starting with art or are a modern master. With Sketchbook, you can draw with different pencils, pens, brushes, watercolor, acrylic, ink brushes, and more — all digitally.

Create your art in separate layers and then edit, combine, and manipulate the layers. You can even name and save them.

# Dashlane Password Manager

Dashlane is a popular password manager you can use to store the login credentials for your various internet sites (for example, online banking, online shopping, and other high-value sites where having strong, unique passwords is vital for your security and privacy). You can also store additional high-value information in Dashlane, such as bank account and credit card numbers.

The free version is sufficient for single-user use, and the paid version unlocks more features.

# Speedtest

When things on your Chromebook slow to a crawl, you'll first wonder: Is it my Chromebook, my internet connection, or the service I'm using? With Speedtest by Ookla (refer to Figure 22-2), you'll instantly know whether your internet connection is the culprit (and when you see Speedtest working, you also know that your Chromebook is more or less okay). Personally, I pin the Speedtest app to the Shelf so that I can instantly know how my internet connection is performing.

**FIGURE 22-2:** The Speedtest app quickly shows internet reachability and performance.

*Illustration courtesy of Peter H Gregory*

# Microsoft Word Online

Google Docs, the word processor from Google, is impressive. But if you come from a lifelong career of working in Microsoft Word, Word Online may be the right option. Create documents of all sorts, from letters to research papers and autobiographies. Word Online is a near replica of the desktop experience, just online. Share your documents and invite collaborators to edit documents with Word Online; then save your documents in OneDrive or download them for storing elsewhere. Word Online is an excellent option if you aren't ready for Google Docs.

Do note that you need a Microsoft 365 account to use Word Online. Also, Microsoft Word Online is technically not an app you download from the Play Store — it's browser-based, like so many others.

# WeatherBug

The makers of WeatherBug tout that it's the fastest, most accurate weather application currently available. WeatherBug is a ray of sunshine in your Launcher menu. Save multiple locations in your WeatherBug for quick referencing. Check current conditions or long-term forecasts. The virtual window gives you a pleasant visualization of the forecast. WeatherBug also pushes out real-time weather alerts to ensure you know when severe weather is moving into your area. Also, check out local or national radar and plan a long trip with a precise weather forecast.

I especially appreciate WeatherBug's lightning strike detector. For me, as a former frequent air traveler, thunderstorms near airports matter because ramp operations are suspended when storms are too close, which translates into delayed or canceled flights. No planes can come or go, and when you're trying to make tight connections, having this information can make all the difference when it comes to getting to your destination or back home on time.

# Podcast Addict

This popular app lets you listen to podcasts, audiobooks, YouTube, RSS feeds, and more. While this app is written for Android and displays in smaller, vertical smartphone formats, don't let that fool you: You can search for everything under the sun. The user interface is so simple that no directions are needed. Just search in the search field, click the check mark to subscribe, click the Episodes button to review episodes, and click play to listen. You can create bookmarks, write reviews, share podcasts with others, change the playback speed, and cast to an external audio device or television. Podcast Addict has many more intuitive features, and it offers a free version as well as a paid version without ads.

## TAKING ADVANTAGE OF ANDROID APPS

Most Android apps also run on Chromebooks. Whether you're looking for games, tools, utilities, or serious apps like note-taking, book reading, word processing, or finance, chances are you can run it on your Chromebook, too. The easiest way to find out is to fire up the Play Store app and look around.

Browse by category, read reviews, and experiment with new apps to see if you like them. If you do, pin them to your Shelf. If you don't, Alt-click and uninstall to remove them and try out others.

Chapter **23**

# Ten Chromebook Security Tips

ybercriminals are making good money, but I want to make sure that they don't get any of yours! Having a Chromebook is a great start because the design of ChromeOS — the heart and soul of a Chromebook — has security firmly in mind. But the nature of cybercrime makes it necessary for you to be vigilant, even when using the most secure laptop available. The tips in this chapter can help keep you and your data safe.

## Lock Your Chromebook when You're Away

Whenever you're working on your Chromebook where other people are around, an excellent habit to get into is to lock it when you step away, even for a minute or two. You can easily lock it; Chromebooks give you not one, not two, but four ways, as follows:

» Briefly press the Power button and then click Lock.

» Open the Settings window and click the Lock symbol.

>> Press the Lock key on your keyboard.

>> Use a cable lock to prevent theft (described in detail in Chapter 18).

# Use Strong, Complex Passwords

According to NordPass, the top ten passwords in 2022 are 123456, 123456789, guest, password, qwerty, 12345678, 111111, 12345, col123456, and 123123. The next ten are just as lame.

Using such passwords is just laziness, and user accounts with weak passwords like these are broken into *a lot.* Using stronger, complex passwords isn't difficult. Here are some examples of better ones (but *don't use these* because they're in a published book now):

>> ST4R.wars (Star Wars)

>> Loosie.IN.the.sky-withDiamonds (Lucy in the Sky with Diamonds)

>> Run-Forr35t-Run! (Run Forrest Run!)

>> Sea-Sp00t-Run (See Spot run)

The idea is to think of a phrase and then devise some consistent way of adding characters to it or misspelling it that you can remember.

You need to use a different password on each site you use. Here's why: If cyber-criminals can successfully break into a website's user IDs and passwords database (which happens often) and you use the same user ID and password everywhere you go, the cybercriminals who stole these credentials can easily log in to all the websites you use frequently. If this includes online banking or other sites on which you buy or sell, you're in big trouble.

Using complex passwords on your websites, and a different password on each site, is a lot to remember — so read the next tip.

# Use a Web-Based Password Vault

Maintaining security isn't easy, although it's way less hassle than dealing with identity theft (ask me how I know this!). Using different passwords on each site is definitely the way to be more secure, but remembering all those passwords can be challenging. The good news is you don't have to.

Some trusted, high-quality password vaults are available. These securely store your login credentials, so you don't need to remember them all. Some of these vaults can even automatically enter your login credentials when you log in. How cool is that!

The best password vaults are Keeper (at www.keepersecurity.com) and Dashlane (at www.dashlane.com). Others worthy of mention include Roboform and 1Password.

# Use Multifactor Authentication Everywhere You Can

One of the biggest threats on the internet involves the theft of login credentials for popular websites. Even if ChromeOS is resistant to attack, hackers use malicious browser extensions designed to steal user IDs and passwords when you type them in. Also, cybercriminals directly attack popular website databases and, if they can break in, often they go for encrypted password databases and attempt to decrypt them. If they do, they have the user IDs and passwords for many — or all — of the site's users!

Using multifactor authentication is generally pretty easy. Google Authenticator is the most popular app used for this purpose — you install it on your smartphone. When you log in to a website, you read a six-digit code from your Google Authenticator app, or the website sends a code to your smartphone; then, you type in that code on the website to log in. Even if hackers can obtain your user ID and password, they can't log in because they don't have your smartphone. Learn more about Google Authenticator in Chapter 18.

Be on the lookout on your social media, financial services, medical, and other websites where sensitive information about you resides. When you see information about activating multifactor authentication (sometimes called two-factor authentication), please consider enabling it. You'll thwart cybercriminals, and your data will be a little bit safer.

# Get a Screen Privacy Filter

If you work with confidential information on your Chromebook and do so frequently in public places, you may want to consider getting a screen privacy filter. It helps to keep prying eyes that glance at your screen from seeing what you're up to. When using a privacy filter, you can clearly see the screen, but people to your left and right just see black when they look at your screen. Keep your business information, or those cat videos, to yourself! Chapter 18 discusses this, and Figure 18-17 shows what they look like.

# Block Malicious Websites with an Anti-Malware Program

ChromeOS is quite robust and resistant to the kinds of attacks that have plagued Windows computers for decades. Still, hazards are out there, and most of the attacks you face are attacks on your browser in the form of malicious extensions and websites that attempt to steal your data.

Security programs like AVG Online Security or Bitdefender Security are available from the Google Web Store. They are purpose-made for Chromebooks and help protect you from known malicious websites and other threats.

# Update the Security on Your Wi-Fi Access Point

You're only as secure as the Wi-Fi network you usually use. If you have a new Chromebook and your Wi-Fi access point (which may be doing double-duty as your cable modem or DSL modem) is old, you may want to consider replacing it with a newer one.

The two most important security settings on your Wi-Fi access point are the type of encryption (which is usually none, WEP, WPA, or WPA2 — pick WPA2!) and the default password. Be sure to read the instructions for your Wi-Fi access point carefully. Visit the Wi-Fi access point manufacturer's website for help. You can also pick up a copy of the latest edition of *Networking For Dummies* by Doug Lowe (Wiley) for more information on securing and customizing your home Wi-Fi network.

# Back Up Your Local Data

With ordinary use of your Chromebook, most of the data you create and deal with is stored by Google "in the cloud," where it is available on all your Google-enabled devices. Still, you may have local data that matters to you. The best way to find out is to open the Files app and see what data is stored locally. Anything in the Downloads, Images, Audio, or Video folders may exist only there and nowhere else. If this is the case, *and* you care about any of these files, it's best to copy them to your Google Drive: Just drag and drop them into separate folders if you want.

Alternatively, you can back up these files to an external hard drive or SD card if you prefer to maintain complete control over this data. Either way, backing up your local data is easy and takes only moments. Go to Chapter 7 to read more about removable storage.

# Use a VPN If You Use Public Wi-Fi Routinely

If you frequent Wi-Fi networks at coffee shops, hotels, airports, and other public places, I recommend you subscribe to a VPN service. As I discuss in Chapter 18, getting a free VPN service will likely do more harm than good. Instead, go with one of the leading VPN services, such as Nord VPN, ExpressVPN, or CyberGhost VPN.

VPN software encrypts all your Wi-Fi network communications so that snoopy people can't eavesdrop on your communications on a public Wi-Fi network. This issue is less important at home where, hopefully, your Wi-Fi access point is configured to use WPA or, better yet, WPA2, which encrypts your network traffic at home.

# Keep Your Chromebook Up-to-Date

I'm saving the best — and most important — security tip for last. Keeping your Chromebook's ChromeOS up-to-date is vital for your security, as well as for the stability of your Chromebook. Be sure to watch your notifications and promptly update ChromeOS and all the apps you've downloaded from the Chrome Web Store and the Google Play Store.

Although some of the updates fix software bugs, you can be sure that many of the fixes improve the security of your Chromebook and the apps you run. When these security bugs are fixed, criminals have a harder time breaking in and stealing your data.

Unlike Windows, where downloading and installing updates seem to take practically *forever,* security updates to ChromeOS take less than a minute to load, including the reboot!

# Index

# T

Table option, Slides app, 190
tablets, 117
tabs
  Chrome browser, 35–36
  Sheets app, 152
Terms of Service agreements
  Chromebook, 12–13
  Google Assistant, 14
  Google Drive, 14
  Google Play, 14
text
  aligning
    center alignment, 139–140
    justifying text, 139–140
    left alignment, 139–140
    right alignment, 139–140
    Sheets app, 167–168
    Slides app, 206–207
  bold font, 138
  clearing, 140–141
  coloring, 138–139
  cutting and pasting, 132
  desktop publishing point, 137
  italics, 138
  point size, 137
  Sheets app
    aligning text, 167–168
    wrapping text, 169
  sizing, 137–138
  Slides app
    aligning text, 206–207
    bold, 204
    clearing formatting, 207
    coloring, 205
    fonts, 202–203
    formatting, 202–205
    italics, 204
    overview, 196–197
    resizing, 203–204
    strikethrough, 205
    underlining, 204
    strikethrough, 138
    underlining, 138
text boxes
  adding, 197–198
  copying and pasting, 201
  deleting, 198
  moving, 199–200
  resizing, 199
  rotating, 200–201
text styles, Gmail, 84–86
texting and video conferencing
  Google Chat
    incoming message requests, 300–301
    sharing files in, 300
    Spaces, 298–300
    video conferencing, 301
  Google Contacts app and, 315
  Google Meet
    host controls, 306
    joining meeting by invitation, 303
    meeting controls, 305, 307
    overview, 302
    scheduling meetings, 303–305
    screen sharing, 306
    setting up meeting, 303
  Google Voice
    call schedules, 311
    call screening, 311
    one-click dialing, 311
    overview, 307
    phone calls, 310
    sending photos, 311
    setting up, 308
    texting, 308–310
    using on multiple devices, 311
    voice mail, 311
  GoToMeeting, 315
  Microsoft Teams, 314
  overview, 297–298
  Signal, 315
  Slack, 314–315
  Webex, 315

Wi-Fi setting, 26
Wi-Fi signal icon, 12
windows
    Show All Open Windows key,
        414–415
    sizing, 27–28, 34–35
Windows PC
    transitioning to Chromebook from, 16
    uploading files to Google Drive from, 116
Word Online app, 232–233, 421
Wordscapes, 417–418
workbooks, Excel, 233
wrapping text, Sheets app, 169
writing emails, 83–84

# X

Xerox Alto, 21
Xerox Star, 21
X-Windows system, 21

# Y

YouTube
    adjusting volume, 293–294
    casting to smart TV, 294
    full screen mode, 293
    overview, 291–292
    playing and pausing videos, 292–293
    search functionality, 292

YouTube Music app
    album art, 248
    Cast button, 246
    Enter full screen button, 247
    Explore button, 246
    Google Account button, 246
    Home button, 246
    library, 245–246
    Library button, 246
    Mini player button, 247
    overview, 70, 241–242
    Play Controls, 246–247
    playing music on, 246–249
    playing music on external devices, 253–255
    playlists, 251–253
    premium version, 242, 244–245
    Queue button, 247
    radio, 249–250
    Search button, 247
    standard version, 242, 243
    Upgrade button, 246
    uploading music, 250–251

# Z

Zoom
    joining meeting, 312–313
    overview, 311–312
    starting meeting, 313–314

# About the Author

**Peter H. Gregory** is a lifelong technologist, having worked on old-school mainframes, supercomputers, minis, micros, PCs, Macs, Chromebooks, smartphones, and more, up to the present day. Since early in his career, Gregory has been helping others understand how to use computers and software through seminars, university courses, on-site training, and mentoring coworkers, friends, and family. He designed and taught a cybersecurity course for IT professionals for ten years at the University of Washington. Currently, Gregory is a cybersecurity executive at a regional telecommunications provider. He holds several cybersecurity and privacy certifications (CISA, CISM, CRISC, CISSP, CIPM, CDPSE, CCSK, and DRCE), which for Chromebooks means only that he knows information technology, privacy, and cybersecurity inside and out. He enjoys motorcycling, woodworking, metalworking, and gardening in his spare time.

# Dedication

To people everywhere looking for a simpler and safer way to get online.

# Author's Acknowledgments

I am grateful for my wife, Rebekah, who inspires me to greatness, and who put up with a lot of early mornings, late nights, and a few weekends when I was there at home but still far, far away. Many thanks to Jennifer Yee, Kristie Pyles, and Lee Gruhn at Wiley for responding to numerous emails and helping to drive this project to completion. Thanks also to my former colleague John Clark, our technical reviewer, for great and constructive feedback, even before he saw a single written page. Thank you, Christine Pingleton, for helping to organize, refine, and copy edit all this content. Thank you, Gio and Shay, for being live test subjects. I also thank Rebecca Steele, my faithful business manager and research assistant, for being an excellent Chromebook test subject. And finally, thanks to my literary agent, Carole Jelen, for almost two decades of support. Writing a book is not a solo act but a team sport, and I'm grateful for everyone mentioned here and others of whom I'm unaware.

Thanks to Ralph Pratt (God rest your soul) for inspiring and coaching me for my first classroom instruction gig, where I taught programmers, department heads, and business leaders how to use a new computer program known as Mapper, which is a bit like modern-day spreadsheets. Mind you, this was in the early 1980s, before Excel, Lotus 1-2-3, Multiplan, or even Visicalc. Ralph's patient coaching set me on a path that would change my career and lead to my writing dozens of books, helping tens of thousands better understand the incredible complexity of information technology.

## Publisher's Acknowledgments

**Acquisitions Editor:** Jennifer Yee

**Project Manager and Development Editor:** Lee Gruhn

**Copy Editor:** Christine Pingleton

**Technical Editor:** John Clark

**Managing Editor:** Kristie Pyles

**Cover Image:** Courtesy of Peter H. Gregory

**Production Editor:** Saikarthick Kumarasamy

# Leverage the power

*Dummies* is the global leader in the reference category and one of the most trusted and highly regarded brands in the world. No longer just focused on books, customers now have access to the dummies content they need in the format they want. Together we'll craft a solution that engages your customers, stands out from the competition, and helps you meet your goals.

## Advertising & Sponsorships

Connect with an engaged audience on a powerful multimedia site, and position your message alongside expert how-to content. Dummies.com is a one-stop shop for free, online information and know-how curated by a team of experts.

- Targeted ads
- Video
- Email Marketing

- Microsites
- Sweepstakes sponsorship

**20** MILLION
PAGE VIEWS
EVERY SINGLE MONTH

*15* MILLION
UNIQUE
VISITORS PER MONTH

**43%**
OF ALL VISITORS
ACCESS THE SITE
VIA THEIR MOBILE DEVICES

**700,000** NEWSLETTER
SUBSCRIPTIONS

TO THE INBOXES OF

*300,000* UNIQUE INDIVIDUALS EVERY WEEK

# of dummies

## Custom Publishing

Reach a global audience in any language by creating a solution that will differentiate you from competitors, amplify your message, and encourage customers to make a buying decision.

- Apps
- Books
- eBooks
- Video
- Audio
- Webinars

## Brand Licensing & Content

Leverage the strength of the world's most popular reference brand to reach new audiences and channels of distribution.

## For more information, visit dummies.com/biz

 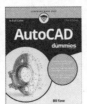     

# Learning Made Easy

## ACADEMIC

9781119293576
USA $19.99
CAN $23.99
UK £15.99

9781119293637
USA $19.99
CAN $23.99
UK £15.99

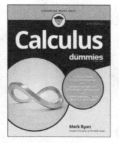

9781119293491
USA $19.99
CAN $23.99
UK £15.99

9781119293460
USA $19.99
CAN $23.99
UK £15.99

9781119293590
USA $19.99
CAN $23.99
UK £15.99

9781119215844
USA $26.99
CAN $31.99
UK £19.99

9781119293378
USA $22.99
CAN $27.99
UK £16.99

9781119293521
USA $19.99
CAN $23.99
UK £15.99

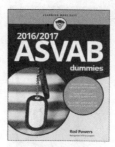

9781119239178
USA $18.99
CAN $22.99
UK £14.99

9781119263883
USA $26.99
CAN $31.99
UK £19.99

## Available Everywhere Books Are Sold

**dummies.com**

**dummies**
A Wiley Brand

# Small books for big imaginations

GETTING STARTED WITH **Coding**
Get Creative with Code!
Camille McCue, PhD

9781119177173
USA $9.99
CAN $9.99
UK £8.99

**MODDING** *Minecraft*
Build Your Own Minecraft Mods!
Sarah Guthals, PhD
Stephen Foster, PhD
Lindsey Handley, PhD

9781119177272
USA $9.99
CAN $9.99
UK £8.99

MAKING *YouTube* VIDEOS
Star in Your Own Video!
Nick Willoughby

9781119177241
USA $9.99
CAN $9.99
UK £8.99

DESIGNING *Digital Games*
Create Games with Scratch!
Derek Breen

9781119177210
USA $9.99
CAN $9.99
UK £8.99

GETTING STARTED WITH *Raspberry Pi*
Program Your Raspberry Pi!
Richard Wentk

9781119262657
USA $9.99
CAN $9.99
UK £6.99

EXPERIMENTING WITH **Science**
Think, Test, and Learn!
Gavin J. Mullins, PhD

9781119291336
USA $9.99
CAN $9.99
UK £6.99

CREATING *Digital Animations*
Animate Stories with Scratch!
Derek Breen

9781119233527
USA $9.99
CAN $9.99
UK £6.99

GETTING STARTED WITH *Engineering*
Think Like an Engineer!
Camille McCue, PhD

9781119291220
USA $9.99
CAN $9.99
UK £6.99

WRITING *Computer Code*
Learn the Languages of Computers!
Chris Minnick and Eva Holland

9781119177302
USA $9.99
CAN $9.99
UK £8.99

## Unleash Their Creativity

**dummies.com**

**dummies®**
A Wiley Brand